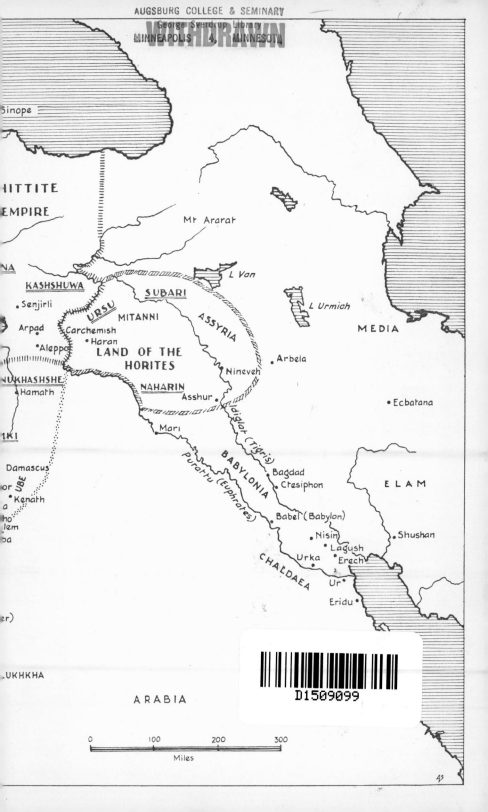

Sinope

HITTITE
EMPIRE

Mt Ararat

L Van

NA

KASHSHUWA

SUBARI

L Urmiah

Senjirli

URSU

MITANNI

ASSYRIA

MEDIA

Arpad

Carchemish

Haran

Aleppo

LAND OF THE
HORITES

Arbela

Nineveh

NUKHASHSHE

Hamath

NAHARIN

Asshur

Ecbatana

IKI

Mari

Idiglat (Tigris)

Damascus

or

UBE

Kenath

a

ho

lem

ba

Purattu (Euphrates)

BABYLONIA

Bagdad

Ctesiphon

ELAM

Shushan

Babel (Babylon)

Nisin

Lagush

Urka

Erech

CHALDAEA

Ur

Eridu

er)

LUKHKHA

ARABIA

| 0 | 100 | 200 | 300 |

Miles

45

A JOURNEY THROUGH
THE OLD TESTAMENT

A
JOURNEY THROUGH
THE
OLD TESTAMENT

by
M. A. BEEK
University of Amsterdam

Translated by
ARNOLD J. POMERANS

LONDON
HODDER AND STOUGHTON

Printed in Great Britain for
Hodder and Stoughton Limited by
The Camelot Press Limited
London and Southampton

Foreword

BY THE REV. PROFESSOR H. H. ROWLEY, D.D., F.B.A.

IT is a pleasure to introduce Professor Beek to English readers. Already before the Second World War his work was known to me, but it was not until after the War that I first met him, when I visited the University of Amsterdam, where he holds a chair. I was then a guest in his home, where I have again found warm hospitality, and from the time of our meeting I have enjoyed the friendship of the author.

That he was trained in the school of Albrecht Alt will be apparent to some readers of this book, who will also observe that he shares with Professor M. Noth, who was trained in the same school, a reluctance to find tangible history in the story of Moses. Professor Beek's own position may be described broadly as liberal, though in the present work he is not primarily concerned with critical questions, which are only occasionally touched on. What he attempts here to do is to take the reader through the Old Testament by describing and commenting on incidents and personalities selected from its pages. The whole of the Old Testament is not covered, and everyone familiar with the Bible will have his own list of what might have been included. The important and dramatic conflict with Sisera in the period of the Judges, immortalised in the Song of Deborah, might well have had a separate chapter, and the prophet Hosea might have claimed another. In fairness to Professor Beek, it should be said that these did have chapters in the Dutch text, but they have been omitted in the English version, which has been somewhat reduced. It should be added that this book is the outcome of a series of broadcast talks on the Bible, designed not for scholars but for ordinary people inside and outside the Church, many of whom are lamentably ignorant of the contents of the Bible. Professor Beek's purpose was to awaken in them an interest in the Bible and to enable them to share his own awareness that the Old Testament is an exciting book, relevant to the modern world and with a message to men today.

The author has published several popular works in Dutch, as well as works of more technical scholarship, and has a reputation in his own country for a liveliness of style which holds his readers, as well as instructs them. It was these gifts which made the talks contained in this book so successful that publication became desirable, and sent it on its way to spread the knowledge of what the Old Testament contains. The author is aware that not all readers will agree with him throughout the volume. Some who are familiar with the Bible will regret that at some points critical questions are not even raised, while others will regret that they were raised at all. Both should reflect that the readers chiefly in the author's mind were they who have ceased to read the Bible because they regard it as an antiquated book, and who do not know its rich treasures. To obtrude critical questions would divert their attention from the author's main purpose; to omit them altogether would mislead by suggesting that there were no such questions, and that a crude literalism would suffice to unlock all the treasures of the Old Testament.

I share Professor Beek's view that the Bible is the most wonderful book in the world. Within the Bible the Old Testament has a range and variety far greater than the New, and the human interest that belongs to its incidents and persons whereby the rich and enduring word of God was mediated to men makes it unique among the world's sacred literature. If readers of Professor Beek's book are stirred to turn to the Bible itself, and then to seek other books which will enlighten them further on the difficulties that undoubtedly attach to it, the author's purpose will be attained, and they will have reason to thank him for setting their feet on a journey that will take them not alone to the Bible, but to God.

H. H. ROWLEY.

9th February, 1959.

Contents

List of Illustrations

Introduction

IT is my firm personal conviction that there is no other book in the whole world as exciting as the Bible. We can devote a lifetime to its study and yet not tire for a single moment. Even so, I have good reason to believe that the Bible has not remained the best-seller it is because of its great message or inspiring contents. Many family Bibles, beautifully bound, and reverently treated, have merely become domestic ornaments and like these, are picked up only for dusting. No matter how often their owners profess that the Bible contains all a man needs for the good life, they still lack the key to its mysteries. Surely they must realise that no book can shape their lives by its mere presence?

The Bible is in fact a very difficult book for the unwary, and those who read it without circumspection do not usually get far. I have little faith in the power of the mere word. Many believe that a simple creed is the "Open Sesame" to the wonderland of the Bible. If they succeed, their road from Genesis to Revelation is usually as straight as a modern highway, and just as comfortable and safe. But to my mind this road is a little monotonous and devoid of all scenic beauty. I prefer to roam along the by-ways, the little alleys and in mysterious out-of-the-way haunts. Admittedly, to do so is more risky, and it is more difficult to find one's way. But then such difficulties are more like life itself than any cut-and-dried scheme could ever be.

I know that there is no lack of commentaries on, or of guides to, the Old Testament. If anything, there is a surfeit of books on this subject, and I do hope sincerely that no reviewer will try to flatter my book by saying that it "fills a need". The book fills no other need than my own: to order and put on paper what material I have gathered over the years. I can say quite truthfully that I do not pretend to have written a better, or even a more original, book than any of the many excellent works that have already been published.

I have come more and more to consider as experiments the radio talks on which this book is based. There is just one little fact that has emerged from them that might serve me as an excuse for offering the public yet another new book on so old a subject. In my talks I wished to stress not only how exciting a book the Bible really is, but also that its problems are in fact our own. Now I know that I have surprised many listeners into realising that, though the Bible was written very very long ago, and though it is set in the Near East, we can nevertheless speak with every justification of "the Bible in our time". There is no need for sophistry or for mental acrobatics if we wish to demonstrate how real the Bible can become in our everyday life. We have only to heed what is written and we cannot help being filled with a warmth that leads straight to reverence.To tell its story frankly yet reverently, critically and yet lovingly, is the noblest task I know.

I cannot conclude this brief introduction without expressing my gratitude to my many friends in Enschede, the last congregation I served as parson. During the most difficult period of the war, my church warden, Mr. H. van Heek, organised a Bible course in which I found all the inspiration I could have wished for. It was there that I learnt anew to be moved by the greatness of the Book of Books. This feeling has never left me since. It is for this reason that I dedicate my book with such gratitude to those who, at the time, helped to make our Bible evenings such a great event.

M. A. BEEK

A. *The Dawn*

In the Beginning . . .

THE first book of the Bible is called Genesis—a Greek word meaning "the creation". Actually the title is misleading, since the Creation is but one of many topics discussed. The ancient Hebrews simply referred to the book by its opening words, and called it: "In the Beginning." Such was the custom of the time and place, the author's name being a matter of no importance and literary fame unheard of. This is borne out also by the Assyrian clay tablets from the library of King Ashurbanipal (668-626 B.C.). One of these tablets, which are kept in the British Museum, was called Enuma Elish, meaning "When the Heavens Above", and it begins:

> "When the heavens above were unnamed and below on earth no name was yet recorded, the primeval ocean was the father of them; and the wild sea their mother. The waters were joined together, the cornfield was not grown and no reed was seen. When as yet the gods had not come forth any of them, nor were called by name. Order did not exist. . . ."

Enuma Elish is believed to be well over four thousand years old and no one knows who wrote it.

Now, the fact that Israel's account of the Creation was called "In the Beginning", must not mislead us into thinking it the oldest book of the Bible. Many scholars have in fact argued that it was a fairly late addition. How else explain that the prophets and psalmists hardly ever mentioned the Creation, or when they did, in words that had no bearing on Genesis? They may have preferred to dwell on the exodus from Egypt as more inspiring, but then again they may simply not have considered Genesis as Holy Writ.

The story of the Creation lends itself to misunderstanding, not least because its authors equated the beginning of the world with the beginning of their national history. We are more modest and usually start our history with Caesar's conquest of Britain in 55 B.C. But the pious Israelite saw all history as one continuum; for him Adam and Eve were as much a part of it as David and Bathsheba, and Cain and Abel no less real than Amnon who was killed by Absalom in King David's time. All history was thought to be equally authentic, the Fall as much as the Exodus from Egypt.

Now, some modern scholars read the Book of Genesis as if it were a scientific textbook, but they are bound to get into deep water. For science steps gingerly where they would have certainty, and adheres to a theory of gradual evolution, in the place of immediate Creation. These scholars have to juggle about with facts and figures, prolonging the six days of the Creation into millennia, and equating the Biblical account of the order in which fish, birds, beasts of the field and man were created with the origin of species. Such an approach inevitably does violence to the Bible and gives the Book a significance it was never intended to have. It cannot be emphasised too strongly that Genesis 1 is not an alternative to modern science, and we must admit frankly that its account of the Creation is no longer our own. For us the earth has long ceased to be a flat disc, floating in a primeval ocean, and the Universe is no longer what the Hebrews thought it to be.

It is only when we compare the Old Testament with other accounts of the Creation (for example, the Assyrian Enuma Elish epic) that its unique character and real importance emerge. Not that I wish to claim Genesis 1 is inherently greater than the myths of other peoples and religions. We are always inclined to be a little unfair to traditions other than our own, but even making allowances for our prejudices, there is no doubt that the Biblical account of the Creation is more moving than other myths with their epic struggles between gods, their dragons and various dark powers of destruction. And surely no other has the beautiful simplicity of the opening lines of the Old Testament:

"In the beginning God created the heaven and the earth. And the earth was without form and void; and darkness was upon the face of the deep. And the Spirit of God moved upon the face of the waters. And God said, Let there be light; and there was light. And God saw the light, that it was good; and God divided the light from the darkness. And God called the light Day, and the darkness he called Night. And the evening and the morning were the first day" (Genesis 1:1-5).

True, not every word is unequivocally clear. Some have argued that "without form and void" is no proper translation of the Hebrew *tohu-va-bohu*, while others have been at a loss to explain why "the Spirit of God moved upon the face of the waters". Was it some mysterious allusion to the Trinity, a first mention of the Holy Ghost? Indeed, the text contains these and many other difficulties, but to dwell upon them might well be reading more into the text than was intended. To us it may be a matter of great consequence to probe into the origins of the world, but to the children of Israel history simply began when God bade the chaos cease. They never lost any sleep about the nature of the chaos itself, but were more concerned with the central message: God gave man dominion over the fish of the sea, the fowl of the air and the beasts of the field, and He saw that it was good.

No, the Creation is no scientific hypothesis, but it is historical in that, to the children of Israel, history began with their acceptance of God and with the realisation that without Him all is chaos.

We have seen that the Old Testament hardly ever again refers to its simple and lovely account of the Creation. Now and then a word or two may remind us of it, as for instance when Amos interrupts his blistering attack on the people of Israel to say:

"Seek him that maketh the seven stars and Orion, and turneth the shadow of death into the morning, and maketh the day dark with night: that calleth for the waters of the sea, and poureth them out upon the face of the earth:—Jhvh is his name" (Amos 5:8).

Such reminders are rare and we must not be surprised that this is so. The Creator is a remote and holy God whose lonely Majesty overwhelms and shames us. Yet He is also the God who spoke with Abraham and Moses, who led the suffering children of Israel out of Egyptian slavery. The emphasis has been shifted: God the Creator of heaven and earth has become He who speaks with men and who, speaking, becomes as one of them.

2

The Image and Likeness of God

MOST readers of the Bible must have been struck by the fact that two versions of the Creation of man are mentioned in short succession. The second, better known, account tells how God created man from the dust of the ground, breathing into his nostrils the breath of life, and placing him in a beautiful garden. Not that the garden of Eden was meant to be a land of Cockaigne, a paradise for idlers—far from it: "And the Lord God took the man, and put him into the garden of Eden to dress it and to keep it" (Genesis 2:15). Even the first man had some task, albeit light compared with that of the Palestinian peasant.

But this garden was not God's only loving gift to man, for He saw that man was lonely. And God said: "It is not good that the man should be alone; I will make him an help meet for him" (Genesis 2:18). He then caused a deep sleep to fall upon Adam and made a woman from his rib. Adam woke, and seeing the woman, he exclaimed full of joy and wonder: "This is now bone of my bones, and flesh of my flesh" (Genesis 2:23), and they started to live happily in their garden of bliss. But from the outset, their idyllic life was tainted by man's frailty and weakness: God's breath might have quickened man into life, but still he was fashioned from the dust of the ground: the dust that is blown by the hot desert wind, dust as ephemeral as man himself. Later, the Preacher would once again proclaim the vanity of all life and say: "For that which befalleth the sons of men befalleth beasts; even one thing befalleth them: as the one dieth, so dieth the other; yea, they have all one breath; so that a man hath no pre-eminence above a beast: for all is vanity. All go unto one place; all are of the dust, and all turn to dust again" (Ecclesiastes 3:19-20).

Lovely though the garden was, therefore, life in it was as tenuous as life is everywhere, and it is characteristic of the Old Testament that it never forgets man's precarious position, his frailty that made the Lord God exclaim in anger: "In the sweat of thy face shalt thou eat bread, till thou return unto the ground; for out of it wast thou taken: for dust thou art, and unto dust shalt thou return" (Genesis 3:19).

Now some have looked upon the second version of man's Creation as an elaboration of the first: "So God created man in his own image, in· the image of God created he him; male and female created he them" (Genesis 1:28). I do not think they are wise to have done so. Each version has its own weight—each is quite independent of the other.

Indeed, it is very lucky that the Biblical author did not bother to reconcile the two accounts. A modern writer would doubtless have tried to smooth out the contradictions, thus glossing over the truth of either story and being unjust to both. The story of Paradise stresses the fact that man is just so much dust. But his Creation on the sixth day to crown God's work shifts the emphasis: "And God said, Let us make man in our image, after our likeness: and let them have dominion over the fish of the sea, and over the fowl of the air, and over the cattle, and over all the earth, and over every creeping thing that creepeth upon the earth" (Genesis 1:26).

When geologists speak of the age of the earth, a million years are as nothing to them. The latest investigations in fact mention an approximate age of 3,350 million years, of which human history is but a tiny fragment. Dr. A. Kuenen expressed this fact very graphically when he wrote: "If we condense the age of the earth into one year, the Palaeozoic age with the first fossilised fauna began in the middle of September, coal was laid down at the beginning of November, the dinosaurs were abroad between St. Nicholas's Day (December 6th) and Christmas. Neanderthal man went hunting for mammoth and cave bears on the evening of December 31st, Julius Caesar invaded England at 11.24 p.m., and you yourself were born on the last stroke of midnight." Thus the Biblical story of Creation refers to only a few minutes of our year, but during these few minutes there occurred the climax of God's creation: man was made in His image.

Few expressions have puzzled Biblical scholars more than the phrase: "in God's image and likeness". Interpretations have been many and contradictory, but most Christians believe that Adam was literally made in God's image but that he lost the likeness after the Fall. Only with Jesus Christ did God's image return to earth so that He could say with full justice: ". . . he that hath seen me hath seen the Father" (John 14:9). Now, the Old Testament itself does not support this interpretation. Nowhere does it state that Adam forfeited his likeness to God after the Fall, but on the contrary, it stresses the fact that this very likeness is man's characteristic distinction. Thus we are told that God Himself said to Noah: "Whoso sheddeth man's blood, by man shall his blood be shed: for in the image of God made he man" (Genesis 9:6). Clearly then, the Old Testament maintains that man had still kept his likeness to God even after the Flood. Now, does all this mean that according to the Bible man was once identical with his Creator? This is not so, for we are told that: "God is in heaven, and thou upon earth" (Ecclesiastes 5:2), and that: "All nations before him are as nothing; and they are counted to him less than nothing, and vanity. To whom then will ye liken God? or what likeness will ye compare unto him?" (Isaiah 40:17-18). No, man was not created to be a God, but to stand above nature, above the beasts of the field, the fowls of the air and the fish of the sea, which are not made in God's image. Indeed, man was created to stand halfway between God and nature.

This is borne out by David when, directing his gaze at the heavens, he asked:

"When I consider thy heavens, the work of thy fingers, the moon and the stars, which thou hast ordained; What is man, that thou art mindful of him? and the son of man, that thou visitest him?" (Psalm 8:3-4).

And this is the answer:

"For thou hast made him a little lower than the angels, and hast crowned him with glory and honour. Thou madest him to have dominion over the works of thy hand; thou hast put all things under his feet; all sheep and oxen, yea, and the beasts of the field" (Psalm 8:5-7).

No, man is neither like God, nor like nature, but is miraculously poised between the two. This is precisely the grace that God has bestowed upon him and also the well-nigh unbearable burden man has to bear. When the Bible says that though man is made in God's image he is also the dust of the ground, it stresses a dichotomy that lies at the very root of man.

3

Paradise Lost

PARADISE is irrevocably lost to man. Adam and Eve alone were lucky enough to spend a fleeting moment in it. A few rays of paradise may continue to beautify man's life on earth but these are like streaks of lightning against a sombre sky. And when man lost paradise, he lost eternal life also. Adam's children may, at best, catch an occasional glimpse of eternity in the midst of time. Legend has it that a Cistercian monk, strolling in the shrubbery of his cloister, was held spellbound by the song of a nightingale. He stayed to listen and when he returned, no one could recognise him. Finally, it was discovered that a monk of this name had disappeared a thousand years earlier. Yes, time may stand still, and when we listen to the song of the nightingale, a day, a month or even a year may be as nothing. Only thus have we retained a vague inkling of paradise and of eternity. Why then was man expelled from the Garden?

We can answer this question in two ways. We may say that the Fall was a great tragedy, and that man was the innocent victim of circumstance. This is the most obvious answer, and one that occurred for instance to the Babylonians. They told the story of Adapa, the first man, their Adam. Adapa broke the wings of the South Wind, and was summoned to defend his action before Anu, the father of the gods. He was advised by the treacherous god Ea to rend his clothes as if in mourning, and to refuse all offers of bread and drink, but to accept the cloak and the vial of oil he would also be offered. Adapa obeyed these instructions, and his torn coat did in fact make a good impression on the council of gods. He was allowed to argue his case against the South Wind, who had treacherously attacked him and thrown him into the water as Adapa had gone about his peaceful business of fishing on a calm lake. Anu then offered Adapa the bread and the drink of life and with them, immortality. To Anu's utter astonishment, Adapa refused and accepted instead the cloak of mortality and the oil of human frailty. And so, as the Babylonian story has it, death came into the world. Poor Adapa could do little about it—his own god had betrayed him.

Another traditional account of the Fall is the Assyrian epic of Gilgamesh, the hero, who was so sorely afflicted by the death of his friend Enkidu that he roamed the world in search of the herb of life. At long last he chanced to pluck this miracle herb from the depths of the primeval ocean and, overjoyed, he returned to his home town. Tired and footsore as he was, he paused by a well for refreshment. He laid down the herb by his side, only to find that the serpent, that sly destroyer of life, had reared up and made off with it. With bowed head and heavy step Gilgamesh continued his journey. Now he knew that eternal life was not to be his. He, too, had been tricked out of eternity.

How different in comparison is the answer of our own Bible! True, Adam and Eve lost life everlasting, when they were cast out from Paradise. Nor was this their only punishment: Adam would henceforth have to eat bread by the sweat of his face, and Eve bring forth children in sorrow. But their suffering was not the result of chance events, nor the work of an evil power; it was man's own sin that had caused his downfall. The Almighty had planted a Garden of Eden for man, had given him a wife, and her a husband, and in return he had asked for obedience to but one commandment: Man could do as he pleased except eat the fruits of one tree, the tree of knowledge of good and evil, for that knowledge belongs to God alone. God had told them unequivocally: "Of every tree of the garden thou mayest freely eat: But of the tree of the knowledge of good and evil, thou shalt not eat of it: for in the day that thou eatest thereof thou shalt surely die" (Genesis 2:16-17). And still, they had broken this commandment; the woman, after having been tempted by the snake, and the man at his wife's bidding. It was then that the hidden cloak of God's glory was withdrawn from them, and they had to hide their shame behind the trees of the garden. Their fall was sad, but clearly they had only themselves to blame. Unlike Adapa and Gilgamesh, Adam and Eve were not the victims of an evil fate, but of their own self-willed sin.

And yet, the punishment was far less severe than they deserved. God made them coats of skin, and clothed them, so that they might live on earth. Their cloak was no longer God's invisible glory, nor was their life everlasting as heretofore, but still they were not irretrievably lost. The Garden-gate was shut to them, but not so the world outside with its sorrow, its hard work, and—its challenge.

4

Cain and Abel

THE story of Adam's two sons has no parallel in the literature of the East, and that is rather a pity, for the Biblical text leaves the reader to guess at the background against which the great drama was played out.

We read that Abel was a shepherd and Cain a tiller of the soil. Their very names hint at their future. "Abel" is a derivation of a Hebrew word that is best translated as vanity. Life is as ephemeral as the dew and no man's life more so than that of Abel. "Cain", on the other hand, resembles the Hebrew for smith, and desert smiths were typical wanderers like our own tinkers and gipsies. Thus the destinies of Cain and Abel were symbolised in their names, and later, in the Book of Ruth, we shall realise fully how the Old Testament delights in such symbolism.

Shepherd and farmer—each has his own sacrifice to bring. The Old Testament does not tell us why it pleased God to receive Abel's sacrifice rather than Cain's, and this has worried saints, scholars and Sunday-school teachers through the ages. For instance, we can read in St. Paul's Epistle to the Hebrews: "By faith Abel offered unto God a more excellent sacrifice than Cain, by which he obtained witness that he was righteous, God testifying of his gifts; and by it he being dead yet speaketh" (Hebrews 11:4).

Other commentators have spoken of smoke that rises and smoke that does not rise, and asserted that God Himself set light to Abel's sacrifice. Frankly, we do not know the answer, but we do know that even though Cain slew His favourite, God did not cast him out altogether. Though his brother's blood cried unto God from the ground, Cain was protected by the Lord Himself, for Cain had humbled himself, and the meek find salvation. "And the Lord set a mark upon Cain, lest any finding him should kill him" (Genesis 4:15). The Old Testament does not tell us what sort of mark it was, but some have spoken of the sign of the Cross. I cannot myself believe this, for there was nothing in Cain to remind us of the infinite mercy of Christ, who spoke of forgiving one's neighbour seventy times seven. Quite the

contrary is the case, for we can hear Cain's descendant Lamech
exclaim:

"... for I have slain a man to my wounding,
and a young man to my hurt.
If Cain shall be avenged sevenfold,
truly Lamech seventy and sevenfold."

(Genesis 4:23-24)

5

The Flood

WE shall discuss the Flood but briefly, though the Bible devotes four
whole chapters to it, sparing us no detail. Here are the length, the
breadth and the height of the Ark; the very day, month and year in
which the fountains of the great deep were broken up; the number of
cubits that the waters rose above the mountains, and the date on which
the waters abated again. While the Old Testament is generally distinguished by its concise language, the story of the Flood seems to miss
the wood for the trees of dates and figures.

The story of the Flood was widespread amongst the peoples of the
East. We have authentic documents to prove that the Sumerians knew
of it some 2,500 years before Christ. The names may differ and so may
some of the details, but by and large the story that was told throughout
Asia Minor was one and the same. People have often wondered about
the historic authenticity of this widespread tale. There has been a great
deal of speculation, particularly since ethnologists discovered that even
the Red Indians and the Eskimos told a similar story. Plato's legendary Atlantis was said to have connected the continents in primeval
times, and to this day there are societies that waste much time and
money in looking for the lost continent and for Noah's ark.

In point of fact, there is no scientific proof whatsoever that a flood
actually occurred—its acceptance is a matter of faith. Even so the
story of the Flood is worth while if only to illustrate the central and
distinctive part religion played in the life of Israel. According to the
Babylonian version the gods decided to get rid of all mankind in a fit

of madness. They unleashed so tremendous a flood that they themselves became terrified and took refuge in the highest heaven of their father, Anu. Here, we are told, they cringed like whipped dogs. However, one man, Utnapishtim of Shurrupak, and his family had been allowed to escape in an ark, and he only because the treacherous Ea had betrayed his fellow gods. When the gods learned that their plan to destroy mankind had misfired they roared with anger, but their wrath was quickly assuaged when Utnapishtim brought them a sweet offering round which they collected like so many flies around a honey-pot. For this was the way of the greedy and capricious gods of Babylon, to whom all life was like a bout in which no holds are barred.

The children of Israel must have heard this story along the caravan routes, for at night the traders would sit round the fire and exchange tales. They must have heard it in Assyrian captivity, and in Babylonian exile. There were a hundred and one ways in which the Hebrew peasant must have come into contact with the literature of his powerful neighbours. The children of Israel must have known the story of the Flood, and all the more remarkable, therefore, is their own version of it. Just compare chapter 6 of Genesis with the deplorable behaviour of the Babylonian gods:

"And God saw that the wickedness of man was great in the earth, and that every imagination of the thoughts of his heart was only evil continually. And it repented the Lord that he had made man on the earth, and it grieved him at his heart. And the Lord said, I will destroy man whom I have created from the face of the earth; both man, and beast, and the creeping thing, and the fowls of the air; for it repenteth me that I have made them. But Noah found grace in the eyes of the Lord" (Genesis 6:5-8).

The power of the malignant, divided and reprobate gods has here been swept away by the one God whose decisions are wise, and who in His sadness could not have decided otherwise. Thus did the Old Testament proclaim its message of faith not only to the ancient world, but to men throughout the ages. Nowadays we may have to do a little translating, for faith is reformulated anew by each successive generation. Perhaps our own faith must be couched in the modern idiom, and perhaps it is only thus that we can proclaim our trust in God the

All-Merciful, the Consoler and the Judge. Still we can do worse than follow in the footsteps of the writer of Genesis 6-9, who did not theorise about polytheism, nor argue against superstition and lack of faith, but simply retold an old story, and in so doing said everything that had to be said—implicitly but unequivocally.

The Biblical account of the Flood has a happy ending. When the worst was over, Noah made a burnt offering to the Lord, solemnly entering into a bond with Him. And the Lord set the rainbow in the cloud as the visible token of their covenant, saying: "This is the token of the covenant which I make between me and you and every living creature that is with you, for perpetual generations; I do set my bow in the cloud, and it shall be for a token of a covenant between me and the earth. And it shall come to pass, when I bring a cloud over the earth, that the bow shall be seen in the clouds: And I will remember my covenant, which is between me and you and every living creature of all flesh; and the waters shall no more become a flood to destroy all flesh" (Genesis 9:12-15). Man's history had begun afresh, but the seeds of evil were not uprooted. In his vineyard Noah drank of the ferm-ented juice of the grape, only to be mocked by his son Ham as he lay helpless and naked. Soon men in their presumption would start build-ing a tower, and find that their speech had turned to babbling. Yes, even after the Flood, man continued on his evil way and left none of God's commandments undefiled. Even so, there was a new hope, for up against the dark sky and across the barren and inhospitable earth, there now rose that glorious band of colour, the token of the covenant. And men knew that they could rely on the covenant, for it was eternal, just as eternal as He who had set it there.

6

The Tower of Babel

WE often speak of the conflict between town and country. Some people swear by large cities, for here alone, they claim, can they take part in the true cultural life of a civilised society. Others again prefer life in the country, where things are as peaceful as they can be in our troubled world. If we could have asked the authors of the Old Testament for their decision, they would have exclaimed one and all: the country without a doubt. Their dislike of town life becomes crystal clear from the very first pages of the Bible. For was not Cain who slew his brother also the builder of the first city?

After the Flood, man's misery was once more to be symbolised by the building of a city. Genesis 11 is usually misunderstood to refer to a tower rather than a city, but in verse 4 we can hear the people say to one another: "Go to, let us build us a city and a tower", and in verse 5 we can read that God himself came down "to see the *city* which the children of men builded".

The story actually takes us to the great and proud city of Babylon. Excavations have brought to light not only the city itself but a number of neighbouring towns also. All of them had one thing in common: strange towers, gross and ugly in appearance, dominating the entire landscape. The tower in Genesis 11, therefore, has a symbolic significance: it represents the city which man had built in his presumption. Such impertinence is decried by many Biblical writers, and we may read in Isaiah:

"For the day of the Lord of hosts shall be upon every one that is proud and lofty, and upon every one that is lifted up; and he shall be brought low; And upon all the cedars of Lebanon, that are high and lifted up, and upon all the oaks of Bashan; And upon all the high mountains; And upon all the hills that are lifted up, and upon every high tower, and upon every fenced wall. . . . And the loftiness of man shall be bowed down, and the haughtiness of men shall be made low: and the Lord alone shall be exalted in that day" (Isaiah 2:12-15; 17).

And indeed, presumption is an abomination unto God, for only those who go about their business humbly and modestly are pleasant in His sight. Because of this, the pious of the land had a horror of cities with their walls and gates, castles and towers, all of which were just so many tokens of man's conceit. Some scholars have interpreted this attitude as the obstinate resentment of simple peasants against the refinements of the city, and there is, no doubt, some truth in their interpretation. But even so the resentment was not simply based on jealousy, but on the profound religious belief that God is in His

C

Heaven above, and man on earth below, and that it did not behove man to build into the sky. Hence the sad ending of Babel and its tower, hence the sad confusion of tongues, and the resulting misunderstandings that could only lead to strife and division. Mankind was broken up into tribes and nations, and these waged constant war on one another. This is the irony of man's fate: he sets out to build a bulwark of unity and strength, and in the end he finds himself utterly defeated:

"So the Lord scattered them abroad from thence upon the face of all the earth: and they left off to build the city. Therefore is the name of it called Babel; because the Lord did there confound the language of all the earth: and from thence did the Lord scatter them abroad upon the face of all the earth" (Genesis 11:8-9).

These words, no doubt, meant more to the children of Israel than they do to us. Their world was inhabited by the Sumerians, a people of great talent and profound thought. They too have recorded their attitude to cities and buildings, but unlike the Jews, they admired city life, claiming that cities were created together with the world. Every god had appointed himself protector of a particular city and engaged a king as his earthly representative to rule over it. How different is their attitude from that of the Old Testament, which tells us that the first city builder was his brother's murderer and that a terrible fate befell those who built the proud Babel!

And then how cruel a play on words the Bible enjoys! The inhabitants of Babylon had called their city *Bab-ili*, the Gate of God. Through its gates God would surely enter to speak to the inhabitants. But the Old Testament scoffs at their conceit, as if to say: why, you with your Gate of God, your Bab-ili, are you deaf to the sound of quite another word, the word *balal* and do you not know what it means? Balal means confusion, and it was beneath your tower and under the walls of your city that the great confusion first began. From here marauding bands would attack the unsuspecting wayfarer. Your gates disgorged a never-ending stream of chariots and horsemen, of battering rams and endless columns of soldiery—how dare you speak of a Gate of God! You wished to build a tower of subjugation and force your speech upon all the world but all you managed to achieve in the end was—babble, utter confusion.

B. *The Forefathers*

7

Farewell to Ur of the Chaldees

Ur of the Chaldees was the name of the town in which Abraham was born and bred many thousands of years ago. A lonely pile of rubble still marks the spot, and the modern pilgrim will notice a host of ruined walls which archaeologists have laid bare to the scorching sun. Neither tree nor bush breaks the monotony of the landscape, and only when you climb right to the top of the ruins can you see one or two palms in the east, towards the Euphrates. You will also see a bump in the otherwise perfectly level ground—the hidden ruins of what was once the rich town of Eridu. But westwards all is as barren and desolate as it was before the day of Creation. As far as the eye can see all is inhospitable desert.

A keen imagination is needed to conjure up the busy past amongst these ruins—the milling crowds, the streets and squares, houses, temples, palaces, and the city towers on whose first battlements we can stand to this very day. But even the most imaginative of us will be hard put to it to believe that the city was once criss-crossed by canals. The Euphrates has since changed its course and no longer flows close to the walls of Ur of the Chaldees, and the sea has retreated some sixty miles. In Abraham's time Ur had two harbours, and knew the hustle and bustle of ships and their crews.

The inhabitants of Ur were not only rich but very pious also. Their main deity was Sin, god of the moon, and not surprisingly the heavenly bodies took pride of place in their religious life. The night-sky of these regions is rarely overcast and the stars twinkle more brightly than we in the West would ever believe possible. Abraham, we remember, was led out of his tent and told: "Look now toward heaven, and tell the stars, if thou be able to number them: and he said unto him, So shall thy seed be" (Genesis 15:5). And of all the heavenly bodies, the moon alone could light the path of those who travelled in the night, and night travel was the order of their scorching day. Still, the night was full of danger and the moon had to be flattered into sending her soft, friendly light across the wide desert so to protect the nomads who travelled under her guidance.

Abraham too was a born nomad. The Old Testament is a little uncertain about this, for while at one point it tells us that it was Terah, Abraham's father, who went out from Ur of the Chaldees, elsewhere we are told that Abraham himself was called out of Ur by God. In any case, Abraham's clan could not bear to live within the city walls, among the narrow streets and high buildings. Adventure and the freedom of the desert called them, and bade them trust in the light of the moon-god just as their forefathers before them had done.

By all rights, this step ought to have earned them oblivion, for history is made by townsmen and not by roaming nomads in the desert. But a great miracle happened, and as we stand on the ruins that were once Ur of the Chaldees we do not remember its kings in their palaces, its priests with all their learning, or its goldsmiths, and accomplished poets and writers, but one of its most humble citizens— Abraham the exile.

When we think of Abraham, we remember the great occasion that earned him the title of Patriarch, the hour when he abandoned his moon-god for God the Almighty whose light shines forth as the sun, and whose power is not restricted to any one city alone. We are at a loss to explain why Abraham of all people obeyed the call when it came, or rather why his response to God was the only one the Old Testament thought worth recording.

The story is told in a few words, simple and clear: "Now the Lord had said unto Abram, Get thee out of thy country, and from thy kindred, and from thy father's house, unto a land that I will shew thee. . . . So Abram departed, as the Lord had spoken unto him . . . and Abram was seventy and five years old . . ." (Genesis 12:1 and 4). It reads just like an official deportation order—an old man of seventy-five being told to take his family to an unknown destination. And Abraham went without a murmur. Yes, Abraham ought to have been forgotten by history the moment he passed through the gates of Ur of the Chaldees, for he was deserting civilisation. But Abraham was the beginning of something that has affected all civilisations, something greater than any one of them, and so we remember him, while the town from which he sprang lies a forgotten pile of rubble under the desert sun.

8

The Women of Israel

WE should now be turning our attention to Sarah, wife of Abraham, and mother of Isaac. But Sarah has become a household word; so much so that we tend to forget the other model wives of the Old Testament: Rebecca, wife of Isaac, Rachel, wife of Jacob, and Zipporah, wife of Moses. Wives and mothers one and all, each typifies the role of woman in the ancient East.

Actually the discovery of legal codes from as far back as the twentieth century B.C. makes it clear that the position of women had somewhat deteriorated by the time the Israelites appeared on the scene. Thus under the law of Moses a man could put away his wife for no better reason than that she had ceased to please him. He was required only to hand her a "letter of divorcement" which gave her the right to remarry. On the other hand, by one of the laws of King Bilalama—who ruled near Babylon in about 1950 B.C.—a man wishing to leave a wife who had borne him children was obliged to leave all his possessions to her; and by the code of Hammurabi (eighteenth century B.C.) a wife was allowed to sue for a divorce if she could produce reliable evidence that her husband had committed adultery.

Yet, though the Israelite woman had few legal safeguards, her role must not be minimised. Deborah, for instance, who lived in the time of the Judges, was strong enough and respected enough to dispel the half-heartedness and doubt of the scattered tribes and to unite them in struggle against the common enemy. Women became prophets to proclaim the word of God, they were influential queens, and their tact and kindness went a long way towards mitigating the evil that men did. Thus in II Samuel 14 we can read how the wise woman of Tekoa managed to bring Absalom back to David and in II Samuel 20 how a woman of Abel pacified Joab, thus saving her town and fellow-citizens from certain destruction. Yes, woman's power was still great in the world of the Old Testament, and even the story of her expulsion from Paradise bears this out clearly. The pity is that half her sentence was pronounced quite out of context. I am firmly convinced that her punishment ought to have read like this: "And God said, I will greatly multiply thy sorrow and thy conception; in sorrow thou shalt bring forth children; and thy desire shall be to thy husband, and he shall rule over thee; *even as his desire will be unto thee and thou shalt rule over him.*" You will look in vain for the last phrase in Genesis 3:16, but you need only turn the page to find it at the end of Genesis 4:7, where it is mentioned in connection with Cain's offering and makes no sense at all.

Woman's power is also stressed in the first Book of Esdras, where we read about three young men of King Darius's guard who had to write down whom they thought strongest in the world. The first wrote that wine was the mightiest of all, the second that the king was even stronger, and the third that woman surpassed both in might, adding that truth reigned supreme even over her. Asked to plead their cause before the entire court, the palm went to him who had spoken in praise of women and truth. No wonder, for just listen how eloquently he put his case:

"O ye men, it is not the great king, nor the multitude of men, neither is it wine, that excelleth; who is it then that ruleth them, or hath the lordship over them? are they not women? Women have borne the king and all the people that bear rule by sea and land. Even of them came they: and they nourished them up that planted the vineyards, from whence the wine cometh. These also make garments for men; these bring glory unto men; and without women cannot men be. Yea, and if men have gathered together gold and silver, or any other goodly thing, do they not love a woman which is comely in favour and beauty? And letting all those things go, do they not gape, and even with open mouth fix their eyes fast on her; and have not all men more desire unto her than unto silver or gold, or any goodly thing whatsoever? A man leaveth his own father that brought him up, and his own country, and cleaveth unto his wife. He sticketh not to spend his life with his wife, and remembereth neither father, nor mother, nor country. By this also ye must know that women have dominion over you: do ye not labour and toil, and give and bring all to the women. Yea a man taketh his sword, and goeth his way to rob and to steal, to sail upon the sea and upon rivers; And looketh upon a lion, and goeth in the darkness; and when he hath stolen, spoiled, and robbed, he bringeth it to his love.

Wherefore a man loveth his wife better than father or mother. Yea, many there be that have run out of their wits for women, and become servants for their sakes. Many also have perished, have erred, and sinned, for women. And now do ye not believe me? is not the king great in his power? do not all regions fear to touch him? Yet did I see him and Apame the king's concubine, the daughter of the admirable Bartacus, sitting at the right hand of the king, And taking the crown from the king's head, and setting it upon her own head; she also struck the king with her left hand. And yet for all this the king gaped and gazed upon her with open mouth: if she laughed upon him, he laughed also: but if she took any displeasure at him, the king was fain to flatter, that she might be reconciled to him again. O ye men, how can it be but women should be strong, seeing they do thus?" (I Esdras 4:14-22).

Here the young man drew breath before beginning his hymn to truth, which, to be honest, was not half so inspiring.

Naturally, conditions at the luxurious court of Susa or Persepolis, could not be compared with those in Abraham's tent, but even the less polished Israelites spoke highly in praise of women:

> "Who can find a virtuous woman?
> for her price is far above rubies.
> The heart of her husband doth safely trust in her,
> so that he shall have no need of spoil.
> She will do him good and not evil
> all the days of her life."
>
> (Proverbs 31:10-12)

In the ensuing description of women's tasks, it appears as if nothing at all was left for man to do. And indeed, he had little to complain of, for thanks to his wife he could spend the day sitting by the gate of the town passing weighty judgments, and playing a leading part in public life.

Just look what the good housewife was expected to do:

> "She seeketh wool, and flax,
> and worketh willingly with her hands.
> She is like the merchants' ships;
> she bringeth her food from afar.

She riseth also while it is yet night,
and giveth meat to her household,
and a portion to her maidens.
She considereth a field, and buyeth it:
with the fruit of her hands she planteth a vineyard.
She girdeth her loins with strength,
and strengtheneth her arms.

.   .   .   .   .

She is not afraid of the snow for her household:
for all her household are clothed with scarlet.

.   .   .   .

Strength and honour are her clothing;
and she shall rejoice in time to come.
She openeth her mouth with wisdom;
and in her tongue is the law of kindness.

.   .   .   .

Her children arise up, and call her blessed;
her husband also, and he praiseth her.
Many daughters have done virtuously,
but thou excellest them all.

.   .   .   .

Give her of the fruit of her hands;
and let her own works praise her in the gates."
(Proverbs 31:13-17; 21; 25-26; 28-29; 31)

No, it was no small part that Sarah played by Abraham's side, or
Rebecca by Isaac's, or that the host of women who came in their train
played in the desert and in the Promised Land. We may see them by
the side of judges and kings, priests and prophets, or else shining in
their own light as they stand head and shoulders above the rest. Their
voice commands respect, their word is mighty. And the Old Testament never forgets that woman's rightful place was assured her from
the very beginning by God himself; for is it not written: "So God
created man in his own image, in the image of God created he him;
male and female created he them"? Clearly the children of Israel were
far less loath to acknowledge the profound place of women in the
scheme of things than Synagogue and Church have been ever since.

9

Abraham's Sacrifice

THE Bible tells us that Abraham and Sarah were granted a child very late in life, so late in fact that they could not rightly expect to be given a second one. Isaac therefore was not merely their first child but also their only child; he was the apple of his parents' eye. And yet Abraham, the loving father, was given the cruel and unexpected order to sacrifice his dearest possession:

"Take now thy son, thine only son Isaac, whom thou lovest, and get thee into the land of Moriah; and offer him there for a burnt offering upon one of the mountains which I will tell thee of" (Genesis 22:2).

There follows the laconic report that Abraham rose early the next morning, saddled his ass and, taking two of his servants and Isaac, went out to the place of which God had told him. Not by a single word does the Old Testament betray the emotions that must have choked the distressed parent. God had spoken and Abraham had answered—that was all. Throughout the whole story, the human element is played down; there are no tears of sorrow, there is no one to feel Abraham's heart beat with anxiety or later with relief. The child Isaac himself is made to carry the wood, while his father holds torch and knife ready. They exchange only the barest words, Isaac saying: "My father" and Abraham replying "Here am I, my son". And when the child asks: "Behold the fire and the wood: but where is the lamb for a burnt offering?" his father glibly reassures him: "My son, God will provide himself a lamb for a burnt offering" (Genesis 22:7-8). And still no sign of emotion.

Many people have taken exception to this story. When I was studying in Germany at the beginning of the Hitler régime, we were told that this story was clear evidence of the pernicious Jewish spirit which pervades the entire Bible. Ostensibly the Nazis wished to scrap Genesis 22, but in fact they would have liked to renounce the whole of the Old Testament, though they were not yet ready to say so openly.

I was always incensed by such criticism, coming as it did from men who had little enough regard for the sanctity of human life. Indeed, it astonished me to realise how the story of Abraham's sacrifice seemed to offend those who saw nothing wrong in sacrificing tens of thousands of their own sons on the altar of their god of war. Clearly, they must have had some inkling of the real meaning of this story: the need for absolute obedience to the will of Almighty God.

In point of fact the happy ending of Abraham's trial is implicit from the very beginning: "And it came to pass after these things, that God did tempt Abraham." God, far from wanting human sacrifice, desired only to test Abraham's faith. Throughout the Old Testament there is no other passage in which human, let alone child, sacrifice is demanded, and, indeed, there are a great many passages in which such sacrifices are decried as abominations in the eyes of the Lord. Now civilised man might take it for granted that the Almighty, Omniscient, and Merciful God could not possibly have accepted anything quite so horrible as human sacrifice, but to the ancients this was far from self-evident. The Old Testament tells us of many heathen idols who demanded just such offerings. Thus we can read that Hiel built the foundations of Jericho on Abiram his first-born, and the gates on his youngest son Segub (I Kings 16:34) and that the King of Moab offered up his son for a burnt offering to his god (II Kings 3:27).

Excavations have proved beyond a doubt that such stories were no mere Israelite fabrications. Not only beneath the houses in Jericho, but elsewhere in Palestine, archaeologists have dug up the remains of so-called "building-sacrifices". Remains of children in jars were found under doors and thresholds, the concrete tokens of a horrible custom illustrating the dark side of man's faith. But the Old Testament itself has throughout taken a firm stand against this monstrous custom. For when the people of Judah, during a desperate war against Babylon, were misguided enough to offer up children in the valley of Hinnom, called "Ge-Hinnom" in Hebrew, the valley gained so bad a name that Gehenna, a contraction of Ge-Hinnom, became the Hell of the New Testament. Jeremiah was only one of the prophets to fulminate against this monstrous custom, saying in God's name that such sacrifices made the land unclean. And that was precisely the outcome of Abraham's tribulation also, a voice out of heaven calling out to him: "Lay not thine hand upon the lad, neither do thou any thing unto him: for now

I know that thou fearest God, seeing thou hast not withheld thy son, thine only son from me" (Genesis 22:12).

We must, therefore, turn our attention to the only thing that matters: Abraham's trial. Trials of faith are invariably the most agonising experiences any believer can have, for whenever God apparently breaks the word He has given, the whole world seems to collapse. Now, Abraham was given a son, and with him a promise, for he had been told: "Look now toward heaven, and tell the stars, if thou be able to number them; and he said unto him, So shall thy seed be" (Genesis 15:5). Abraham had placed his trust in this promise, and God had apparently broken it. Where, then, did Abraham gain the strength to obey without despairing? Why did he not rebel and protest unto the Lord, arguing against Him just as Jeremiah and Job had dared to argue against Him? It will always be difficult to answer this question satisfactorily, but the last words on the subject are probably found in the Epistle to the Hebrews, where we can read: "By faith Abraham, when he was tried, offered up Isaac: and he that had received the promises offered up his only begotten son, Of whom it was said, That in Isaac shall thy seed be called: Accounting that God was able to raise him up, even from the dead; from whence also he received him in a figure" (Hebrews 11:17-19).

The Jewish rabbis, too, had roughly the same attitude, and this is borne out by a drawing of Abraham's sacrifice in Beth-Alpha, a spot halfway between Samaria and the Sea of Galilee. Here a sixth-century synagogue was once decorated with mosaics, one of which is shown in Fig. 1. Some readers might object that no Rabbi would ever have tolerated such pictures in a synagogue, because orthodox Jews have always adhered to the letter of the commandment: "Thou shalt not make unto thee any graven image, or any likeness of any thing." In actual fact, those Rabbis must have interpreted the commandment as it was originally meant: images were quite permissible even in the house of prayer, so long only as they were not worshipped like heathen idols.

Similar decorations were discovered in many other places as well and they show us clearly how the Jews in the early Christian era interpreted the Old Testament. Let us therefore look more closely at page 44. From left to right are shown Abraham's servants and the ass, the ram tied in a thicket, and finally Abraham himself holding a knife

The sacrifice of Isaac: after a Jewish mosaic. (VIth century A.D.)

in one hand and Isaac his only child in the other. The altar is already lit, its flames leaping upwards. God's hand is shown to be guiding the entire tableau. The Hebrew letters near the hand of God are the original text of "Lay not thine hand . . ."

The most significant part of the whole picture is the ram, which stands ready to take Isaac's place. Just look again at Genesis 22, one of the most gripping chapters in the entire Old Testament. We are taken along the road from Abraham's house to the distant land of Moriah, we listen to the short conversation between father and child, who "went both of them together". And quite unexpectedly a voice from out of heaven proclaims release, and only then does Abraham see the ram, accidentally caught by its horns in a thicket.

Now the Rabbis of Beth-Alpha clearly thought otherwise. For them it was beyond question that the ram was no accident. Similarly, the Talmud is quite explicit in stating that God had held this ram in readiness, even before the Creation. Men of little faith may well ask in fear and trembling whether the Lord is not an arbitrary despot who plays a cat and mouse game with mankind—the pious know better. Everything is pre-ordained. Therefore—say the Rabbis—the mountain of our terrifying drama was called Moriah, a name derived from the Hebrew verb "to see". God's decisions are neither sudden whims nor accidents; the Lord beholds all things long before they happen.

10

The Ten Righteous Men

I SHALL never forget the evening when I first reached the Dead Sea. On its southern shore I could see the ridge of rock-salt, the Ridge of Sodom, some seven miles long and 300 feet high. The stars and the crescent moon were just rising and I felt as if I had been cast into another, ghostly, world. Next morning it struck me how much the salt wall resembled the wall of a Gothic cathedral, and how, with a little imagination, one could conjure up the picture of a woman turned into a pillar—Lot's wife.

It was desolately still in this "hole in the ground", some thousand feet below sea level; not even the song of a solitary bird broke through the silence. Everything was salt, and even my hands were caked with it. Nothing can grow or flourish here, and even the clouds shun this region. Though no trace of human civilisation has ever been discovered hereabouts, ancient travellers, horror-struck as they passed by, made it the setting of Sodom and Gomorrah, two cities that perished because of the wrath of God.

Once upon a time, the Bible tells us, this sea of salt had been a fertile plain with green pastures and well-filled fields. No wonder then, that when offered a choice of land by his uncle Abraham, Lot immediately plumped for Sodom and Gomorrah. And prosperity may even now return to this region. The modern state of Israel, having discovered that the Dead Sea is rich in potash, has set up an industry to exploit this mineral, though the works have had to be closed because of tension with Israel's Arab neighbours.

It is characteristic of the Old Testament that it does not blame the tragedy on a natural calamity or a war, but on man's transgressions alone. Sodom and Gomorrah were destroyed through the deserved anger of the Almighty.

The climax of the story comes when God makes Abraham privy to His intentions. The dialogue between the patriarch and his God is perhaps the strangest and at the same time the most profound conversation between God and man in the whole of the Bible. "Wilt thou also destroy the righteous with the wicked?" Abraham asked. "Peradventure there be fifty righteous within the city: wilt thou also destroy and not spare the place for the fifty righteous that are therein? That be far from thee to do after this manner, to slay the righteous with the wicked: and that the righteous should be as the wicked, that be far from thee: Shall not the Judge of all the earth do right?" (Genesis 18:23-25). And so convincing were his arguments that the Almighty Judge of the universe was won over, and said: "If I find in Sodom fifty righteous within the city, then I will spare all the place for their sakes" (Genesis 18:26). But Abraham, still dissatisfied, began to bargain, albeit with his tongue in his cheek: "Behold now," he said, "I have taken upon me to speak unto the Lord, which am but dust and ashes: Peradventure there shall lack five of the fifty righteous: twilt thou destroy all the city for lack of five?" (Genesis 18:27-28). And like a typical Eastern trader, he continued to beat the Lord down to forty, thirty, twenty, and finally to only ten righteous men. His attitude strikes us as a little too mercenary and unbecoming. But God listened with the utmost patience, for to God man may safely divulge his deepest desires. And in the end, the Lord agreed to spare the city for the sake of only ten.

What follows is not really of equal importance. Apparently Sodom and Gomorrah lacked even ten righteous men, and they were laid waste. The crux of the whole matter is the problem of the righteous men. Though thousands may go their godless ways, though nations may defile God's every commandment, so long only as ten righteous men remain, honest and brave, the sinners are as nothing. On the scales of divine justice, ten righteous men weigh far heavier than thousands of transgressors.

This train of thought runs throughout the whole of the Old Testament. Prophets, poets, and historians keep reiterating the fact that a handful of pious men can save whole nations. Through the bruises of the Lord's servant we are healed, for our deserved chastisement was upon him (see Isaiah 53:5).

II

The Ladder that Reached up to the Sky

WHILE the Bible tells us but little about Isaac, the son of Abraham, it devotes a great deal of attention to Jacob, and particularly to two critical nights in his life, and the years between them, during which he became a servant for Rachel's sake. The first night (Genesis 28) takes us to Bethel and the second describes the wrestling with a stranger near the ford of Jabbok (Genesis 32).

Let us first examine Jacob's vision near Bethel. At the time, Jacob was on his way to Haran, the land of his mother across the Euphrates. This was a dangerous mission, for who could tell if the local gods would protect one across the border? Abraham's simple faith in God's omnipresence was not inherited by Jacob, for faith must be born anew with each generation. This is precisely what his vision was about.

On the night in question, then, the sun having set, Jacob was forced to sleep in the open, a stone as his pillow. That night he had a strange dream. He saw a ladder stretching right into the sky and God's angels dancing upon it. This vision is of great importance to Biblical scholars and psychologists alike, and we must leave it to them to fathom the meaning of each element of the dream. We shall instead examine one fact only: when God revealed Himself it was night. All religions know that night brings divine counsel and that its stillness and stark mystery strike man with the blinding light of revelation.

And this is what Jacob was told:

"I am the Lord God of Abraham thy father, and the God of Isaac: the land whereon thou liest, to thee will I give it, and to thy seed; And thy seed shall be as the dust of the earth, and thou shalt spread abroad to the west, and to the east, and to the north, and to the south: and in thee and in thy seed shall all the families of the earth be blessed. And, behold, I am with thee, and will keep thee in all places whither thou goest, and will bring thee again into this land; for I will not leave thee, until I have done that which I have spoken to thee of" (Genesis 28:13-15).

D

This solemn pledge makes up the spiritual weight of the whole story; the rest was but the setting, colourful and fitting though it may have been.

For Jacob, who had tricked his brother out of his birthright and out of his father's blessing, Jacob, whose brother's tears would for ever pursue him, knew that he was not cast out by God and that the Lord would go with him to even the farthest corners of the world. Much pain and trouble still awaited him. Soon, in the house of Laban, he, the deceiver, would himself be deceived. But pain and trouble would henceforth purify and strengthen Jacob for his work. In Bethel the future had lost all its threat, for Jacob knew that God was travelling with him, as once He had travelled with Abraham and Isaac.

12

Seven Short Years

THE Bible gives an unusually vivid account of Jacob's first meeting with Rachel. The story puts us in mind of a pastoral poem. They met by the well, that centre of village life. Here the womenfolk would come at dawn or dusk, and fill their pitchers, while the shepherds watered their charges. It was by just such a well that Abraham's servant found Isaac a wife, and it was by a water-hole that Moses found the daughters of Jethro. Christ's meeting with the Samaritan woman, too, took place by a well. In general the wells were very deep and the pitchers had to be lowered into them on a rope. To this day we can still see some of the stone-work into which the ropes have cut deep grooves in the course of centuries. Here shepherds fought bloody feuds, here men and women fell in love, here village scandals flourished, and here, on his first day in Haran, Jacob met the woman with whom he would fall in love and for whom he would gladly sacrifice many years of his life. The Old Testament never tries to analyse feelings of hatred and love, suffering and joy; it simply tells us the facts. Rachel took Jacob back with her to the house of her father Laban, where he was received with characteristic hospitality, and made a welcome guest for a month. Then Laban made a business-like suggestion: Jacob was to work for him, and he had but to name his price. Jacob's reply came quite unexpectedly: he would gladly serve seven years for his beautiful cousin Rachel, Laban's younger daughter. "And Jacob served seven years for Rachel; and they seemed unto him but a few days, for the love he had to her." This was the first Biblical hymn to earthly love although the Old Testament has many such. For what else is the Song of Solomon but a number of jubilant verses that sing of a love such as Jacob's, who served seven years for a woman, and yet felt that they passed as a few days. People have tried to make these songs more palatable to nice people, by explaining them away as allegories, as allusions to Jesus Christ, the bridegroom, and the Church, His bride. But all such interpretations, no matter how profound, pious and learned, pervert the down-to-earth zest for life of the Old Testament.

Monogamy was not the rule of the Old Testament, and Abraham, Jacob and Moses all had more than one wife each. We hear that Solomon went very much further than this, but here the Bible draws the line, and ascribes his idolatry to the influence of his countless foreign wives. Monogamy, however, became more common in practice, though some backward Jewish communities continue polygamy to this day. Not so long ago the Israel government was placed in a dilemma when a great number of polygamous Jews from the Yemen were flown in by air-lift. A law had to be passed whereby no women could be taken away from their husbands, though no new polygamous marriages could be contracted. Polygamy does not necessarily mean the denigration of love or marriage, and this was certainly not the case with the Israelites or any other Eastern people. Indeed, the famous code of the Babylonian King Hammurabi (about 1700 B.C.), provided full safeguards for every one of the many legitimate wives a man might have. The idea that men might see their wives unveiled only after marriage arose out of the story of Isaac and Rebecca (Genesis 24:65), yet the story of Jacob and Rachel makes it clear that this custom was not the rule, for who would have served seven years for a woman he had never seen?

When the seven years were up and the wedding ceremony over, Jacob found that he had been wed to Leah, Rachel's elder sister. Laban excused his scandalous deceit by saying that the custom of his land did not allow the younger daughter to marry first. This was true enough, but it was somewhat late in the day to tell Jacob. Still, Jacob forgave Laban immediately when he was told that Rachel, too, could become his wife, and what is more, immediately, if he but served another seven years. There is a great deal of tragedy in the story of Rachel and Leah: the tragedy of Leah the unloved wife who would have to spend a life of sorrow by the side of a husband who had never wanted her. The Authorised Version actually calls her a "hated" woman, but this is an exaggerated translation. All the same, Leah's lot was hard, nor, for that matter, was Rachel's life entirely untroubled, and to make things worse Jacob's relationship with Laban was becoming more and more strained. Now, why had Laban gone out of his way to cheat Jacob? No doubt because he had realised that his son-in-law seemed to have been born under a special star. All his works prospered, and he was clearly one of God's blessed few. Laban would gladly have shared in this blessing, and no doubt this was the reason why he tried to enslave him. But Jacob was longing for his freedom and for the far-away land of Abraham and Isaac. He was ready to answer God's call when it came, and took his wives back to his own land, confident that the Lord would be with them.

13

Joseph and His Brothers

OF the thirteen children that Jacob fathered, one was destined to play a most important part. His name was Joseph, and he overshadowed all his brothers and his sister. His path to glory and power was anything but smooth, and it was only after many trials and tribulations that he gained a position of power and trust in the land of Egypt. When we first meet him (Genesis 37) he is a seventeen-year-old boy, spoilt by his father, hated by his brothers, and given to speaking ill of others. To make things worse he has an insufferable conceit and dreams of himself as the elect of his house. Dreams are a recurrent theme in the story of Joseph. Joseph dreams, and later, in Egyptian captivity, the Pharaoh's butler and baker dream, and even the King himself is given to dreaming. Now, we may say that dreams are liars, but the ancients looked upon these nocturnal visions as revelations of a higher and divine reality. While we may sometimes marvel at the vanity of life, thinking it but a dream, the ancients believed that dreams revealed the true meaning of life. Modern depth-psychology is beginning to reconcile these views, for when psychologists carefully analyse their patients' dreams, they do so in the hope of learning something about the hidden life that goes on below the threshold of consciousness. Though their methods and objects are quite unlike those of Pharaoh's soothsayers, psychologists, too, know that dreams are not always deceptive.

They would have had little difficulty in interpreting the meaning of Joseph's dreams, and particularly the meaning of the dream Joseph told to his brothers: "Hear, I pray you, this dream which I have dreamed: For, behold, we were binding sheaves in the field, and, lo, my sheaf arose, and also stood upright; and, behold, your sheaves stood round about, and made obeisance to my sheaf" (Genesis 37:6-7). Surely it was bad enough for Joseph to have dreams like this without having to boast about them! But Joseph's vanity was so great, and he so naïve that he noticed nothing of the antagonism he was arousing and saw nothing wrong with recounting further dreams as well.

"Behold, I have dreamed a dream more; and, behold, the sun and the moon and the eleven stars made obeisance to me."

This was too much even for his doting father, who told him reproachfully:

"What is this dream that thou hast dreamed? Shall I and thy mother and thy brethren indeed come to bow down ourselves to thee to the earth?" (Genesis 37:9-10).

Wisely Joseph forebore to reply, and his father did just what the Virgin Mary did after the birth of Our Lord: he kept these things locked in his heart with the secret suspicion that they might be true, after all.

Joseph's dream of the sun, the moon and the eleven stars also has great psychological significance, though some scholars have said that the eleven stars simply represented the twelve signs of the zodiac, one of which was invisible. Now, the contemplation of the heavens could not have been the mainspring of this dream. It might have been that in Babylon, the home of astrology, but not in Israel. No, the theme of Joseph's dreams was his tremendous egocentricity, the idea of his own shining light surrounded by his father, mother and eleven brothers. His self-adulation was such that the heavens alone could supply its proper symbols. While we must sympathise with Joseph's brothers, we must also remember the rabbinical dictum that man can serve God with both the good and the bad sides of his nature.

The second act of our drama was played out in the vicinity of Dothan. We can still find this little place on the map, north of Samaria, the former capital, now called Sebastye. Here lay the great caravan route connecting Egypt with Asia Minor and Mesopotamia. Here traders would come and go, and water their beasts. In Joseph's time, they probably did not use the camel, for as far as we can tell it had not yet been domesticated. The camel, which is capable of going without water for three consecutive days, was to cause a revolution in transport, from which King Solomon was later to profit greatly. But in earlier times traders had to make do with the vagaries of asses and it surprises us how widespread trade was despite this unreliable and unpredictable means. Thus, for instance, amber from the far-away Baltic could be sold to the royal palace of Nineveh.

But to return to Dothan. What happened there is too well known to need retelling. Bloodshed was barely avoided, and the "master-dreamer" thrown into a dried-up well instead. The Bible stresses the callousness of Joseph's brothers, by relating that when the evil deed was done, and the helpless Joseph left to starve at the bottom of the well, "they sat down to eat bread" (Genesis 37:25). Could there be a more ironical and yet more poignant description of the crass indifference into which jealousy may turn brotherly love? Or a clearer warning against fathers showing marked preference for one of their children? Fortunately a caravan passed by—the Old Testament speaks of it interchangeably as being Ishmaelite and Midianite—and Judah suggested they sell Joseph for twenty pieces of silver. It is difficult to convert this sum into modern currency, but by comparison with, for instance, Leviticus 27:1-7, Joseph must have been sold very cheaply indeed.

This act of our drama ends with the tale of Jacob's woe as he is shown Joseph's bloodstained coat. About Joseph's emotions the Old Testament says nothing. It is the father's grief alone that we are allowed to feel.

We must look upon chapter 38 of Genesis as an interlude, for it is only in chapter 39 that we get another glimpse of Joseph, now a servant of Potiphar, one of the Pharaoh's officers. Betrayed and falsely accused by Potiphar's wife, whose love he had refused, Joseph is thrown into gaol. At this point, and in later passages, the Old Testament gives us an excellent account of Egyptian conditions. The mention of names and titles and the description of the political organisation of that strange empire together with all sorts of less important details make it clear that the writer was either very well acquainted with local conditions, or else that he copied freely from Egyptian sources. Actually, the story of Joseph and Potiphar's wife bears a striking resemblance to an Egyptian story about two brothers. This story was discovered in 1862, on the papyrus now kept in the British Museum. It dates from about the thirteenth century B.C., a time not too remote from that of the Patriarchs, and tells of two brothers, one married, the other single. The single brother served in his brother's house, and his great strength and virility so inflamed his sister-in-law's passion that she approached the young man in roughly the same way that Potiphar's wife approached Joseph. But he, too, rejected the woman's love and returned instead to his work in the field. When the elder brother came home in the evening he found his wife in a pitiful state. "She poured not water on his hands as had been her wont, nor did she kindle the light so that his house lay in darkness, and she herself a broken woman." Hearing her false accusation against his brother, her husband, like Potiphar, became terribly enraged and decided to put his brother to death. But when the younger brother returned home in the evening, quite without any suspicions, the cattle warned him of his impending danger as he locked them up for the night. He decided to flee from his brother, and called on the god Ra to protect him. "And Ra heard his prayers and caused a great water to rise up between him and the elder brother, and the water was full of crocodiles, and one brother stood on the hither side of the river and the other on the yonder side, and the elder beat his hands in rage." From then on the story grows wings, until in the end the younger brother's son becomes Pharaoh of Egypt. The rest has little bearing on the story of Joseph, but clearly this Egyptian fable runs a close parallel to the Biblical account. The revenge of women crossed in love must quite obviously have been a general theme, but we must return to our specific case.

While still in prison, Joseph managed to make a name for himself by interpreting the dreams of courtiers and even of the Pharaoh himself. Then, we are told, he rose quite unexpectedly to very great heights of power. Now his meteoric career is not borne out by any existing Egyptian records, though, surely, so miraculous a rise on the part of a stranger was bound to have attracted the attention of historians. In my considered opinion, then, we must look on Joseph's career as a Biblical illustration of God's loving-kindness, rather than as strict historical fact. Be that as it may, the story is certainly told in a masterful way. The first encounter in Egypt between Joseph and his brothers, who had long ago given him up for dead, is told with breathtaking dramatic skill. Joseph suddenly realises the truth and can hardly restrain himself from revealing his identity. The suspense is kept up until after the brothers' second visit to Egypt. Here, the writer wanted his readers—or probably his listeners—to hang on his every word, and so, just before the denouement he interrupts the story with a wordy repetition of perfectly well-known events, straining the reader's patience almost to the limit.

Egyptian paintings give us a very fair idea of what Joseph's brothers must have looked like. The Egyptians had good reason to look down on the people who inhabited Palestine during the years 2000 to 1500 B.C., for one Sinuhe, who had cause to flee from Egypt in about that period, took refuge with a Bedouin sheik, and recorded his impressions for posterity. While praising the hospitality of his hosts, he felt impelled to deplore their bad manners and loud voices. And the selfsame Sinuhe waxed almost lyrical when, in his old age, he was allowed to return to his homeland. He could not give thanks enough for at last being able to take a bath again, to anoint his body with good oil, and to wear a decent linen coat. Excavations in Palestine have confirmed many of Sinuhe's findings, and we can understand why the Egyptians refused to share their tables with such barbarians and why they segregated them to a special province—the land of Goshen. All the more strange, therefore, is the story that Joseph had no difficulty in presenting his father and some of his brothers to the Pharaoh himself, so that Jacob, when asked by the Pharaoh how old he was, could reply: "The days of the years of my pilgrimage are an hundred and thirty years: few and evil have the days of the years of my life been . . ." (Genesis 47:9).

After their father's death, the brothers were convinced that Joseph would be revenged upon them, but they were quite wrong. "Ye thought evil against me," he reassured them, "but God meant it unto good." A pious thought, no doubt, but not altogether human and devoid of all signs of feeling. We get the impression that Joseph was simply thumbing his nose at his brothers.

But then it appears that our chronicler rather than Joseph himself was responsible for this impression, for Joseph, by bursting into tears, showed that he was full of brotherly love. For the writer of the story Joseph was but the divine means of saving Israel from starvation. All his faults were as nothing before the great aim: to tide the chosen people through the most perilous times, and to protect the seed that would soon bear a rich harvest. Hence the emphatic conclusion of the Book of Genesis that all was meant "to bring to pass, as it is this day, to save much people alive".

C. The Exodus from Egypt

14

Israel and Egypt

Two mysteries surround Israel's stay in the land of the Nile, one of which is the silence of the Egyptians about events which ought to have made a deep impression on them. Joseph's position of viceroy, the ten plagues and the catastrophic defeat of the Egyptian army could surely not have gone unnoticed by all local historians. Of course their silence could have been due to the inglorious outcome of the episode, and it was, indeed, considered the task of the historian to ignore anything that might reflect badly on his nation. In fact both Egyptians and Mesopotamians kept strictly to this rule, and the Old Testament set quite a new fashion by daring to report Israel's defeats and the weaknesses of its kings, including even those of King David. All the same, some obscure reference to the Exodus ought surely to have crept into the Egyptian records.

The second mystery lies in the converse fact that the culture and religion of Egypt failed to make any apparent impression on Israel. So long a stay in a foreign land ought surely to have left some traces on the visitors, yet while there was a great deal of cultural absorption from other peoples such as the Assyrians, the Babylonians and some of the inhabitants of Palestine (Canaan and Phoenicia), Egypt alone left not a mark. There is not even the slightest Biblical reaction against, or discussion of, the profound and highly symbolic religion of the Egyptians.

It is a pity that so great a man as Sigmund Freud, who dealt with both problems, came to such far-fetched conclusions. According to him, Moses took over the idea of monotheism from Akhenaten, the Pharaoh famous for having instituted a religious and aesthetic reformation in his country. The assumption that Moses was an Egyptian and that he was taught to worship Jehovah by Akhenaten is very tempting but it must be false. This becomes clear when we compare the Jewish idea of the God of their Fathers with the Egyptian idea of Aten, god of the sun. The God of the Fathers always appeared associated with fire, but with fire rising up from the earth towards the sky. The burning bush, the pillar of fire which accompanied the departing Israelites, and the smoke on Mount Sinai—all of them rose up towards Heaven while Akhenaten's sun did quite the opposite. Furthermore, Akhenaten's so-called monotheism never renounced its belief in the divinity of the Pharaohs. Clearly, the worship of Aten is something so radically different from the worship of the God of Israel as to make Freud's explanation a poor answer to the great mystery of Israel and Egypt.

Meanwhile we have closed the pages of the first book of the Old Testament. How the conditions of Jacob's seed have changed! At the end of the Book of Genesis we were told that Joseph had died, respected by the Egyptians and by his family, and that he had been embalmed as befitted his high position. Yet on the first page of the Book of Exodus we find the children of Israel in great distress. The Egyptians had begun to fear them for, we are told, "the children of Israel were fruitful, and increased abundantly, and multiplied, and waxed exceeding mighty; and the land was filled with them" (Exodus 1:7). Actually this is a typical piece of Oriental exaggeration, for only a little later do we learn that this fruitful people could muster a total of only two midwives. Clearly, we must take the impressive account of Israel's fertility with a pinch of salt, and consider it rather a reflection of the Pharaoh's state of mind. This Pharaoh was afraid of strangers and had forgotten his obligations to the descendants of a man who had helped Egypt through its years of hunger. His fear caused him to persecute these foreign barbarians with their queer religion and impudent bearing. Now, nothing could have been simpler than to take the strangers beyond the border and to abandon them to the desert. Instead Pharaoh sent them to specially set up labour camps where they had to do the work of slaves, and to build the store-cities of Pithom and Raamses. Here the Bible mentions one of the few historically verifiable facts in this whole story. Egyptian texts from the time of Rameses II speak of the so-called " 'pr-people", i.e. people "who hauled the stones for the great fortress of the city of Pi-Ramses". The term " 'pr-people" did not refer to a specific ethnic group, but simply to a class of strangers serving as slaves, yet it is highly probable that the seed of Jacob was included in this class.

It was during this time that Moses, the son of a Levite, was born in mysterious circumstances. For the first three months of his life he was hidden in his parents' house, and then placed on the Nile in a basket of bulrushes. He was discovered by Pharaoh's daughter, who took pity on him and unwittingly handed him back to the care of his own mother. The legend of Moses' birth has many parallels in ancient history, and must be considered as evidence of a particular style rather than of historical truth. Thus the Biblical account is very similar to the story of Sargon inscribed on the clay tablets of Mesopotamia.

Sargon I of Akkad was the first Semitic ruler over vast regions between the Euphrates and the Tigris roughly 4,500 years ago. The clay tablet begins with the following words: "I am Sargon, the powerful king, the king of Akkad." He goes on to say that he knew nothing of his father or his relatives except that they lived in the mountains. The text continues: "My mother, a temple prostitute, conceived me and bore me in secret. She laid me into a basket of reeds and sealed me in with pitch. She placed me on the river, and the river bore me safely to Akki the waterman. Akki the waterman drew me out of the water with his pail. Akki the waterman adopted me and brought me up. Akki the waterman made me his gardener." Later, he continues, he became the king's butler and finally was crowned king himself. While the two stories differ in many ways the birth legends are so alike as to preclude any question of chance.

We are on better historical ground when we read that Moses, though brought up at the court of the Pharaoh, missed no opportunity of seeking the company of Semitic slaves. When it became known that he had killed an Egyptian overseer, he was forced to flee to Midian. Here he was handsomely received into the house of Jethro the Kenite, whose daughter Zipporah he later married. This story of Moses' flight and marriage is very reminiscent of the story of Jacob and his arrival in Laban's house. Some authorities look upon Moses' stay with Jethro the Kenite as an event that decided not only his own religious life but that of the whole of the people of Israel. But we must read between the lines if we wish to infer any Kenite influence on Moses— the Bible itself says nothing on this point. All it tells us is that during his stay in Midian, Moses was called by God from out of a burning bush, revealing that He had not abandoned the seed of Abraham, Isaac and Jacob. And He chose Moses as the instrument of His great task—to lead out His people from Egyptian bondage.

15

God's Call to Moses

WHILE Moses was still staying in the desert of Midian there was nothing to herald the great events that were about to happen. He had impressed Jethro's daughters from the start with his courage and kindliness. After his marriage to Jethro's daughter, he had joined the household, living happily with his wife and child, with never a thought for Egypt, the land from which he had fled. It was during this time that he happened to take his father-in-law's sheep as far afield as Horeb, the mountain of God. The exact location of this mountain is unknown and though elsewhere it is called Sinai, it is by no means certain that it was in fact the Mount Sinai of today. The writers of the Old Testament thought it a matter of utter indifference where they placed the scene of God's revelations, and showed respect to but one place: Jerusalem and Mount Zion, on which part of the Holy City was built.

It was near Mount Horeb, then, the mountain of God, that Moses had the strange vision of a bush that was on fire and yet was not consumed by the flames. And out of the burning bush a voice said to Moses: "Draw not nigh hither: put off thy shoes from off thy feet, for the place whereon thou standest is holy ground. . . . I am the God of thy father, the God of Abraham, the God of Isaac, and the God of Jacob" (Exodus 3:5 and 6). It is an often forgotten, but nevertheless very important fact, that God expressly made Himself known as also being the God of Moses' own father—Amram. In this way the Bible stressed the connection between Moses and the Patriarchs and made it clear that it was no strange God who was revealing Himself. Moses reacted by hiding his face in terror. He knew that all those who see God must die.

Then there came the overwhelming demand: "I have surely seen the affliction of my people which are in Egypt, and have heard their cry by reason of their taskmasters; for I know their sorrows; And I am come down to deliver them out of the hand of the Egyptians, and to bring them up out of that land unto a good land and a large, unto

The mosque Al Aksa in the Temple Court of Jerusalem.

Court of Temple in Jerusalem.

Plate 1

The Tigris flowing past the ruins of Asshur.

A *guffa* in a Babylonian canal. This is how the author of Exodus 2 pictur
Moses' basket of bulrushes.

Plate 2

a land flowing with milk and honey. . . . Come now therefore, and I will send thee unto Pharaoh, that thou mayest bring forth my people the children of Israel out of Egypt" (Exodus 3:7-8, 10). Moses protested. There are demands that flatter our own vanity and ambition and that are obeyed no matter how difficult and onerous they are, but we often feel too puny to carry out God's commandments. And this is in fact what Moses felt when he said: "Who am I, that I should go unto Pharaoh, and that I should bring forth the children of Israel out of Egypt?" (Exodus 3:11). Moses' reply was humble enough. He was a man who knew his own limitations only too well, a man who felt himself far too small for so great a task.

It was a long conversation that the unfortunate man had with his God, but God was very patient with him. They discussed many subjects, not all entirely to our taste. We might object, for instance, to the magical tricks Moses was taught, no doubt in order to impress the magicians at the court of Egypt: to change his rod into a serpent, and the serpent back into a rod; to put his hand into his bosom and to take it out as "leprous as snow", and to turn water into blood. But other things that emerge from the conversation between God and Moses touch us with their deep simplicity, for when Moses said: "Lord, O my Lord, I am not eloquent, neither heretofore, nor since thou hast spoken unto thy servant: but I am slow of speech, and of a slow tongue", the Lord replied: "Who hath made man's mouth? or who maketh the dumb, or deaf, or the seeing, or the blind? have not I the Lord? Now therefore go, and I will be with thy mouth, and teach thee what thou shalt say" (Exodus 4:10, 11-12).

Still, the most important subject was raised right at the beginning of their conversation, when Moses asked: "Behold, when I come unto the children of Israel, and shall say unto them, The God of your fathers hath sent me unto you; and they shall say to me, What is his name? What shall I say unto them?" (Exodus 3:13). But God refused to divulge His name, for in the ancient world to reveal one's identity was tantamount to relinquishing one's powers. All He told Moses was: "I AM THAT I AM", which we may translate as, "What is this to you?". Moses had to submit—the God of the Fathers had given him his orders.

E

16

The Historical Relevance of Passover

THOSE who have had the privilege of spending the night of the *seder* in an hospitable Jewish household will surely remember it as long as they live. The seder-service is held on the first two nights of the Jewish Passover, which roughly coincides with Easter. The Hebrew word "seder" means "order", and the celebration always follows a rigid order, or service as we might call it. The name itself tells us little about the unique significance that the seder has had for Jews over the centuries of the Diaspora. Its basis is the Biblical account of the exodus from Egypt, so much so that many scholars have suggested that the Book of Exodus was in fact written as the Passover liturgy of the Jewish people.

Here we have a characteristic example of the developments religious festivals can undergo. Originally, the Passover celebration was a harvest and livestock festival, and the Biblical injunction to eat matzos, unleavened bread, on the Passover can only be explained by the fact that the barley harvest in Palestine always falls in the spring. Later on the harvest festival became a feast of thanksgiving for the historical miracle: matzos became the symbol of the haste with which the people of Israel stole out of Egypt by night. Even so, the symbol has little bearing on historical reality when we remember that the eating of matzos was—at least in the times of the Temple—always associated with the offering of a Paschal lamb. Now according to Exodus 12:3, 4 it takes four days to prepare the Paschal lamb—no symbol of haste this! Here we can see clearly how two festivals—one celebrating the barley harvest and the other associated with livestock—were made the occasion of a great memorial service for the exodus from Egypt. We may compare such history-making with our own sanctification of heathen festivals which explains why we celebrate Easter by eating Easter eggs.

While we know little about the original harvest festival, the historical celebration continues to be held year after year, keeping the memory of the liberation from Egyptian bondage ever fresh in the minds of orthodox Jewry. One of the most delightful aspects of the seder evening is the fact that the children take part in the celebration and that the youngest is expected to ask his father a number of set questions in Hebrew or, to be more exact, in Aramaic. "Why," the child asks, "is this night unlike all other nights? On other nights we may eat leavened or unleavened bread; tonight we may eat only matzos. On other nights we may eat all kinds of herbs, tonight only bitter herbs. On other nights we do not dip our food into our drink; tonight we must dip it twice. On all other nights we eat sitting upright or inclined forward; tonight we must recline."

In answer, the child is told that unleavened bread is a reminder of the haste with which the children of Israel left Egypt, that bitter herbs are symbols of the bitter fate of the bondsman, and that reclining is the privilege of the free—slaves have to stand up. And so the child's simple questions become the occasion for a retelling of the whole story of Exodus. The seder evening with its mixed mood of solemnity and joyousness becomes the re-enactment of the flight from Egypt before the eyes of the entire Jewish household—each year anew. And during the many centuries of their exile, far from their beloved Jerusalem, Jews have put into the festival all their longing for Zion. Both at the beginning and at the end of the seder-service, they sing a Hebrew hymn with the following words: "Now we are here; next year we shall be in Jerusalem. Now we are oppressed; next year we shall be free."

Christians would do well to reflect on the Jewish seder-service, for Our Lord's Last Supper was probably just such a celebration. True, some scholars have argued that Jesus was simply giving a banquet to his friends as was the custom of the time and they base this opinion chiefly on the fact that there was no mention of a Paschal lamb. But we must not forget that the Disciples had no need of a Paschal lamb, for was not Jesus Himself the Lamb of God who had washed away the sin of the world? This was expressed clearly by St. Paul when in I Corinthians 5:7 he wrote: "Purge out therefore the old leaven, that ye may be a new lump, as ye are unleavened. For even Christ our passover is sacrificed for us."

And in describing the Last Supper, the Gospels mention other elements of the seder-service also. At the time, the temple of Jerusalem was still undefiled and thousands of pilgrims would come from far and wide to worship in the Holy City. Many would lodge in the villages and hamlets near the city, such as Bethany, but the Passover service was always held in the city itself. The Talmud calls it a miracle of God that room was always found for each member of this milling crowd so that all could celebrate the seder in the company of their friends. The service then was simpler than it is today, consisting as it did of the breaking of the matzos, the passing of the wine, the saying of prayers and the singing of psalms of praise. That is how the Jews celebrated their redemption from the yoke of Egypt. But Jesus was celebrating quite another redemption, the redemption of which St. Paul said: "Stand fast therefore in the liberty wherewith Christ hath made us free, and be not entangled again with the yoke of bondage" (Galatians 5:1).

And, indeed, the story of the Last Supper in Jerusalem comes to life on the night of the seder. The service brings it home how deep-rooted Christianity is in Judaism, and how little we really understand of the New Testament if we do not know the Old. Jews and Christians alike can here remember their suffering and their redemption, the Jews the martyrdom and redemption of their whole people, the Christians the martyrdom and resurrection of one who was the son of this people, Jesus Christ our Lord.

Now, just because the Passover was originally a harvest festival, we must not deny it all historical truth. What probably happened is that a small number of Israelites escaped the watchful eyes of their Egyptian guards, took refuge in the desert of Kadesh-Barnea and then tried to join some tribes of relatives in Canaan. Legend must have turned this handful of refugees into a gigantic army. If the Biblical account were taken literally, and if we assume an army marching in columns of four, one yard between each column, the front line of this army would have reached Damascus by the time the rear was still crossing the Egyptian border. This is clearly an impossible exaggeration, but the real truth does emerge during the recital of the Passover epic. Thus Exodus 14:5 speaks of flight rather than resounding victory, and Exodus 14:25 tells us that the Egyptian chariots simply became stuck in the mud so that they could not continue the pursuit.

But no matter whether the Exodus from Egypt was a gigantic evacuation or the headlong flight of only a few, their escape through the swamps of the Gulf of Suez—not of the Red Sea!—was felt by the children of Israel to be a miracle of God. And so Moses could sing, together with the children of Israel:

> "I will sing unto the Lord,
>   for he hath triumphed gloriously;
>   the horse and his rider hath he thrown into the sea."
>   (Exodus 15:1)

When the refugees from Egypt finally rejoined their old tribes, their story was turned into popular legend. Their fate became the fate of a whole people, and tradition stressed the miraculous nature of their salvation. Thus harvest festival and national history fused into Israel's Passover legend. In this legend, Moses—whose name probably meant "Deliverer"—became the founder of a religion and its saviour. He became a myth and so the real truth about his life will never be known.

17

The Journey Through the Desert

THOSE of us who have known the German yoke, who knew the joy of liberation and later the many setbacks and disappointments that followed it, could do worse than read the Book of Exodus, and particularly chapters 15, 16 and 17. Miriam's song of victory is still ringing in our ears, when we read that there is no water. And when water is finally found it is bitter and undrinkable. And just as the people began to murmur against Moses and to ask him: "What shall we drink?" (Exodus 15:24), they came to Elim with its twelve wells of water and threescore and ten palm trees.

But hunger followed upon thirst. Many of us who have known what hunger is like, have yet thought that, if only we were free, we could bear everything, even hunger and thirst, that nothing is as bitter as bondage. But then we noticed that hunger and thirst also were unbearable, even in freedom. Alas, we are but frail creatures, and we have no right to despise the children of Israel for their behaviour in the desert, for not having borne their privations with greater strength.

In the vast desert of Sin, between Elim and Mount Sinai, they murmured against Moses and Aaron, their leaders. "Would to God", they said, "we had died by the hand of the Lord in the land of Egypt, when we sat by the flesh-pots, and when we did eat bread to the full; for ye have brought us forth into this wilderness, to kill this whole assembly with hunger" (Exodus 16:3). These were the words of slavish souls, afraid of the wide open spaces, and unwilling to take even the slightest risk. Little could be done with such men, and the Old Testament makes it clear that the crossing of the desert was no epic feat. But we must bear in mind that the people had suffered in the wilderness for a whole generation, and that the Lord Himself had brought them salvation by causing manna to rain down from the heavens, by sending quails for their meat and by working wonder upon wonder as His people, tired and embittered, continued to move towards the Promised Land.

But miracles rarely awaken a lasting faith. Once the people had left the desert of Sin, and pitched camp in Rephidim, they lacked water again. What could be worse than lack of drinking water in the desert? Again they raised their voices against Moses and said: "Wherefore is this that thou hast brought us up out of Egypt, to kill us and our children and our cattle with thirst?" (Exodus 17:3). Heroes may say: "Liberty or death", but ordinary, frightened, and careworn people say "Anything rather than death". And we are bound to admit that the sad and depressing story of the Israelites' weakness is closer to everyday life than any epic poem. Heroes are unusual, and a whole people of heroes an impossibility.

Nor can we say that Moses himself stood out as a rock of comfort in the midst of his people. He, who in his youth had killed an Egyptian, remained a quick-tempered and passionate man haranguing his people and his God with flaming anger. At times he too could no longer bear the burden of his murmuring people, and himself rebelled against the heavy burden God had placed upon him. For unlike his people, Moses could not blame any one man for his trials and tribulations and in his lonely majesty he could only turn against God.

It is strange to realise with what mixed feelings the Jewish religion looks back on this period in the desert. On the one hand the memory is one of horror. Thus Deuteronomy (1:19) speaks of "that great and terrible wilderness"—quite understandably so, since, apart from thirst and starvation, the children of Israel were in constant danger from marauding tribes who infested the neighbourhood, stealing and murdering wherever they could. We remember the struggle against the Amalekites, a struggle that could only be won by Moses holding up his miraculous rod. And when Moses tired and sat down on a stone, Aaron and Hur had to stand on either side of him to support his arms.

But there is another, later, attitude to the time in the wilderness, more human and more attractive. We too can now think back on the last war as a time in which we grew in spirit, in which we lived more deeply and intensively and less selfishly. Sometimes we long to live with just that intensity once again. Similar feelings must have inspired the prophets when they idealised the journey through the desert, depicting it in the most romantic colours. Thus the prophet Hosea compared the journey with a time of sweet courtship: God had discovered his people as a bridegroom discovers his bride, and life in the desert was a life of love, faith and happiness. It was their subsequent stay in the towns that rang the death knell to the idyllic life of this pastoral people. It was then that they ceased to live with their one God and chose to whore with the false gods of the Canaanites and the Phoenicians instead. Hence Hosea had his battle-cry—Back to the desert!, and summoned the people to return to that happy time when, though suffering from hunger and thirst and though surrounded by enemies, they had been at one with their God. And hence also the rise of such sects as the Rechabites who preferred a life in tents to the safety and comfort of the walled city.

Indeed, their journey through the desert kept a constant hold on the people's imagination. But even so, their most important achievement was not the journey itself but the fact that they were given the clear commandments that would help man to steer an even course through the maze that was his earthly life. However, we are now touching upon events to which we may safely devote a separate chapter.

18

Mount Sinai

No single event has had so profound an effect on the history of Israel as God's revelation to Moses on Mount Sinai. According to the Book of Exodus, God's appearance then was not altogether unexpected, for when Moses had been called from the burning bush, and while he had still been in two minds whether he should go or not, the Lord had said to him: "Certainly I will be with thee; and this shall be a token unto thee, that I have sent thee: When thou hast brought forth the people out of Egypt, ye shall serve God upon this mountain" (Exodus 3:12).

What happened on Mount Sinai was so awe-inspiring, so deeply moving, that the Old Testament could only describe it by hints and allusions. Later generations would not tire of harking back to the terrifying signs of fire and smoke and to the voice of the trumpet that accompanied God's revelation, and remember how, for a short period, the whole mountain became sanctified territory, the holiness of God having passed into the place of His revelation. Now, modern man may not be aware that holiness is a very dangerous thing when placed in the wrong hands. To him the idea of sanctity is connected with virtue, morality and goodness. But the holiness of the Old Testament had very little connection with goodness or virtue. Here it is simply one of God's attributes, and God is beyond virtue and goodness. Here, holiness is charged with a potency that may well prove fatal to ordinary mortals.

For a better idea of this Biblical attitude, we must turn to II Samuel 6, where we can read the tragic story of the ark of God. King David set the ark upon a new cart in order to convey God's holy shrine to Jerusalem. On the road the draught animals faltered, and the ark began to shake. A man called Uzzah immediately put out his hand to stop the ark from falling, but as he did so he was struck dead as if by lightning. The susceptibilities of modern man are likely to be offended by the fact that Uzzah, who had meant so well, was made to pay for his good intentions with his life. However, in order to understand the story we must try to identify ourselves with the religious feelings of the children of Israel—to them God's holiness was so great that it became defiled by man, however good his intentions.

Mount Sinai was therefore declared holy territory for a short time. Actually the mountain became an open temple, the word temple being derived from the Greek word *temenos*, a sacred enclosure. A temple is a sacred enclave in a profane world. Whoever enters here must step lightly and change his attitude as indeed we change our outward manner as we enter a church, no matter how often we aver that the church is but of this world. And, conversely, returning to the world out of the temple, man must be careful, too, for it is no small matter to have been close to the Majesty of God.

And so the people of Israel were kept at a proper distance from Mount Sinai, a voice having told them:

"And thou shalt set bounds unto the people round about, saying, Take heed to yourselves, that ye go not up into the mount, or touch the border of it: whosoever toucheth the mount shall be surely put to death: There shall not an hand touch it, but he shall surely be stoned, or shot through: whether it be beast or man, it shall not live" (Exodus 19:12, 13).

Again we are astonished by the severity of these instructions, but the same harsh and strict laws prevailed in the Temple of Jerusalem even in Jesus' days. The forecourt of the temple held a barrier of stones with a Greek inscription. One of these stones, preserved to this day, warns every non-Jew not to pass this barrier at the risk of his life. Only those who had a right to do so could enter, and similarly only Moses, Aaron and the priests were allowed on Mount Sinai, while the people had to keep away until the sound of the trumpet gave them tidings that the danger was past.

And as Moses was enveloped in a dark cloud on top of the mountain, the people, full of fear and trembling, heard rumblings of thunder, and saw flaming torches and black clouds appearing on the mountain, while the sound of trumpets was so loud that the crowd became terrified. "And Mount Sinai", we read, "was altogether on smoke, because the Lord descended upon it in fire: and the smoke thereof ascended as the smoke of a furnace, and the whole mount quaked greatly" (Exodus 19:18). In terror the people would later say to Moses:

"Speak thou with us, and we will hear: but let not God speak with us, lest we die" (Exodus 20:19). What really happened on and around Mount Sinai will always remain a mystery. Many have tried to give an explanation, but their attempts are necessarily contradictory. Those who start with the dogmatic belief that each word of the story is a literal account of historical events, cannot have too easy a time of it, for if they had read the Book of Exodus from beginning to end they could not have helped noticing that far from being a chronological account it is a series of disjointed impressions. We could do far worse than let these impressions give us a taste of the moving, awe-inspiring events around Sinai which united the amorphous mass of men into a people, and—we may well say—a very great people indeed.

The holiness of Sinai was reflected in Moses. In Exodus 34:35 we can read how Moses came down from the mountain, the skin of his face shining with a wonderful radiance. Therefore, the story tells us, Moses had to place a veil upon his face, lest the people were blinded.

But even Moses was not allowed to see the Lord in all His Glory, for no man may see God just as no man may look into the midday sun. And when Moses ardently begged the Lord to be shown His glory, he was told to go into the cleft of a rock. As the Glory passed by, a hand covered Moses' face—all he was allowed to see was the retreating figure of God. Surely, this is the way it must be between God and man. We may be allowed to hear a word, perhaps a mere whisper or echo of a word, for He is the Holy God whom no one may see and whom no one may touch. All discussions about the Lord's person must be tentative, yet our words may reflect our deep reverence before His Majesty, and this, in essence, is the story of Moses on Mount Sinai.

19

The Golden Calf

No doubt, the hardest of all the commandments God gave to Moses on Mount Sinai was the injunction: "Thou shalt not make unto thee any graven image, or any likeness of any thing that is in heaven above, or that is in the earth beneath, or that is in the water under the earth:

Thou shalt not bow down thyself to them, nor serve them" (Exodus 20:4-5). Now, why were the Jews forbidden to have any images of God? When answering this question, it would be false to think of Greek sculpture with its beautiful gods and goddesses. We must rather think of those spine-chilling idols displayed in museums: distorted gods without arms or else with a superabundance of limbs, and goddesses with their feminine charms so exaggerated as to look like caricatures of Venus. Religion was never concerned with representing gods as men, but with giving symbolic expression to man's innermost longings and fears. For this very reason the gods were often depicted as animals, and particularly as bull-calves, those symbols of virility and power.

The commandment not to make graven images was therefore not due to the fear that God might be turned into man's likeness. The ancients had no wish to humanise God, nor yet to turn His spirit into flesh; to them images were but the constant and concrete reminders of a spiritual reality. And here lay the great danger: man, who is always so given to spiritual laziness, is inclined to worship the image as if it were God Himself, to call eternal what is transitory, divine what is profane, and absolute what is limited. This is precisely the danger that the second commandment is meant to guard against. In a sense it is merely an amplification of the first commandment: "Thou shalt have no other gods before me" (Exodus 20:3). Images have a way of becoming what they were never intended to be—false gods.

The history of Jewry, of Christianity and of Islam, is riddled with outbreaks of idolatry in one form or another. Nor was this idolatry always successfully vanquished. The Greek Orthodox Church, for instance, continues to hold its *festum orthodoxiae*, a celebration in memory of the victory of A.D. 842 when the Byzantine Church saved its icons from those who had wanted to destroy them. Icon worshippers have always claimed that they are not making "other" gods but that they are merely conjuring up visions of God's reality. We may disagree with them, but even so we can sympathise with the very human need for some concrete symbol or token.

There is another, equally dangerous, way of satisfying this need. In preferring dogmas to images, man has found a different means to serve the same end: the expression of the inexpressible. Thus he constructs religious systems based on the supposed thoughts of Him whose thoughts must be quite unlike his own, and whose ways must transcend all his understanding. Even though we realise the futility of this striving of ours, we do not tire of proclaiming our message, continually trying, as we do, to keep God's reality before us. But here lies the same threat to purity of religion that we discovered in idolatry —fatal errors easily creep into our interpretation of the Truth, and these errors are then identified with the Truth itself. Our dogma is no longer a servant to the Truth but has become a pitiless tyrant over it.

The Old Testament makes it clear how great a temptation idolatry has always been, and excavations in Palestine, however disappointing in other respects, have never failed to bring to light a surfeit of graven images. These, we may assume, were largely the work of the Canaanites amongst whom the children of Israel lived, and either served as charms to be worn on necklaces or else as signs affixed to doorposts for warding off the evil eye. Some had extraordinary, almost comical shapes, while others could rival the best in modern sculpture. Both the cultured peoples of Mesopotamia and Egypt and the less cultured tribes that inhabited Palestine had idols. The people of Israel were alone in their refusal to make images of God and must have found it difficult indeed to maintain this spiritual isolation. Many kings, therefore, succumbed to temptation, and we can read that King Jeroboam, who reigned over the ten northern tribes of Israel after King Solomon, erected golden calves in the two temples he had built. One of these temples stood in Dan and the other in Bethel, and in both bull-calves were worshipped as the footstool of God. As such they might be compared to the cherubim in the Temple in Jerusalem, yet the writer of the Book of Kings does not tire of expressing his revulsion for them, despite the fact that Jeroboam had meant no disrespect to God.

Only against this background can we understand the story of the dance round the golden calf. The Book of Exodus tells us that, as Moses and Joshua descended from the mountain, they were met by the sound of song and dancing. The waiting people had collected their golden ornaments and had melted them down and fashioned them into that greatest of all fertility symbols: the bull-calf. Now, it is improbable that these nomads could have mustered enough gold between them for this and so many scholars have looked upon this story as being not so much an historical account as a plaint against Jeroboam I and his idolatry in the shrines of Dan and Bethel. When the Book of Exodus tells us that Moses was so enraged by his peoples' weakness that he ordered the Levites to massacre the people, we may assume that the Book was trying to emphasise the beginning of the long and arduous spiritual struggle which Moses, and the Prophets after him, had to wage against the people's idolatry. They were not always successful and Isaiah raised up his hands in horror when he saw the people hewing down trees to fashion idols. "And the residue thereof he maketh a god, even his graven image: he falleth down unto it and worshippeth it, and prayeth unto it and saith, Deliver me, for thou art my god. They have not known nor understood", the prophet concluded, "for he hath shut their eyes that they cannot see; and their hearts, that they cannot understand" (Isaiah 44:17-18).

20

The Ten Commandments

It is by no means certain that the Ten Commandments were in fact written on only two stone tablets. The reports in Exodus and Deuteronomy are neither clear nor do they agree with each other. We may, however, assume that the commandments were carved on stone and, further, that the stones contained more than just the Ten Commandments. In any case the stones have disappeared. They were probably kept in the ark of Solomon's Temple, and carried back as trophies to Babylon when the temple was laid waste by Nebuchadnezzar. We cannot be sure, but we do know that the second temple, that stood in Jesus' time, contained neither ark nor stone tablets.

Most likely the stones containing the Law of Moses were first set up in a prominent place. Laws carved on stone seem to have been the rule even in earlier times, and so we know that the code of Hammurabi (roughly 1700 B.C.), was erected in the Sun Temple of Sippar, not far from Babylon. The tablet was dug up in Susa, far from its original home, and it, too, was taken away as a trophy and can today be seen in the Louvre in Paris. There are, furthermore, some trivial tablets that date from even before that time, and people may well ask why it is that possessing as we do tablets from the year 1950 B.C. we cannot recover the Law of Moses. However, the chance of such a tremendous find is extremely small. A great king such as Hammurabi would have given orders for many copies of his work to be made, while there was only one copy of the Law of Moses. Looking for it is therefore like looking for a needle in a haystack. Even so it is far more profitable to search for it than for Noah's ark which some treasure-hunters seem to be busily doing.

Comparisons of Moses' law with the other codes discovered in Asia Minor emphasise the unique character of the Ten Commandments. In Hammurabi's code, for instance, each phrase begins with the set formula: "If . . ." followed by a given transgression and its penalty. In other words, the code of Hammurabi was a penal code. The Law of Moses, too, contains many penal clauses, and, for instance, in Exodus 21:18-19 we may read, "And if men strive together, and one smite another with a stone, or with his fist and he die not, but keepeth his bed: If he rise again, and walk abroad upon his staff, then shall he that smote him be quit: only he shall pay for the loss of his time, and shall cause him to be thoroughly healed." Such rulings invariably conjure up the picture of a Kadi, an Arab judge surrounded by a gesticulating crowd of plaintiffs, defendants and witnesses, as he passed sentence according to the custom of his land. True, the code of Hammurabi was ostensibly handed down to the King by Shamash, the sun-god, but the legalistic "if" betrays its real origin—the Kadi's daily practice by the city gates. Hammurabi simply lent his laws the authority of Shamash, the all-seeing one who dispenses justice, who protects the poor and weak, who succours the widow and the orphan and who preserves peace and order.

In contradistinction to Hammurabi's code, to the codes of Lipit-Ishtar and Bilalama and to many others, the Law of Moses is far more than a penal code, for it contains categorical and positive injunctions the like of which are found nowhere else in the Middle East. The commandments: "Honour thy father and thy mother . . . Thou shalt not kill . . . Thou shalt not steal" (Exodus 20:12-15), are quite categorical and do not begin with *ifs* or *buts*. Nor are the Ten Commandments the only examples of categorical laws in the Old Testament. Thus Deuteronomy 27 contains the so-called Tablet of Curses which begins with: "Cursed be he that setteth light by his father or his mother. And all the people shall say, Amen. Cursed be he that removeth

his neighbour's landmark. And all the people shall say, Amen"
(Deuteronomy 27:16-17). We gain the impression that these curses
were recited by the priests or Levites for the edification of the people,
the congregation assenting with the words Amen, Amen.

We could give many more examples of such categorical injunctions
throughout the Books of Exodus, Leviticus and Deuteronomy, but
shall merely quote Leviticus 19:11-16:

"Ye shall not steal, neither deal falsely, neither lie one to another.

"And ye shall not swear by my name falsely, neither shalt thou
profane the name of thy God: I am the Lord.

"Thou shalt not defraud thy neighbour, neither rob him: the
wages of him that is hired shall not abide with thee all night until
the morning.

"Thou shalt not curse the deaf, nor put a stumbling-block before
the blind, but shalt fear thy God: I am the Lord.

"Ye shall do no unrighteousness in judgment: thou shalt not
respect the person of the poor, nor honour the person of the mighty:
but in righteousness shalt thou judge thy neighbour.

"Thou shalt not go up and down as a talebearer among thy
people: neither shalt thou stand against the blood of thy neighbour:
I am the Lord."

Yet of all the many laws and codes in the Old Testament the Ten
Commandments are the most concise, and hence no other code can
offer man clearer guidance along the path of righteousness. No wonder,
for is not its divine origin vouchsafed by the opening words: "I am
the Lord thy God, which have brought thee out of the land of Egypt,
out of the house of bondage"? (Exodus 20:2).

21

Balaam's Ass

THE story of Balaam and his ass is an integral part of the journey
through the wilderness. Inexorably the children of Israel were drawing
closer to the Promised Land overcoming all opposition on the way.

No wonder then, that the king of Moab, who ruled over the fertile plains of Transjordania, was gripped with fear. As he saw this great army of emaciated people approaching, he said in his picturesque Eastern way: "Now shall this company lick up all that are round about us, as the ox licketh up the grass of the field" (Numbers 22:4).

In his anxiety he sent for one Balaam who had the reputation of being a man of powerful words. "Come now, therefore, I pray thee", the King asked him, "curse me this people; for they are too mighty for me . . . for I wot that he whom thou blessest is blessed, and he whom thou cursest is cursed" (Numbers 22:6). Clearly this Balaam was worthy of his hire, and the King was willing to pay him handsomely.

To this day the Near East is full of magicians who will sell you magic words for money. While I was in Jerusalem, I met a Temanite rabbi who thought nothing of writing and selling charms to any who could pay for them. He was a highly respected man and made a good living from his penmanship. No one seemed to object to his trade, but I had the distinct impression that the learned rabbi himself had far less faith in his miracles than had his customers.

Now the odd thing about the Biblical story is the implicit assumption that Balaam did in fact have this terrifying power though—and this is after all the core of the whole story—he was by no means free to pronounce blessings and curses as he chose. His powers were strictly limited, and the limits were set by God Himself. No wonder then that Balaam refused to accompany the King's messengers, for God had given him no authority to curse Israel and all the gold and silver in Moab could not prevail against God's wishes.

But the messengers returned with another request from the king: "Thus saith Balak, the son of Zippor, Let nothing, I pray thee, hinder thee from coming unto me: For I will promote thee unto very great honour, and I will do whatsoever thou sayest unto me: come therefore, I pray thee, curse me this people" (Number 22:16-17). Still Balaam remained firm: "If Balak would give me his house full of silver and gold, I cannot go beyond the word of the Lord my God, to do less or more" (Numbers 22:18). But then, in the dark of night, Balaam thought he heard the voice of God commanding him to "rise up, and go with them". The Bible leaves it an open question whether Balaam did in fact hear the voice of God, or whether he had a dream inspired

[Palestine Archaeological Museum

A trough from Solomon's stables in Megiddo.

[British Museum

The minaret of Samarra. In ancient times this minaret was thought to have been the tower of Babel.

Clay tablet with an outline map of the regions of the world and text relating to the conquests of Sargon of Agade, who reigned about 2300 B.C.   Plate 3

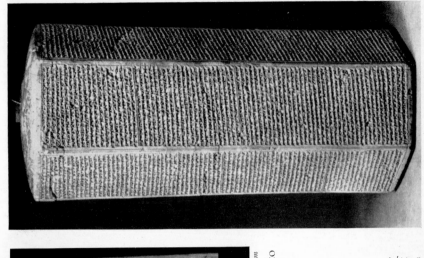

A panel from the "Black Obelisk": Jehu, King of Israel, doing homage to Shalmaneser III, King of Assyria.

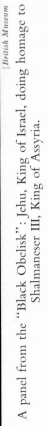

Baked clay prism inscribed with the annals of Sennacherib, King of Assyria, describing especially his siege of Jerusalem under its king, Hezekiah.

by the great treasures and impressive honours that awaited him. In any event he now felt free to go to the King and to curse Israel.

But he had a bad conscience and in our story his conscience spoke in the form of his ass which could see what poor misguided Balaam did not see or would not see: the angel of God barring the way, sword in hand. Those who read the text in the original Hebrew will make a most surprising discovery: they will read that the angel was Satan in whose disguise God Himself was barring Balaam's way. Now the Satan of the Old Testament was not what Christians were later to understand by that name: God's adversary, the evildoer and the prince of darkness; no, he was the form that God Himself assumed whenever men did not listen to His voice or obey His commandments.

This is precisely what Balaam had done, and so, as his journey took him through the vineyards and hills of Moab, his ass drove him against the needle-sharp rock walls that served as fences in these parts. And when he began to belabour the poor beast, the Lord opened Balaam's eyes, and Balaam saw that it was the angel of the Lord who would not let him pass. His way was barred until he had promised not to utter a single word that might offend the Lord.

And Balaam, the great magician, bowed down to the Lord's will:

"How shall I curse, whom God hath not cursed?
or how shall I defy, whom the Lord hath not defied?"

(Numbers 23:8)

"How goodly are thy tents, O Jacob,
and thy tabernacles, O Israel!"

(Numbers 24:5)

"Blessed is he that blesseth thee,
and cursed is he that curseth thee."

(Numbers 24:9)

And so the story ends. Balaam and the king each went their separate ways. The Bible did not deny that Balaam was a man with mighty and powerful words at his command—quite the contrary. But all human power is as nothing compared with God's. The moral of the story is: If God be against us, who can be for us? If God be for us, who can be against us?

F

22

The Death of Moses

IF you should ever visit Palestine you will be struck by the great many graves in which the men and women of the Old Testament lie buried. A little south of Jerusalem, close to the city wall, you may be shown the grave of King David, and a colourful train of pilgrims can often be seen ascending the path to Mount Zion in order to pay homage to their great King. Here, in an empty vault, you will find a gigantic stone coffin of which sceptics say in whispers that it is completely empty. But these whispers cannot stop a host of pious Jews from spending days on end in the gloom of David's so-called tomb, and swaying their bodies to and fro while they monotonously recite the psalms.

Near Jerusalem, also, on the way to Bethlehem, you may visit Rachel's grave, or Abraham's to the north of it. In Nineveh lies the prophet Jonah, and Daniel in Kirkuk. But there is one grave for which you will look in vain, that of the greatest of all the leaders, law-givers and prophets of Israel, their deliverer from Egyptian bondage: Moses. Even the children of Israel wondered why "no man knoweth of his sepulchre unto this day" (Deuteronomy 34:6). In the circumstances, all sorts of fantastic tales were woven about the mysterious death of the greatest Jew of all time.

In the Book of Deuteronomy we read that Moses was not allowed to enter the Promised Land, and that he died on Mount Nebo. This mountain lies in Transjordania to the north-east of the Dead Sea. Its high peak affords a wonderful view over the whole Jordan valley, and on bright days the Sea of Galilee can be made out in the distance. Here the stony and unfertile regions of the Promised Land are hidden behind a lovely green landscape. All this Moses was allowed to see. When he died, the goal of this journey was within easy reach.

Today we may well ask ourselves whether his death in exile was a tragedy or a blessing. We know the disappointments that awaited those who entered the Promised Land and who observed that the people there were no better than elsewhere, and just as obsessed by unfulfilled longings and desires. Moses, at least, was allowed to keep his illusions about the Promised Land.

But the Bible never doubted that Moses, who had roamed the desert with his people for forty years, died a bitter death. And the Biblical writer found the reason for Moses' punishment in his alleged impatience, and bitter anger against God by the waters of Meribah. So it is written in Deuteronomy 32:49-52 and in Numbers 20:12, but the unsuspecting reader is never told exactly what Moses was punished for. The Old Testament does not mention a single disrespectful deed or rebellious word on his part.

And so Moses was buried somewhere "in a valley in the land of Moab, over against Beth-peor" (Deuteronomy 34:6). Later generations were dissatisfied with this account and preferred to surround Moses' death with legend. Fragments of these have been handed down to us, and one of them can be found in the Epistle of Jude.

In verse 9 we read: "Yet Michael the archangel, when contending with the devil he disputed about the body of Moses, durst not bring against him a railing accusation, but said, The Lord rebuke thee." The story was taken by Jude from a non-Biblical source, the *Assumptio Mosis*, rediscovered in a library in Milan during the nineteenth century. Unfortunately the references in it to the dispute between Michael and the devil about the body of Moses are irrevocably lost.

Great writers, too, have speculated about Moses' fate. Both Goethe and Freud devoted their attention to this problem, one saying that Moses, unable to face his murmuring people, committed suicide, the other that Moses was murdered by them. We can see how this gap in tradition, this mystery, has aroused man's curiosity and how he has tried to fill in the missing parts.

As for the Bible, it is content with considering Moses one of the mighty, an unbroken man even in old age: ". . . his eye was not dim, nor his natural force abated" (Deuteronomy 34:7). Never again was Israel to have a prophet to come face to face with the Lord. And when we think of Moses, we remember him as that unique man who lived a life of great loneliness and who died in loneliness, in terrible isolation.

D. *In the Time of the Judges*

23

Joshua's Entry into the Promised Land

THE Book of Joshua begins with the promise of a full account of the conquest of all Palestine: "From the wilderness and this Lebanon even unto the great river, the river Euphrates, all the land of the Hittites, and unto the great sea toward the going down of the sun, shall be your coast" (Joshua 1:4). But the promise is never fulfilled, and instead the reader is only told what happened in and about Jericho. Even here there are contradictions, for according to one version Jericho fell because of Rahab's betrayal of her kinsmen, while according to another the city walls collapsed through a miracle.

Neither account is borne out by excavations. On the road between Bethel and Jericho lie the ruins of Ai, a city mentioned in the Book of Joshua. Jewish scholars, in an attempt to reconstruct its story, have come to the conclusion that it was walled in about 2100 B.C. and abandoned about 1600 B.C. Thus the ruins must already have stood there when the Israelites invaded the region. Similarly, Jericho must have been destroyed long before the coming of the Israelites. In any case Dr. Kenyon's recent excavations have proved beyond a shadow of doubt that its ruins in Tell-es-Sultan do not bear out the historical accuracy of the Book of Joshua.

Nor is it easy to get any sort of reliable picture of Joshua himself, the successor of Moses. In all probability there must have been another book, the Book of the Just, on which the author of the Book of Joshua drew freely and to which he referred on many occasions. But the Book of the Just is irretrievably lost, and so all we can safely say is that Joshua was Moses' close companion in the desert, that he was a military leader, that he accompanied Moses on to Mount Sinai, and that he was one of the twelve spies who were sent into the land of Canaan. We also know that he must have been a very brave man for, while ten of the spies came back saying: "We be not able to go up against the people. . . . The land, through which we have gone to search it, is a land that eateth up the inhabitants thereof; and all the people that we saw in it are men of a great stature" (Numbers 14:31, 32), only he and Caleb stood firm.

The reason Joshua has remained such an enigma is due to the fact that the Book named after him deals with only three specific events. The first is the battle of Gibeon in which Joshua with a small army managed to beat off the advancing Canaanites. As the enemy was in full flight, God sent down first a hailstorm that killed more of them than even the sword of the Israelites had done.

And then, to rout the Canaanites completely, He bade the Sun stand still:

> "Sun, stand thou still upon Gibeon;
> and thou, Moon, in the valley of Ajalon.
> And the sun stood still,
> and the moon stayed,
> until the people had avenged themselves
> upon their enemies."
> (Joshua 10:12, 13)

Now this story has become a favourite bone of contention between Bible critics and apologists, many of the latter explaining the miracle away in astronomical terms. I must frankly confess that this type of explanation has always struck me as being far more incredible than the miracles themselves. The Bible, I must reiterate, is not a scientific textbook, and its miracles are miracles of God and not experiments that can be repeated in the laboratory. Nobody should delude himself into thinking he is doing the Bible any service by trying to justify it on pseudo-scientific grounds; on the contrary this merely negates one of the central points of the Bible's message. I myself believe that an ancient song gave rise to the poem about the sun that stood still over Gibeon, but shall gladly relinquish my opinion the moment I hear of a better one. In any case, all that is historically established is that Joshua won a decisive battle and that his compatriots were so grateful to him that they appointed him judge over them.

Clearly, therefore, Joshua was a personality to be reckoned with. It was he who united the tribes of Israel round the sanctified ground in Shechem. Here, at the end of his life, he renewed those bonds between Israel and God that Moses had forged on Mount Sinai, and that his people were for ever in danger of betraying. In their long history the

Israelites could never wholly withstand the temptation of worshipping the idols of the heathens amongst whom they lived, and only their leaders' constant perseverance and courage could keep them in the path of the Law.

And we shall always remember Joshua for doing just that, and for continuing the great work that Moses had begun. "Now," he told his people, "therefore fear the Lord, and serve him in sincerity and in truth: and put away the gods which your fathers served on the other side of the flood, and in Egypt; and serve ye the Lord. And if it seem evil unto you to serve the Lord, choose you this day whom you will serve; whether the gods which your fathers served that were on the other side of the flood, or the gods of the Amorites, in whose land ye dwell: but as for me and my house, we will serve the Lord. And the people answered and said, God forbid that we should forsake the Lord to serve other gods" (Joshua 24:14-16).

24

Gideon and His Three Hundred Men

GIDEON was undoubtedly one of the more attractive judges. We first meet him threshing wheat by a wine-press, and if we know anything about the period we see at once that this was a humiliating position for him to be in. Wheat is normally threshed on high ground where the wind can blow the chaff away. A walled vineyard in a valley between large terraced hills is the last place for threshing grain, and Gideon could only have been there for fear of the Midianites. The Midianites were a nomadic people, who had managed to penetrate deep into Israel because of the anarchic conditions prevailing there at the time. In fact, they roamed through the length and breadth of Judah and Israel, managing even to reach the Mediterranean coast. They would suddenly descend upon the land like locusts, robbing and plundering, and peasant boys like Gideon had to keep out of their way.

But Gideon was called by God to free his people. Like others before and after him he hesitated when the call came, asking God for a sign that would allay his doubts. This hesitation, this demand for a visible sign, makes us like Gideon all the more. Many have thought they were thus chosen, but few have been able to satisfy later generations about the genuineness of their call. Not so Gideon. When he was given the sign for which he had asked, the sign was so unmistakably clear that poor Gideon went in fear of his life—he had been allowed to see the angel of the Lord Himself.

Gideon's great day came when with three hundred men he won a towering victory over the Midianites. The Book of Judges is convinced that God specifically kept this army so small, and that Gideon might equally well have set out with thirty-two thousand men. The Lord, we are told, said to Gideon: "The people that are with thee are too many for me to give the Midianites into their hands, lest Israel vaunt themselves against me, saying Mine own hand hath saved me" (Judges 7:2).

And so Gideon whittled down his army, but by a most peculiar method. Dismissing first those who were afraid he was still left with ten out of the original thirty-two thousand, and ten thousand were still too many. Then he sent home all those who knelt down to drink water, and only the rest, a mere three hundred, were allowed to remain. To be quite frank, I have never been able to fathom what sort of criterion this was. True, I have often heard sermons purporting to show that the way in which the three hundred drank water gave incontrovertible proof of their stout hearts and of their readiness to follow their leader without hesitation, but if that was indeed the case, I, for one, cannot for the life of me say why. Far better say that it was the Almighty who chose this means of indicating to Gideon who was to stay with him, since Gideon himself could far more conveniently have made the choice by letting his men draw lots.

Gideon's army was greatly helped by a dream. Gideon and his servant Phurah overheard a Midianite soldier telling his friend: "Lo, a cake of barley bread tumbled into the host of Midian, and came unto a tent, and smote it that it fell, and overturned it, that the tent lay along." The other replied: "This is nothing else save the sword of Gideon" (Judges 7:13, 14). Gideon took the dream to be a sign of the Lord, and, dividing his army into three groups, he gave each of his men a trumpet, an empty pitcher and a lamp. Then at a given signal, all the trumpets were sounded, all the pitchers broken and all the lamps flourished. The Midianites were thrown into such utter confusion that

Gideon easily routed them. If we follow the Biblical text closely, we gain the impression that it is made up of two separate stories. At first we are led to believe that the army of the Midianites was to be shattered by the simultaneous blast of three hundred trumpets alone. The pitchers and lamps were apparently added as an afterthought; clearly the writer was trying to combine a number of different versions but failed to hide the traces of his work.

Still, this story of victory by stealth may well rest on historical fact, and many episodes during the Israel-Arab conflict of 1948 are reminiscent of Gideon's victory. Thus, outside Jerusalem, I was shown a hill of strategic importance which had been taken from the Arabs by only a handful of Israelis who, following Gideon's example, had imitated the sounds of a huge army, not, admittedly, by means of old-fashioned trumpets, but with three . . . loudspeakers! And this was by no means the only such anecdote I was told.

But to the Book of Judges, Gideon's victory over a far superior army was not the result of his brilliant strategy—it was God's will. Even had Gideon commanded thirty-two thousand men, they would have achieved nothing had God wished it otherwise. This theme will be repeated when we come to David's fight against Goliath, and is put into words by St. Paul: "My grace is sufficient for thee: for my strength is made perfect in weakness" (II Corinthians 12:9).

Even so, victory earned Gideon the gratitude of his people; so much so that they offered him the crown. But Gideon was adamant: "I will not rule over you, neither shall my son rule over you: the Lord shall rule over you" (Judges 8:23). Here we have the first mention of a king over Israel, and clearly the Book of Judges was strongly opposed to the idea of an hereditary monarchy, considering, as it did, that in any form a human kingship detracted from the Majesty of the Supreme Ruler.

And so the day on which Gideon, with a handful of men, delivered his people from the Midianities became yet another occasion for giving praise to God, of whom Gideon was but the instrument. We may admire Gideon's courage and resourcefulness, but all the glory of the victory is the Lord's alone.

25

The Story of Jotham

IN the ninth chapter of the Book of Judges we can read the parable of the trees that had learnt to walk and to talk like men. Having decided to choose a king, they approached the olive tree, whose fruit is so highly prized by all. Now, the olive tree, conscious of its own worth, rejected the offer out of hand. It could not become king and remain true to its nature: the peasant must till his land, the scholar pursue his studies, the merchant follow his trade. No wonder, then, that the olive replied: "Should I leave my fatness, wherewith by me they honour God and man, and go to be promoted over the trees?" (Judges 9:9).

Next they turned to the fig tree. Now the fig tree is no less worthy than the olive tree, so much so that Jesus saw fit to use it as an image of the Kingdom of God: "Now learn a parable of the fig tree; When his branch is yet tender, and putteth forth leaves, ye know that summer is nigh: So likewise ye, when ye shall see all these things, know that it is near, even at the doors" (Matthew 24:32-33; Mark 13:28-29).

And just like the olive, the fig tree too, was fully aware of its worth, and so replied: "Should I forsake my sweetness, and my good fruit, and go to be promoted over the trees?" (Judges 9:11).

But still the trees of the wood would not give up their quest, and they turned to the vine, which is not, properly speaking, a tree at all. Now the vine had always felt at home amongst the mountains and hills of Judah, and had no desire to descend into the plains: "Should I leave my wine, which cheereth God and man, and go to be promoted over the trees?" (Judges 9:13). So the trees had to climb even lower down the scale, and to approach the bramble, that curse of the land, the destroyer of barley and wheat. Now the bramble, good for nothing except being weeded out and burned, was very willing indeed to become king. Moreover, it was fully convinced of its fitness for the job, and so it replied: "If in truth ye anoint me king over you, then come and put your trust in my shadow" (Judges 9:15). How vainglorious to assume the airs and graces of a real tree beneath whose leaves the weary traveller may take refuge from the heat of the midday sun! Yes, the bramble had no hesitation in accepting an office which olive, fig and vine had scorned as being unsuitable for them.

This parable refers to an important phase in the history of Israel. The Israelites were then scattered throughout the length and breadth of the country, and their common ties were loose. They might gather to discuss topics of common interest, but then they would return home again, independent and proud, despising all those who would renounce the useful life of the farmer to play the overlord. Only boasters and idlers chased after these phantoms, and such men were like the bramble that had wanted to rule over the cedars of Lebanon.

Now the man who told this parable was Jotham, the son of Gideon, whose own father had refused to become king, but whose step-brother had thought fit to accept the proffered crown. His name was Abimelech, the son of a woman from Shechem, and he was therefore a kinsman of the Canaanites. While Abimelech could count on the support of the Canaanite heathens, he had first to eliminate Gideon's seventy sons, each one of whom was a pretender to the throne. With seventy pieces of silver, presented by the heathen priests of Shechem, Abimelech hired assassins who fell upon his father's house, killing all the sons but one: Jotham, who escaped to proclaim his parable from a safe distance. And this is the rider he added:

"If ye then have dealt truly and sincerely with Jerubbaal and with his house this day, then rejoice ye in Abimelech, and let him also rejoice in you: But if not, let fire come out from Abimelech, and devour the men of Shechem, and the house of Millo; and let fire come out from the men of Shechem, and from the house of Millo, and devour Abimelech" (Judges 9:19-20).

In the end, even the men of Shechem rebelled against Abimelech. They first set up ambushes in the mountains, plundering all passers-by, and then, having drunk too much during the harvest festival, they cursed Abimelech aloud in the very temple whose treasury had provided the money for Abimelech's assassins.

Abimelech decided to hit back at once, and to take Shechem by surprise. In the struggle, all the inhabitants were slain, some being burned to death in the temple where they had taken refuge. With characteristic ruthlessness Abimelech then marched against Thebez which had made common cause with Shechem. Here this evil man

met his doom for, during the siege of the city, a woman dropped a
millstone on him and cracked his skull. His last words to his armour-
bearer were: "Draw thy sword and slay me, that men say not of me,
A woman slew him" (Judges 9:54). And so, Abimelech, the man who
knew no scruples, and whose wickedness was matched only by his
ruthless ambition, came to an ignominious end. He failed, says the
Book of Judges, because God's righteousness could not let him succeed.
Jotham's prophetic parable had heralded his impending doom. And
Abimelech was the reason why the question of kingship was not to be
raised in Israel for another fifty years.

26

Jephthah's Vow

ONE of the most tragic Biblical figures was Jephthah, the judge.
Even his youth was unhappy, for, though Gilead, his father, was a
man of some importance, he was not born of Gilead's legitimate wife.
And so his brothers said to him: "Thou shalt not inherit in our father's
house; for thou art the son of a strange woman" (Judges 11:2). Men
like Jephthah normally became servants, but Jephthah had too much
spirit for this, and preferred the free life of the outlaw instead. With
a gang of other desperadoes he fell to robbing caravans and to
attacking outlying villages.

We must bear in mind that brigands in those days were not the
worst of men, and were, in fact, often admired. Farmers could enter
into treaties with them and buy safety at a relatively small price.
They had a very strict code of honour: those under their protection
were kept safe and the caravan that had paid its due could travel on
unmolested.

And so, in times of great national need, highwaymen were the
natural leaders in the struggle against the enemy, against the Ammonites who were infesting Trans-jordania. Jephthah was hardened in
battle, and knew the land like no other. If anyone could vanquish the
hated foe, it was he.

But Jephthah was loth to accept the flattering offer of leadership when it was made, for he had not forgotten the bitterness of his youth. "Did not ye hate me, and expel me out of my father's house?" he asked. "And why are ye come unto me now when ye are in distress?" (Judges 11:7). And why indeed should he have pulled their chestnuts out of the fire, only to be dismissed once he had done their bidding? Not until he was solemnly appointed leader not only in war, but also in peace, did Jephthah fall upon the Ammonites and defeat them in battle. Alas, his triumph was short-lived. Before going into battle, he had made this vow to God:

> "If thou shalt without fail deliver the children of Ammon into mine hands, Then it shall be, that whatsoever cometh forth of the doors of my house to meet me, when I return in peace from the children of Ammon, shall surely be the Lord's, and I will offer it up for a burnt offering" (Judges 11:30-31).

And when the hero returned home, it was his own daughter who came out to meet him with timbrels and dances. In dire distress and rending his garments in mourning, Jephthah exclaimed: "Alas, my daughter! thou hast brought me very low, and thou art one of them that trouble me: for I have opened my mouth unto the Lord, and I cannot go back" (Judges 11:35). And his daughter, his only child, appreciating the full significance of a vow to God, told him with great composure: "My father, if thou hast opened thy mouth unto the Lord, do to me according to that which hath proceeded out of thy mouth" (Judges 11:36). All she asked was two months' grace to go up into the mountains where her companions might "bewail her virginity". And when she returned on the agreed day, her father fulfilled his vow. Jephthah's fearless daughter was long remembered by the maidens of Israel. Each year they would go up into the mountains for four days to honour her memory.

The Old Testament deprecates this whole episode, for the God of Israel has always abhorred human sacrifice, and His teachers have for ever warned the people not to be reckless in their promises to God. "Be not rash with thy mouth," the Preacher said, "and let not thine heart be hasty to utter any thing before God: for God is in heaven, and thou upon earth: therefore let thy words be few. . . . When thou vowest a vow unto God, defer not to pay it; for he hath no pleasure in fools: pay that which thou hast vowed. Better is it that thou shouldest not vow, than that thou shouldest vow and not pay. Suffer not thy mouth to cause thy flesh to sin; neither say thou before the angel, that it was an error: wherefore should God be angry at thy voice, and destroy the work of thine hands?" (Ecclesiastes 5:2, 4-6).

Jephthah is only one of many people whose foolhardy promises have caused misery to themselves and to others. From the New Testament we know the story of Herod who, seduced by his step-daughter's dancing, called out in ecstasy: "Ask of me whatsoever thou wilt, and I will give it thee. And he sware unto her, Whatsoever thou shalt ask of me, I will give it thee, unto the half of my kingdom" (Mark 6:22-23). Goaded by Herodias, Salome demanded the head of John the Baptist, and Herod, the King, had to accede to her wishes. Both Jephthah and Herod may serve as a warning how silly it is to write blank cheques to fate or to people, for such cheques can only be met with life-long remorse.

While the Book of Judges relates only this one episode from the life of Jephthah, he is chiefly remembered as the man who made suspected strangers pronounce the word *shibboleth*. Those who said "s" instead of "sh" were known to be Ephraimites and killed on the spot. The historical accuracy of this story has often been doubted, though the Arabs of this region to this day confuse the two sibilants. In any case *shibboleth* has become part and parcel of the English language, the Oxford Dictionary defining it as "a test word or principle or behaviour or opinion", though in the original Hebrew it meant an ear of grain.

The Bible tells us little more of the life of Jephthah. "And Jephthah judged Israel six years. Then died Jephthah, the Gileadite, and was buried in one of the cities of Gilead."

27

Samson's Strength and Weakness

JERUSALEM is joined to Tel-Aviv by a single-track railway line, inherited from the Turks. Since those days very little money has been spent on it and the little train still meanders down the coast. The journey is uncomfortable, but as the traveller who knows his Bible looks out of the window, he cannot help being reminded that it was here, amongst these vineyards, that Samson waged his epic struggle against the Philistines.

When the Philistines first settled near the coast, their relations with the Israelites were cordial. Samson moved amongst them quite freely, and even had a romance with a Philistine maiden.

The son of parents who had long ago given up all hope of ever having a child, Samson was divinely destined to become a Nazirite, a servant of God. Nazirites were not as other men. Not for them the fruits of the vine, or the barber's blade—their locks were charged with divine strength. The children of Israel were not alone in attributing magical properties to hair and nails and many primitive peoples continue to do so to this day. Long ago, soldiers going to war would let their hair grow, the better to confound their enemies.

The Old Testament mentions two famous Nazirites, Samson and Samuel, but only in the story of Samson was there any mention of this strange power. Possibly this lends credence to the belief that the story of Samson was based on an ancient sun-myth. His hair, some people have held, was symbolic of the strong rays of the summer sun, but all we can say with certainty is that the name of Samson was derived from the Hebrew word for sun, and that the Bible placed his home near Beth-Shemesh, the House of the Sun, where a sun-temple had once stood.

The stories of Samson's feats were legion. On one occasion, while on his way to marry a maiden of Timnath, he was met by a lion, whom he rent with his bare hands, and on another occasion he caught three hundred foxes, and, tying them tail to tail, he put a firebrand between each pair of tails. Then he set fire to the brands and chased the foxes into the standing corn of the Philistines so that their corn, their vineyards and their olives went up in flames. And in the many struggles that followed, Samson always emerged victorious against overwhelming odds, though sometimes he had no weapon save the jawbone of an ass.

The Book of Judges revels in these stories, and once again the reader may be astonished to find that the Bible thought fit to relate much that sounds improper in our ears. But then the Old Testament is always realistic, taking life as it is and not as it ought to be. This

G

realism coupled with a truly Eastern delight in story-telling, make the
story of Samson a veritable treasure-house of sparkling humour and
dramatic incident. Yes, there is a great deal of rough humour in these
stories of Samson, the man who even in death defeated more enemies
than other warriors destroy during their lifetime.

But the Book of Judges includes the story of Samson not only
because it was he who began the successful struggle against the Philistines, but mainly because he used his strength in the service of God.
Even so, the Old Testament was not carried away by blind admiration
for him. On the contrary, the greatness of the story lies in the description of the weakness and the waywardness of a giant.

For Samson, this tower of strength, failed on three critical occasions.
We are told that during the preparation for his wedding to a Philistine
maiden from Timnath he set a riddle for his unwanted bodyguard of
thirty young Philistines. If they found the answer, each of them would
win a sheet and a change of garments, but if they did not they would
have to give Samson thirty sheets and thirty changes of garments.
Now, Samson was being most unfair, for his riddle could not possibly
be answered by anybody:

> "Out of the eater came forth meat.
> and out of the strong came forth sweetness."
> (Judges 14:14)

He was actually referring to the lion that he had killed on his way
to Timnath, and to the swarm of bees and some honey that he had
later discovered in the carcass. Never having breathed a word of this
to a soul, Samson was confident that he would have the better of his
hosts.

When, after three days, the Philistines realised how fruitless all their
attempts had been, they began to threaten Samson's wife, saying to
her: "Entice thy husband, that he may declare unto us the riddle, lest
we burn thee and thy father's house with fire: have ye called us to
take that we have? is it not so?" (Judges 14:15). And so the girl, jealous
of her happiness, came crying to Samson, and pleaded with him to
give her the answer which she repeated to her persecutors. We can
still see them standing there beaming with malicious self-satisfaction,
as they tell the unhappy bridegroom:

> "What is sweeter than honey?
> and what is stronger than a lion?"
> (Judges 14:18)

Samson had lost—in a moment of weakness he had surrendered his secret to his bride. He thundered:

> "If ye had not plowed with my heifer,
> ye had not found out my riddle."
> (Judges 14:18)

Then he killed thirty Philistines from Ashkelon, and gave their garments to the winners. This was Samson's first defeat.

Much better known is Samson's love for another daughter of the Philistines, Delilah, the maiden from the valley of Sorek. It was her task to lure Samson into revealing the secret of his strength. Her compatriots had promised her eleven hundred pieces of silver if she succeeded. Three times he resisted her blandishments, but in the end her feminine wiles prevailed. When Delilah had shorn off the seven locks of his head, the Philistines put out Samson's eyes and took him away to Gaza in brass fetters.

And so Samson became a blind prisoner monotonously slaving away at the treadmill. But when his hair had grown again, God gave him his last chance. During a banquet in honour of the god Dagon, to which the Philistines had flocked in their thousands, Samson, the vanquished foe, was brought in to amuse the crowd. He asked his guide to lead him towards the supporting pillars of the house so that he could lean against them. And saying a short prayer that began with the words: "O Lord God, remember me, I pray thee, and strengthen me, I pray thee, only this once, O God . . ." (Judges 16:28), he was filled with new strength. Grasping the central pillars and calling out: "Let me die with the Philistines" (Judges 16:30) he pulled the house down on all the thousands assembled within it. Misusing his superhuman strength in a last blind orgy of destruction, Samson perished together with his enemies.

And so ends the story of one of the most famous of all the judges, Samson the mighty man, who was yet so weak towards the maiden from Timnath and towards Delilah, the maiden from the valley of Sorek, and weaker still when he used God's last gift to him to wreak blind vengeance on his foes.

28

The Story of Ruth

AFTER these bloodthirsty tales of war and strife, the serene story of Ruth's life comes as a very pleasant contrast. This story is, indeed, one of the loveliest in the whole of the Old Testament. In the Hebrew Bible we find it as part of five stories, the so-called Festal Rolls which continue to be read in synagogue during certain festivals. The Book of Ruth is read during the Jewish Pentecost, which nearly coincides with Whitsun, and the time of the wheat harvest, for the harvest fields of Palestine are the backcloth of the Book of Ruth. The story begins with the words: ". . . in the days when the judges ruled . . .", and that is the reason why the Authorised Version has appended the story of Ruth to the Book of Judges.

"Now it came to pass," we read, "in the days when the judges ruled, that there was a famine in the land" (Ruth 1:1). And so a family from Bethlehem, in Judah, left for the fields of Moab, beyond the Jordan and the Dead Sea. They were Elimelech and his wife Naomi, and their two sons Mahlon and Chilion, both of whom were to marry women of Moab: Ruth and Orpah. The symbolic nature of the whole story becomes perfectly clear from these names alone. Mahlon means "the ailing" and Chilion "the weak" and both were to die early in life. Their Moabite widows, too, bore symbolic names: Orpah resembling the Hebrew for "traitor", and Ruth meaning "the faithful". And when Naomi returned to her native Bethlehem, it was Ruth who insisted on accompanying her. Back there, all the women said: "Is this Naomi?" (which means loveliness), and she replied: "Call me not Naomi, call me Mara [the bitter] for the Almighty hath dealt very bitterly with me" (Ruth 1:19, 20). Here too we can see how names are an integral part of the story.

While still in far-away Moab, Naomi heard that the Lord had heeded His people and had given them bread. The famine was over and Naomi longed for her country and her people. She tried to persuade her daughters-in-law, both childless widows, to remain in their own land and with their own families instead of choosing the rigours of life in a foreign country. But Ruth, unlike Orpah, would not desert her mother-in-law, and she pronounced these unforgettable words: "Entreat me not to leave thee, or to return from following after thee: for whither thou goest, I will go; and where thou lodgest, I will lodge: thy people shall be my people, and thy God my God: Where thou diest, will I die, and there will I be buried: the Lord do so to me, and more also, if ought but death part thee and me" (Ruth 1:16-18). Ruth knew that leaving her country meant not only breaking all bonds with her family and people, but also serving another God. Yet she did not hesitate to choose the God of Israel, and to abandon the gods of Moab.

Arrived in Bethlehem, Ruth worked hard to support her mother-in-law and herself by gleaning ears of corn in the fields belonging to one Boaz, whose name implied that he was "a man of strength". The gleaning of corn was the traditional privilege of the poor specifically granted them by the Law of Moses. It was part of the social code of ancient Israel, and served to protect not only the poor, the widow and the orphan but the stranger also. Now when Boaz came to inspect his fields, he was greatly struck by this strange girl. His servants told him that she had laboured incessantly from early morning. Boaz then addressed her in kindly words, and she replied with great humility— a poor defenceless woman facing one of the mighty of the land.

Back home, she told Naomi of their meeting. Naomi was delighted, for Boaz, she knew, was a near relative, and as such bound to marry his closest kinsman's widow. This custom was later referred to in the famous discussion between Jesus and the Sadducees about the resurrection. What, they asked, would happen to a woman, who, according to the Law of Moses, had successively married seven brothers and then died herself? If she entered the Kingdom of Heaven, which of the seven brothers would be her real husband? Jesus replied that "in the resurrection they neither marry nor are given in marriage but are as the angels of God in heaven" (see Matthew 22:23-30).

But to return to Ruth and Naomi. Boaz would gladly have done his duty by marrying this attractive girl, but for the fear of offending an even closer kinsman. It was only when this man had publicly proffered his shoe to Boaz in the customary gesture of renunciation that Boaz felt free to marry her. In due course they had a son whose name was Obed and it was Obed who was destined to become the grandfather of David, Saul's successor and King of Jerusalem. Thus it came about that the most famous of all Jewish kings, the founder of a glorious dynasty, the author of the Psalms, had a Moabite great-grandmother, a fact whose importance cannot be stressed enough.

For in the fifth century B.C., shortly after the Babylonian exile and mainly under the influence of Ezra and Nehemiah, the Jews thought fit to wage a bitter struggle for racial purity. They had become an exclusive club, attaching importance to family trees and racially pure ancestors. Yet the story of Ruth ends with the laconic recital of the family tree of the greatest ruler, David, the king whose own racial "purity" was by no means impeccable!

And perhaps this is the most important lesson of the Book of Ruth, this and the example of a faith so great that the Lord Himself was moved by it.

E. *The Kings*

29

The Tabernacle of Shiloh

FROM the desert, the children of Israel brought home their shrine: the Ark of the Covenant. It was quite usual for tribes or even whole nations to worship at a shrine; what was strange about the Israelite Ark was its mobility. Still this was only to be expected in a nomadic people, who believed that their God accompanied them on all their journeys.

The plan of the Ark was revealed to Moses by God Himself on Mount Sinai (Exodus 25-27), and though it played an important part in the journey through the desert, and in the conquest of the Promised Land, the Book of Judges does not mention it at all. However, it reappeared in the First Book of Samuel, having meanwhile been guarded faithfully by the priests. Now it stood in the tabernacle of Shiloh, in central Palestine, its external appearance no more impressive than that of the other little temples which excavations have brought to light. But it was only Shiloh that held the glorious Ark of the Lord, and so Shiloh became the focal point of Jewish worship. To Shiloh, people would bring their sacrifices and at Shiloh offer up their most fervent prayers, for here prayer was said to be more effective than anywhere else on earth.

The temple was guarded by Eli the priest and his two sons Hophni and Phinehas. Eli must have been a good man, yet too weak to curb the wickedness of his sons, who would steal the best part of the sacrifice, and misbehave with the temple prostitutes. Through their misdemeanour they were clearly asking for trouble, and trouble was not slow in coming. The Philistines had meanwhile gone over to full-scale warfare, and when things looked very black indeed for Israel, Hophni and Phinehas decided to avert disaster by bringing the holy Ark to the battlefield. But the Ark had been so defiled that it had lost its power: it was captured, Hophni and Phinehas were slain, and Eli died of grief.

This defeat at the hands of the Philistines might well have spelt the end of Israel, had not Samuel, his people's chosen leader, come to the rescue.

30

Samuel's Call

THE Old Testament gives a detailed description of Samuel's youth, his call and his relations with Eli. His mother, the pious Hannah, was granted a son by God after years of childlessness. Throwing herself before the Ark in anguish and with bitter tears she promised God that, if only He would grant her a son, the child would become Eli's servant in Shiloh. While she was still praying and lamenting, Eli entered and thought that a drunken woman had come to defile his tabernacle. This was not altogether unheard of for the sacrificial wine would often go to people's heads, but when Eli heard what was troubling Hannah, he sent her away with renewed courage. And when a son was born to Hannah, she called him Samuel, meaning "God has heard", and she took him to Eli as soon as he was weaned. But though the child grew up in the company of a weak old man and his two wicked sons, his environment seems to have left him quite untouched. And, like Jesus after him, Samuel gained favour in the eyes of God, and the Lord spoke to him at dead of night. At first, Samuel failed to respond to God, for when he heard his name called twice he thought that Eli was summoning him, and he rushed to the old man's assistance. Twice more Samuel was to hear his name called, and twice more he failed to recognise God's voice.

The Bible tries to explain this strange lapse: the word of God had long been silent and visions of God almost forgotten. In the end it was Eli who realised what was happening to his servant Samuel, and so he instructed him to reply:

"Speak, Lord; for thy servant heareth."

And God's reply spelled the doom of the house of Eli:

"Behold, I will do a thing in Israel, at which both the ears of every one that heareth it shall tingle. In that day I will perform against Eli all things which I have spoken concerning his house: when I begin,

I will also make an end. For I have told him that I will judge his house for ever for the iniquity which he knoweth; because his sons made themselves vile, and he restrained them not. And therefore I have sworn unto the house of Eli, that the iniquity of Eli's house shall not be purged with sacrifice nor offering for ever" (I Samuel 3:11-14).

Thus did Samuel become a prophet amongst his people.

31

The First King

IN Samuel's days the people of Israel had again begun to ask for a king. Samuel had appointed his sons to be judges under him, but his sons had taken bribes and had brought dishonour to the law. No wonder, then, that the people felt no attachment to the house of Samuel and that they told the prophet: "Behold, thou art old, and thy sons walk not in thy ways: now make us a king to judge us like all the nations" (I Samuel 8:5).

Samuel was deeply hurt when he heard this, not only because of the slight to his own pride, but also because of his clear knowledge that God alone was fit to be king over Israel. And when he prayed to God, the Lord confirmed his worst suspicions: "Hearken unto the voice of the people in all that they say unto thee: for they have not rejected thee, but they have rejected me, that I should not reign over them" (I Samuel 8:7).

We often forget how absolute was the power of Oriental kings. Their word was law, their favour man's greatest blessing. The law of Moses made some attempt to curb this power, and in Deuteronomy 17:14-20 we are told that no king may own too many horses, too many women, or too much gold and silver. He must keep a copy of the law and read from it every day "that his heart be not lifted above his brethren". But apart from this, the king could decree how much taxes the people must pay, how many soldiers they must supply for his army, and what wars were to be waged. In none of his decisions was he bound to consult the people, although wise kings would make a point of asking the advice of competent counsellors. Samuel explained all these drawbacks to the Israelites, but they persisted in their desire for a king, and insisted that Samuel proclaim and anoint the Lord's choice.

Now the people pressed so insistently for a king simply because they needed a supreme commander in the field, like other nations. In this respect they were not to be disappointed, for Saul and David put an end to the deep humiliation their people had suffered at the hands of the Philistines. But though the enemy was driven back it was not without grave opposition that the kings managed to consolidate their position.

Their history begins with Saul, the first of the kings. While still a young lad, he had gone out with a servant to look for his father's asses. Just as he was about to turn back empty-handed, the servant suggested that he consult the prophet Samuel, who lived in nearby Ramah. When Saul objected that he did not carry enough money to pay the prophet, the servant offered to lend him the fourth part of a shekel. It is always difficult to assess the true value of ancient currency, but we do know how much the Philistine smiths charged for repairing sickles and ploughshares (see I Samuel 13:20-22). Comparing their charges with the fee of the prophet, we must conclude that his demands were not at all excessive.

Saul met Samuel by the gates of the town. The prophet had been warned by God to prepare for his meeting with the future king, and when Saul appeared the Lord said to Samuel: "Behold the man whom I spake to thee of!" (I Samuel 9:17). After having assured Saul that his asses had meanwhile been found, Samuel began to praise Saul's family. But Saul interrupted him with: "Am not I a Benjamite, of the smallest of the tribes of Israel? and my family the least of all the families of the tribe of Benjamin? wherefore then speakest thou so to me?" (I Samuel 9:21). But Samuel paid no attention and took him into his house and seated him in the place of honour amongst the guests. And next morning he escorted him personally to the gate. It was then that the seer proclaimed the word of God, and told Saul that he was destined to become King over Israel. As a sign Samuel prophesied a number of events that would befall Saul on his way home. At Rachel's tomb, two men would tell him that his asses had been found. By the plain of Tabor he would meet three men carrying sacrifices to Bethel. In

Gibeah he would meet a band of prophets, and be so carried away that he would begin to prophesy with them. It was only when all these predictions had come true that Saul began to believe the prophet's words. Even so, when the people were told of God's choice, the embarrassed Saul hid among the baggage and could only be found with difficulty, for so great was the humility of the youth who had set out to look for his asses and had found a crown instead.

Meanwhile the Philistines had so weakened the Israelites that even the smallest of tribes felt strong enough to invade the country. And so Nahash, king of the Ammonites, laid siege to Jabesh in Gilead. Asked for his surrender terms, he instructed the unhappy inhabitants to pluck out their right eyes. When Saul heard of this he was so incensed that he took a yoke of oxen and cutting them into pieces, sent them throughout all the coasts of Israel, saying: "Whosoever cometh not forth after Saul and after Samuel, so shall it be done unto his oxen" (I Samuel 11:7). Then the people united behind Saul to free Jabesh and to wipe the stain from Judah and Israel. Only after the Ammonites had been beaten off could Saul make his full authority felt and his supporters feel strong enough to threaten his opponents with death. However Saul proved that his wisdom in peace matched his prowess in battle, when he told them that this day, when Israel had been saved by the help of God, no man must be put to death. Instead, he and Samuel would go up to Gilgal to renew the kingdom there, so that all the people could swear loyalty to their new king.

Thus the kingship of Saul seemed to rest on two strong pillars: his divine vocation and a military prowess that had led his people to such great victories. And, indeed no cloud was to mar his glory during the first years of his reign.

32

Saul's Tragedy

SAUL's life was to become embittered by his conflict with Samuel. Characteristically, the Old Testament does not theorise about their struggle, but tells us anecdotes that are far more telling and colourful than any dissertation might have been.

In I Samuel 13 we hear of the first clash between Saul and the priest who had once anointed him. It was during one of the many wars between the Israelites and the Philistines, and Saul's army was on the point of running away. Only a sacrifice to the Lord could avert disaster, but Samuel had not arrived. Now a priest had the right to perform religious ceremonies and no unauthorised person, not even the king, could act as a substitute. But anxious to win the battle Saul decided to offer up the sacrifice himself. Had he looked further than the military needs of the moment, he would not have precipitated the inevitable conflict with Samuel. There followed the so-called "Holy War" against the Amalekites. For us, all wars are unholy, but this must not blind us to the fact that the ancients did wage "Holy Wars", often on the sinister advice of an oracle.

In this instance it had been Samuel who had instructed Saul, in God's name, to smite the Amalekites and to destroy them utterly. The order was horrible, for it meant that no one was to be spared, neither man nor woman, infant or suckling, ox or sheep. The whole thing strikes us as one great senseless slaughter, an unbridled massacre. Still Saul obeyed Samuel's order, though he spared Agag, the king of the Amalekites, and also the best of his sheep and oxen. It would be wrong to believe that Saul was swayed by humanitarian considerations —he probably spared Agag because it pleased him to have a king dancing attendance upon him, for such was the custom in the Middle East. In any case, Samuel was so offended by this act of disobedience that he decided to turn his back on Saul for ever. Saul made a desperate attempt to hold him back, and laying hold of Samuel's robe, he unwittingly ripped it. Samuel was quick to call out: "The Lord hath rent the kingdom of Israel from thee this day, and hath given it to a neighbour of thine, that is better than thou" (I Samuel 15:28). But still Saul would not relinquish his hold, for if Samuel left now, he, Saul, would have lost the last shred of his divine authority. He begged Samuel to stay, if only for external appearances, and strangely enough, Samuel complied for the moment. While Saul remained king, Samuel would try to save his face.

It is very difficult for us to understand Samuel's behaviour. He who was so pitiless to Agag, the king of the Amalekites, and who cut him to pieces with his own hands, could not help mourning for Saul when they eventually did part. Perhaps he realised that Saul had never wanted to be king, and that he had been wrong to coerce the young man. Clearly Saul's lapses were the outward signs of God's rejection of him. No contrition, no prayer, no sacrifice, could alter this fact, and there was no point in Samuel's continued presence at the court. The cup of Saul's bitterness was full, for with Samuel the whole priesthood withdrew from him, and left him a pitifully lonely man. No one would offer up sacrifice in wartime, and even the oracle was silent. The priesthood had never forgiven him for usurping their function, and this was their revenge.

At that time there lived a woman in Endor, who could ask questions of the dead, and though King Saul had done his best to put an end to witchcraft, it was with her that Saul took refuge during the last night of his life. I do not think the Old Testament could have described his tragedy more tellingly than it did. Disguised, and approaching at the dead of night so that even the witch would be deceived, he knocked at her door. Yet the witch recognised him in a vision and the king had to put her mind at rest before she would tell him the rest of her vision: she had seen an old man, covered with a mantle, who could only be Samuel. And Saul asked the witch to tell Samuel how worried he was that God and the prophets had forsaken him, and that not even the oracle would answer him any longer. "Then said Samuel, wherefore then dost thou ask of me, seeing the Lord is departed from thee, and is become thine enemy" (I Samuel 28:16). David would be made king, and Saul together with his sons would next day be killed in battle.

On hearing this, Saul fell unconscious to the ground. We can still see him in all his helplessness, tended by the witch of Endor and supported by his two faithful servants as he went out into the night a broken man.

33

Saul and David

WHEN David was first introduced to the court of Saul, he was already known as a great harpist and an even greater hero, handsome, and experienced in matters of war. True, Saul's armour would not fit David, Saul being of heavier build, but this must not mislead us into thinking David a weakling. It is characteristic of all mythologies that the hero relies more on his presence of mind, his shrewdness and skill, than on mere brute force. And so David preferred to go to battle against the giant armed only with a staff, a bag, a sling and five smooth pebbles.

The fight itself began with curses and much abuse. This was a favourite literary device for prolonging the reader's excitement, or for making him laugh. So, when the Philistine saw the handsome youth bearing his staff and his bag, he exclaimed: "Am I a dog, that thou comest to me with staves? . . . Come to me, and I will give thy flesh unto the fowls of the air, and to the beasts of the field" (I Samuel 17:43, 44). David replied in fitting terms, and, flinging his stone, he felled the giant. The struggle was over before it had even begun, the Philistine army took to its heels, and David was given the king's daughter in marriage.

So far this is a tale like many others, but now we come to another, more important, and typically Biblical aspect: faith in God. Next to God's, man's power is as nought, and God cares neither for Goliath's strength nor for David's courage and resolution. And so the Bible makes David appear much smaller and weaker than he really was. This Biblical message of human frailty pervades the whole story, and was put into David's mouth when he ended his boast of courage in the face of wild animals with the following remark: "The Lord that delivered me out of the paw of the lion, and out of the paw of the bear, he will deliver me out of the hand of this Philistine" (I Samuel 17:37). And to Goliath he said: "Thou comest to me with a sword, and with a spear, and with a shield: but I come to thee in the name of the Lord of Hosts, the God of the armies of Israel, whom thou hast defied" (I Samuel 17:45).

And this was David's glory: that he knew his debt to God. His victory was not won by the sword, nor yet by his courage and shrewd-ness, but by God's will alone. Through his deeds, Israel proclaimed His Majesty to mankind, teaching men to place less trust in human might and greater faith in the power of the God of Israel.

The story of David and Jonathan, the son of Saul, is the story of an unforgettable and lasting friendship. Jonathan, the son of Saul, the king, felt drawn towards young David from the very start. As a token of his affection, he presented David with his robe and garments, his

sword, his bow and his girdle, believing, as was the custom, that part
of his being attached to his clothing and weapons. In the course of the
ensuing years, their friendship was to be put to many a hard test, and
Jonathan's heart must often have wavered between his father and his
friend, as Saul's jealousy of David became quite unmistakable. The
climax came at the time of the new moon, which was always celebrated with a ceremonial meal. But on that day, just as on the day
before, David's seat had remained empty. When Saul wanted to know
why, Jonathan had his excuse ready: David had gone to Bethlehem to
celebrate the new moon with his own family. Saul knew that Jonathan
was lying, and so he turned on him: "Thou son of the perverse rebellious woman, do not I know that thou hast chosen the son of Jesse to
thine own confusion, and unto the confusion of thy mother's nakedness?" (I Samuel 20:30).

Then Saul revealed the real reason of his hatred: David was the pretender to the throne, and Jonathan would not rule while David lived.
Saul must have heard the people sing:

> "Saul hath slain his thousands,
> and David his ten thousands"
> (I Samuel 18:7)

and drawn the right conclusion—David must die. But Jonathan protested, and his indifference to the future of the dynasty so enraged Saul,
that he threw his javelin at Jonathan, who left the table in fierce
anger.

From then on Jonathan did his utmost to protect David from his
father's wrath. Of course, he had to work secretly and to keep his
eyes wide open, but then his friendship had come to mean much
more to him than his father's goodwill. And when David had to take
refuge in the wilderness, Jonathan sought him out and said: "Fear not;
for the hand of Saul my father shall not find thee; and thou shalt be
king over Israel, and I shall be next unto thee; and that also Saul my
father knoweth" (I Samuel 23:17). Yes, he would rather play second
fiddle to David, than be the first in the land without him.

Yet Jonathan's wish was not to come true: he fell in the battle of
Gilboa by his father's side. When David was brought the news, he
lamented loudly:

H

"How are the mighty fallen in the midst of the battle!
O Jonathan, thou wast slain in thine high places.
I am distressed for thee, my brother Jonathan:
very pleasant hast thou been unto me:
thy love to me was wonderful, passing the love of women.
How are the mighty fallen, and the weapons of war perished!"

(II Samuel 1:25-27)

No one else was ever to take Jonathan's place in the heart of David, and this was only right, for each friendship is unique, and a true friend irreplaceable.

After the defeat of Abner, the captain of Saul's army, and the death of Ishbosheth, Saul's other son, David was made king over both Judah and Israel. It was then that he made his greatest decision: Jerusalem was to be the capital of his kingdom.

34

David Founds Jerusalem

THERE are many reasons why David's decision to make Jerusalem his capital was wise and good. In the first place the walled fortress on Mount Zion was easily defended, and, furthermore, inhabited by strangers as it had been, it belonged to none of the tribes of Judah or Israel, and no one could feel slighted by David's choice of capital. We must remember that the people of Judah and Israel were made up of a large number of families and tribes, each with their own leaders and all prizing their independence. They would never have allowed any one tribe to rule over them, and only common danger would force them to band together temporarily. Once a battle was over and the immediate danger averted, each tribe would return home and forget about its neighbours. It was a sign of David's political sagacity that he made no attempt to subject the tribes to force of arms but won them over by tact and diplomacy instead.

David's capital was by no means a large city. Its streets were narrow and the houses close together, just as they were in our own mediaeval towns. We are told that Mount Zion, and David's city, lay on the western hill of modern Jerusalem, but in fact David founded his city east of it, close to the Temple Hill of today.

Of the forty years that David reigned, he spent thirty-three in Jerusalem. Through its gates he would take his army each spring to protect and extend his borders. David's military career consisted of a series of successful forays, all based on Jerusalem. From one of these, he brought back the Ark to Jerusalem, thus turning his capital at one and the same time into a Holy City and a House of the Lord. The Ark entered the city to the strains of festive song, psalteries, harps, timbrels, cornets and cymbals, and it was this festive procession which was responsible for the permanent estrangement between David and his wife Michal, the daughter of Saul. She objected strongly to David's leaping and dancing before the Ark, clothed only in a linen ephod, the priests' loose robe. And so she scolded him bitterly: "How glorious was the king of Israel today, who uncovered himself today in the eyes of the handmaids of his servants, as one of the vain fellows shamelessly uncovereth himself!" (II Samuel 6:20). And David rebuffed her with proud words, for which she could never forgive him. He was not to be the father of her children, for she "had no child unto the day of her death".

The presence of the Ark turned a nation of roving nomads into a settled people. Their God who had previously dwelled amongst the cherubim had become the God who lived on Mount Zion. In David's time the Ark was still housed poorly in a tent, but soon Solomon would build it a temple so glorious that its praises would be sung throughout the length and breadth of the East. From far and wide pilgrims came to pay homage to the holy shrine, and Jerusalem became the spiritual centre it was to remain throughout the centuries, in prosperity and adversity alike. David's dynasty was to come to an end, but not so the glory of his city; the Ark itself was to be seized, so that the shrine of the Second Temple had to remain empty, but still the Temple was sanctified by its lost glory. By the time the Temple itself was laid waste, never to be rebuilt, Jerusalem and Mount Zion had become engraved in the hearts of the pious. The sanctity of the Ark and the Temple had passed into the spirit of this holy city and its holy mountain, and in the minds of Jews and Christians Jerusalem is for ever associated with the greater glory of God.

This love for Jerusalem, this reverence for Mount Zion, have become political realities in modern Israel. When the author of the Second Book of Samuel wrote of the city's simple beginnings in about 1000 B.C. he could hardly have suspected that, thirty centuries later, Jerusalem would still be a fount of spiritual strength.

35

Nathan the Prophet

DAVID ruled over Jerusalem like any Oriental potentate. The king's will was law, and he responsible to no one. But David knew his own weaknesses, and could never forget how he had acted over Bathsheba, the wife of Uriah the Hittite.

The events are described in such detail, that we feel they must have been reported by an eyewitness who, though he loved his king, made no attempt to whitewash him. Possibly the author was one who was himself deeply involved in the events: Nathan the prophet. David had remained home that spring, sending Joab to lay siege to Rabbah, an Ammonite town. And so the devil found work for the King's idle hands: David became infatuated with Bathsheba, and could not wait for Uriah the Hittite to divorce her. Uriah had to be put out of the way at once.

No doubt Joab would have pleaded that he was acting under orders, a favourite defence of all war criminals, then as now. In any event when Uriah the soldier came to him with his own death warrant, Joab had no hesitation in doing David's bidding. For Uriah bore a letter from the King, in which David told his commander: "Set ye Uriah in the forefront of the hottest battle, and retire ye from him, that he may be smitten, and die" (II Samuel 11:15), and Joab hastened to oblige his Lord and Master. Knowing full well how impatient the king must have been to hear of the outcome, Joab sent a messenger with tidings of an unsuccessful attack on the besieged city. Should the king become angry, the messenger was to say: Uriah the Hittite, too, had fallen. And this indeed is what happened. At first David ranted against Joab for his recklessness in battle, but when he heard that Uriah had been killed, he told the messenger: "Thus shalt thou say unto

Joab, Let not this thing displease thee, for the sword devoureth one as well as another: make thy battle more strong against the city . . ." (II Samuel 11:25). A mighty king had used all his powers to destroy one of his humble servants, so that the servant's wife could join the royal harem and make David the legitimate father of the child she had conceived. Who would now dare raise his voice against the king? But there was one who did, one who dared say aloud what was on everyone's mind—Nathan the prophet. He came to the king, ostensibly to consult him on a point of law. There lived a rich man who had sheep and cattle in plenty, and a poor man who had but one ewe lamb which he had bought and reared, which had grown up with his own children, had eaten of his own food, had drunk of his own cup, had slept in his own arms and which he had loved as a daughter. Yet when the rich man had brought a visitor to his table, he would not kill one of his own cattle, but had slaughtered the poor man's ewe lamb instead.

Just man that David was, he became infuriated and said to Nathan: the lamb shall be restored fourfold and the rich man put to death. Only then did Nathan tell him simply: "Thou art the man." And all David could say was: "I have sinned against the Lord" (II Samuel 12:7 and 13). Thereupon Nathan forgave him in the Lord's name, for he had humbled himself. Rarely has sin been confessed and forgiveness been proclaimed in so short and effective a way. No drama, no histrionics, just a poor sinner facing his God in all his nakedness. And on the other side no reproaches, no sermons, but simply the conviction that there is no sin so black that God would not forgive it, if only repentance was deep and sincere enough. The sequel to the story is strange and difficult to understand. The child Bathsheba had given him fell ill and the king fasted and prayed throughout the seven days of the child's illness. He was wrestling with God for its life, but all was in vain, for the child died. And then the strange thing happened: David actually felt relieved, for he washed and anointed himself and was ready to eat once more. He accepted the child's death as just punishment for the crime he had perpetrated against its mother's first husband, and so he grieved no longer.

36

Absalom's Treachery

KING DAVID was to have little joy from Absalom, his favourite son. The King's love for Absalom had so blinded him to his son's knavery, that he had failed to act in time.

Absalom wanted nothing better than to be Crown Prince, and so he courted popular favour. In this he was helped greatly by his appearance: he was said to be the best-looking man in all Israel, and without any blemish. His magnificent shock of hair had to be cut every year, for else it would have weighed him down. It was this that was one day to cause his downfall.

But not by his good manners and his noble figure alone did he impress the populace. He was a born demagogue and knew how to handle people. At the break of dawn he would proceed to the city gates, there to cast doubt upon the king's legal pronouncements by agreeing with plaintiff and defendant alike. He realised, however, that it was not enough to ingratiate himself, and that he had to impress the mob by his regal bearing. So he drove about in a chariot, ostentatiously preceded by fifty heralds. The populace was particularly awed by his many horses, for horses were a novelty in David's day.

By this time, Absalom was nearly thirty years old, and feeling that time was running short, he had himself proclaimed King of Hebron. Hebron was the old royal city and its inhabitants had not forgiven David for having moved his capital to Jerusalem.

Absalom could also count on the fact that many supporters of the house of Saul had not forgotten their grudge against his father, that the ten northern tribes had never liked being ruled by the south, and that everyone objected to the high taxes David had levied to pay for his many wars. But despite Absalom's open insurrection, his father continued to shut his eyes to Absalom's treachery, no doubt because he refused to admit to himself how corrupt his own son really was. It was only when Jerusalem was lost and David, together with his faithful band, had to leave the city, that he decided to hit back.

His victory was a foregone conclusion from the moment that

Absalom's ministers were foolish enough to prefer the advice of Hushai the Archite to that of Ahithophel, one of Absalom's staunchest supporters. Ahithophel was an exceptionally intelligent man, and his contemporaries knew him as such, for whenever he spoke, his wisdom was apparent to all. When David heard that the wisest of his counsellors had deserted him, he realised that only this weighty enemy had to be silenced for there to be any hope of success. And so he instructed Hushai the Archite to insinuate himself into Absalom's confidence and to advise him badly.

Hushai, therefore, went up to Jerusalem and vied with the populace in shouting: God save the King! Hushai managed to dispel all Absalom's doubts about his sincerity by saying: "Nay; but whom the Lord, and this people, and all the men of Israel, choose, his will I be, and with him will I abide. And again, whom should I serve? should I not serve in the presence of his son? as I have served in thy father's presence, so will I be in thy presence" (II Samuel 16:18-19). And Absalom believed him, and made him a counsellor.

Now when Ahithophel asked to be given twelve thousand men to march against David that very night while David was still weak and tired, Hushai knew that this plan would most certainly have utterly destroyed his master. He would have to do his utmost to dissuade Absalom, but his task was an almost impossible one, for he was still treated with some suspicion and lacked the authority of his opponent.

We can still feel the delight with which the Biblical story-teller revelled in Hushai's success against such odds. "The counsel", the Book makes him begin, "that Ahithophel hath given is not good at this time" (II Samuel 17:7). Everyone must have been dumbfounded by his impertinence. What next would he say? And so the whole council listened with bated breath as Hushai warned them not to underestimate David. He went on to describe the authority that David still enjoyed amongst the people and that David was surely lying in ambush for Absalom's army. The only remedy was for Absalom to gather all his men about him and to be vigilant day and night.

And the people knowing David to be a shrewd warrior, said: "The counsel of Hushai the Archite is better than the counsel of Ahithophel" (II Samuel 17:14). Only men whose judgment was clouded would have behaved as they did, and Ahithophel realising that all was lost, saddled his ass and rode home to put his affairs in order, before hanging himself.

And so Hushai helped King David gain precious time to close his ranks. But even when David felt strong enough to recapture the Holy City, his love for Absalom was so great that he ordered his commanders to spare him. But this time Joab ignored his master's wishes. When he found Absalom caught by his beautiful hair in the branches of a tree, he killed him outright. When King David heard the news, he called out: "O my son Absalom, my son, my son!" (II Samuel 18:33). And so ends a chapter of the Bible that tells how a civil war was decided in the council chamber rather than on the field of battle. Ahithophel appealed to man's reason, and was therefore bound to lose, while Hushai, who played on man's stupidity, was bound to win.

<h1 style="text-align:center">37</h1>

Rizpah, the Antigone of Israel

STUDENTS of Greek mythology are familiar with the story of Antigone who could not rest while her brother Polynices lay unburied in the fields. So she called upon the whirlwind to cover him with sand and for this act of disobedience King Creon ordered her to be buried alive. Israel too had her Antigone, and her name was Rizpah.

Rizpah's story begins with a famine that lasted three years. Famines in Palestine were always due to drought, and droughts were sent by God, and so David consulted the oracle to discover in what way God had been offended.

And the oracle told him that the blood of the Gibeonites was still on Saul and his house, and that God demanded seven sons from the house of Saul so that the Gibeonites could hang them, to the honour of God, as it were. Now we cannot possibly agree that the sacrifice of seven innocent lives could ever redound to God's honour, and so we must look upon this story as just another illustration of the way in which man can corrupt his religion.

Among the seven men delivered up to the Gibeonites were the two sons of Rizpah, one of Saul's concubines. They were put to death

during the first day of the barley harvest, and their bodies left in the
fields as prey to the beasts and the birds. Now this was the worst fate
that could have befallen them, for the people believed that only burial
could bring peace and rest to the dead. This is why "Rizpah the
daughter of Aiah took sackcloth, and spread it for her upon the rock,
[and lay there] from the beginning of harvest until water dropped upon
them out of heaven, and suffered neither the birds of the air to rest on
them by day, nor the beasts of the field by night" (II Samuel 21:10).

Now, the wheat harvest takes place in April and the rainy season
starts in October, and all the while the sun has sent down its blistering
rays. During those months the land is dead, the flowers faded, the
grass withered. In the heat of day people escape into the shade, but all
the while Rizpah sat in the open, ceaselessly beating off the birds of
prey by day, and the wild beasts by night.

And when King David was told of Rizpah's doings, his judgment
was far more humane than that of King Creon: he gave orders to
bury the corpses. And he did more than that. He remembered that the
bodies of Saul and Jonathan had still not been taken to the sepulchre
of Kish, Saul's father, and he made good the omission. Only then, the
story has it, did God relent, and send down rain on the thirsty land.
Thus did Rizpah's great love open King David's eyes and so save the
whole country.

38

David the Psalmist

THE Bible tells us that David was a gifted poet whose songs were
often set to music and called Psalms, a word derived from a Greek verb
meaning "to pluck".

Now it is a mistake to think that all the Psalms were written by
David himself. Psalm 90, for instance, is called "A Prayer of Moses,
the man of God", and Psalm 137 with its nostalgic longing for Jerusalem stems clearly from the sad days of the Babylonian exile in the
sixth century B.C. and long after David's death. The Book of Psalms
was therefore written in the course of at least seven centuries.

The Psalms have probably made a deeper religious impression on man than any other part of the Old Testament. Not only are many Christian hymns based on them, but they have inspired composers and poets to works of great beauty. Watts's famous "O God, our help in ages past" is based on the Psalms and so is "God save the Queen".

The Psalms were written in accordance with a time-honoured poetic device of the Hebrews: parallelism. In parallelism we have a correspondence of successive passages, the second quite often simply reformulating the first. Thus Psalm 15 begins with the double question:

> "Lord, who shall abide in thy tabernacle?
> who shall dwell in thy holy hill?"

And the answer, too, comes in two similar lines:

> "He that walketh uprightly, and worketh righteousness,
> and speaketh the truth in his heart."

More rarely, the second line is used to emphasise the first by contrast, as in the ending of Psalm 1:

> "For the Lord knoweth the way of the righteous:
> but the way of the ungodly shall perish."

The reason why many Psalms seem to lack logical cohesion is that various voices were used to recite the different verses, and that it is no longer possible to reconstruct the way in which the parts were arranged. A good example of this type of part-song is the Second Psalm, recited at coronations. Verses 1-3 were obviously spoken by the people as they decried the plots of the heathen against the Lord. Then the priest chimed in to tell how God in His omniscience derides the vain counsel of the nations and sets his king high up on Mount Zion (verses 4-6). In verses 7-8 the king himself makes known what God has told him, and in verse 9 he is once more the listener: "Thou shalt break them with a rod of iron; thou shalt dash them in pieces like a potter's vessel." Then the Psalm returns to its original theme of admonishing the heathen, and concludes with the general benediction: "Blessed are all they that put their trust in him."

People have often asked why some psalms are repeated. Psalm 70, for instance, is very similar to Psalm 40:14-17, and Psalm 108 consists of Psalms 57:8-11, and 60:7-12. Now these repetitions arise from the fact that the Book of Psalms was collected by more than one man, and that there were at least five original sets of Psalms. Each set ended with the customary liturgical formula: "Blessed be the Lord God of Israel from everlasting, and to everlasting. Amen, and Amen" (Psalm 41:13). Similar endings are found in Psalm 72:18-19; Psalm 89:52; Psalm 106:48 and more elaborately in the entire last psalm. From Psalm 72:20 we may also gather that each set had a title of its own, the second book being called: "The prayers of David the son of Jesse." And so the mystery is solved except for the fact that the repetitions are not literal but show small discrepancies. These must have crept in as the various writers committed to paper the songs they had learned by heart.

It is rather difficult to date the Psalms, for only a small number refer to specific historical events. Psalm 137 is clearly a song about the Babylonian exile (586 to 539 B.C.) and in other cases a close scrutiny of the ideas on which the song is based may sometimes, if rarely, help to date it very approximately. By this method the well-known Psalm 118 can be dated before the exile, for it speaks of a popular procession to the horns of the altar. Now this must have happened before the exile, for afterwards only the priests were allowed to approach the Holy of Holies.

Ever since excavations have brought to light the literature of the ancient world, there have been suggestions that the Psalms were in fact copied from other nations. Babylon, in particular, knew many songs that bore a striking resemblance to the Psalms, so much so that the great expert on Babylonia, Friedrich Delitzsch, thought he could speak of downright plagiarism. Few would agree with him now; we prefer to think that the similarities were due to what anthropologists call the convergence of related cultures.

This is best illustrated by the example of Psalm 104 which resembles the sun-hymn of Akhenaten who ruled over Egypt in the fourteenth century B.C., and who elevated Aten, the god of the Sun, to supremacy amongst the gods. In his honour Akhenaten composed a hymn which contained the following verses:

"Thou goest down to rest behind the western mountain of light, and cloakest the earth with the darkness of death; the sleeper retireth to his chamber, his mind veiled, and his eye clouded over; yea, though all his gold be stolen from under his pillow, he knoweth it not. The lion cometh forth from his den. . . . But when thou returnest from behind the mountain of light, brightness is cast over the earth, and darkness is set to flight; thou sendest forth thy rays and both lands rejoice, the sleeper awaketh and springeth to his feet. . . .

"How numerous are thy works; albeit they are hidden from the face (of man), thou who art the one god beside whom there is no other. It hath pleased thee to create the earth, with its men, cattle and the other beasts. . . .

"Thou hast set each man in his place; thou providest for his needs, feeding the hungry whose days are numbered. . . .

"The world is in thy hands, for thou hast created it. When thou risest, man liveth, and when thou settest, he dieth. Thou art life: man liveth through thee."

Now though these verses bear a strong resemblance to Psalm 104, the sun-hymn to Aten differs from the Psalm in that its revered god of the sun is not the invisible God of Israel, who can only be served by man's submission to His moral laws. And it is precisely this unique point of view which distinguishes the Psalms from all other writings, however similar they may be, and which makes the Book of Psalms one of the most inspiring of all.

39

The Reign of Solomon

THE First Book of Kings never tires of extolling Solomon's wealth and wisdom, so much so that the reader is inclined to tire of all his gold and ivory. In fact, Solomon's whole story strikes us as so fabulous that we feel we must be reading the story of the Thousand and One Nights rather than the Bible which otherwise is so sober. But if we read between the lines, we cannot help noticing that, all his glittering gold notwithstanding, Solomon was by no means the perfect guardian of the kingdom he had inherited.

He had first of all many enemies, also inherited from King David. One of these was Hadad, King of Edom in the South. Hadad, together with some of his officers, had managed to escape King David's wrath and had taken refuge with the Egyptian Pharaoh. He had but one desire: to return home and to take vengeance. Together with the King of Aram in the north, he crossed the borders and Solomon, who was no warrior, could do little to stop them. The enemy was at the gate, and at the slightest sign of internal strife he would fall upon the capital.

And there was, indeed, great danger of such internal strife developing into full-scale rebellion. Under King David the nation had been united in worshipping God, but during Solomon's reign, temple and ritual were becoming more important than obedience to God's will, and idolatry was again rearing its ugly head. According to the Book of Kings this change was largely wrought by Solomon's harem of foreign princesses, with their strange customs and false gods. As King Solomon grew older, not only did he grow more tolerant of all this idolatry, but himself became influenced by it: "For it came to pass, when Solomon was old, that his wives turned away his heart after other gods: and his heart was not perfect with the Lord his God, as was the heart of David his father" (I Kings 11:4). The moral is clear: nations are strong not through the might of their arms alone, but above all through their spiritual unity. When that has gone, no amount of social benefits, gold reserves, and up-to-date weapons will be able to halt the nation's downfall.

Solomon's reign, therefore, despite his fabulous wealth, bore the germs of its own destruction. What had always distinguished Israel from all other nations was in danger of disappearing. The God of Israel had become one god amongst the many gods of the Canaanites, the Temple but one shrine amongst other shrines. And what was almost as bad, the bond between the twelve tribes, that had always been a little tenuous, was in danger of fast breaking up altogether. Their unity had enabled the tribes to keep the common foe at bay, but it had had to be paid for in heavy taxation, and all the taxes now went to Jerusalem as a matter of course. True, Solomon's lavish expenditure was partly met by the profits from his trading in horses and carts, and also from sheep-farming, but his extravagance was such that the people had to make up the balance, and a staggering balance it was. No wonder the poor peasants in the north murmured as they saw caravan after caravan laden with gold, making for Jerusalem. The Holy City had become a millstone around their necks, and while they sweated, Solomon had so much gold that he had to hide it in the forest of

Lebanon, whence the Pharaoh of Egypt would one day take it all with a minimum of trouble.

And so Solomon left his successor with an impossible heritage: an empire weakened within and with strengthened foes without, and a population that needed little encouragement to break away. All the wisdom of Solomon would have been hard put to it to preserve unity under such circumstances.

40

The Wisdom of Solomon

THOUGH the First Book of Kings devotes most of its attention to Solomon, he never really comes to life. He is like one of the many stylised figures known from Egyptian and Babylonian sculpture— impressive and great but not at all flesh and blood. King David had been quite the opposite, for despite his greatness and glory, he had been every inch a man. The Bible never tired of speaking of the many deeds that had endeared him to his people. But not so Solomon, whose only great quality was the wisdom that God had given him in Gibeon. Here, at the altar, God had appeared to the king in a vision, and told him that He would grant his dearest wish. And when Solomon had asked to be made a wise judge over his people, he had shown that he had never been altogether devoid of wisdom, even before his vision.

Though Solomon's actions were often quite ruthless—he had given orders for Adonijah, his rival to the crown, to be murdered, for Joab, King David's commander, to be assassinated while taking refuge by the horns of the altar, for the high priest to be dismissed, and for old Shimei to be put away—he was humble towards the Lord, and only desired an understanding heart to distinguish between good and evil, the better to judge his people. And his wish was good in the eyes of God, for Solomon had not asked for long life or riches nor for vengeance, usually man's dearest desires, but for wisdom instead. And when God granted him wisdom, all the rest came as a matter of course.

Kings had to be wise, indeed, in those days, for it was they who had to judge all the most difficult lawsuits in the land. Simpler cases might be judged by the town gate, but when justice was long in coming, only the king could put things right, and woe to the ruler who was slow of wit and understanding. But Solomon quickly proved his worth. All Israel knew his shrewd decision in the case of the two women who had claimed the same child, and the people realised that only God could have granted him so much understanding.

His fame was not confined to Judah and Israel, but reached far beyond the borders. Nor was it his shrewdness alone that the people admired, but his proverbs and songs also. Full of respect for him, the Book of Kings tells us: "And he spake of trees, from the cedar tree that is in Lebanon even unto the hyssop that springeth out of the wall: he spake also of beasts, and of fowl, and of creeping things, and of fishes. And there came of all people to hear the wisdom of Solomon, from all kings of the earth, which had heard of his wisdom" (I Kings 4:33-34). No wonder then, that the report of Solomon's wisdom reached the ears of the Queen of Sheba who decided to set out on a long journey simply to match her own wits against the king's. Their meeting is described very briefly in I Kings 10, but neither is her name given nor her country located accurately. This is why she has given rise to so many legends, some of which have even found their way into the Koran, the Holy Book of Islam. Here we can read that Solomon had learnt the language of wild animals and taught them obedience to his will. One day he decided to summon all the animals to a meeting but only the hoopoe, a bird revered by the Arabs, disobeyed the summons. For this insubordination, it was sentenced to death, *in absentia*. The bird was reprieved, however, when it finally appeared to explain that it had been delayed by the wonders of the land of Sheba, a country so incredibly rich, that its very soil was more precious than gold and silver. Thereupon the hoopoe was instructed to fly back to the queen with an invitation to King Solomon's court. Afraid of offending the mighty King, the queen set out on a journey that was to last many years. Solomon received her in his glass palace, and as she approached his throne she thought she was wading through a pool of clear water and so lifted her skirt to prevent it from getting wet.

Nor were the Mohammedans the only people to have paid attention to this meeting, and the greatest of modern Hebrew poets, Bialik, has collected a host of Jewish legends about the riddles the queen asked of Solomon and his brilliant answers to them. But the Old Testament itself says nothing of these riddles, nor does it mention

Solomon's marriage to the queen, a marriage from which the present royal house of Abyssinia claims to be descended.

All these non-Biblical legends make it clear how interested Jews, Christians and Mohammedans alike have been in the Queen of Sheba. Archaeologists believe that they have at last discovered her kingdom and are unearthing the ruins of what they think must have been her capital. Meanwhile she remains a mysterious woman of whom nothing but her wisdom and wealth is known. Her presents to the King, the Bible tells us, excelled everything Jerusalem had ever seen: "And she gave the king an hundred and twenty talents of gold, and of spices very great store, and precious stones: there came no more such abundance of spices as these which the queen of Sheba gave to King Solomon" (I Kings 10:10). So much for her wealth. As for her wisdom, the Bible tells us that it was no match for King Solomon's: "And Solomon told her all her questions: there was not any thing hid from the king, which he told her not" (I Kings 10:3). And so she had to admit: "It was a true report that I heard in mine own land of thy acts and of thy wisdom. Howbeit I believed not the words, until I came, and mine eyes had seen it: and, behold, the half was not told me: thy wisdom and prosperity exceedeth the fame which I heard" (I Kings 10:6-7).

In trying to reconstruct their duel of wits, we could do worse than look at the Book of Proverbs. In my opinion, many of the Proverbs are simply the answers to riddles, and Proverbs 6:16-19 must surely have been the answer to the riddle: What six things does the Lord hate, and which seventh thing does he abominate?

> "These six things doth the Lord hate:
> yea, seven are an abomination unto him:
> A proud look, a lying tongue,
> and hands that shed innocent blood,
> An heart that deviseth wicked imaginations,
> feet that be swift in running to mischief,
> A false witness that speaketh lies,
> and he that soweth discord among brethren."

Some further examples of such answers are found in Proverbs 30:18-19 and 21-31:

A canal in Iraq.

The Temple Mountain of Uruk.

Plate 5

A *wadi* near Jericho.

The Samaritan Pentateuch being displayed during the

Plate 6

"There be three things which are too wonderful for me,
yea, four which I know not:
The way of an eagle in the air;
the way of a serpent upon a rock;
the way of a ship in the midst of the sea;
and the way of a man with a maid.
For three things the earth is disquieted,
and for four which it cannot bear:
For a servant when he reigneth;
and a fool when he is filled with meat;
For an odious woman when she is married;
and an handmaid that is heir to her mistress.
There be four things which are little upon the earth,
but they are exceeding wise:
The ants are a people not strong,
yet they prepare their meat in the summer;
The conies are but a feeble folk,
yet make they their houses in the rocks;
The locusts have no king,
yet go they forth all of them by bands;
The spider taketh hold with her hands,
and is in kings' palaces.
There be three things which go well,
yea, four are comely in going:
A lion which is strongest among beasts,
and turneth not away for any;
A greyhound; an he goat also;
and a king, against whom there is no rising up."

(Proverbs 30:21-31)

We can open the Book of Proverbs on any of its pages and be inspired by its sparkling wit and elegant expression. The book is also full of humour and rightly so, for once man has seen himself in all his vanity he will be able to laugh at himself, with a laughter that may well be a reflection of God's own mirth.

Though the Book is headed: "The proverbs of Solomon, the son of David, king of Israel", we must not think that all the proverbs

I

were written by Solomon, just as we must not think that all the Psalms were written by David. Both kings had a reputation, the one for his proverbs and the other for his psalms, and ancient writers preferred to attribute their own contributions to the acknowledged leaders in the field. A wise writer would rather enhance his sayings by giving them the weight of Solomon's authority than have people congratulate him on his own cleverness. Even so there is no doubt that many of the proverbs were written by Solomon himself, thus reflecting his own great wisdom. And perhaps the greatest lesson that can be learnt from him, is that virtue and wisdom need not be the boring topics that many preachers make them.

On the other hand, the Book of Proverbs can be criticised for its priggishness and for the way in which it represents the point of view of the successful. While the prophets defended justice and the rights of the poor, wisdom now proclaimed the advantages of prosperity and a settled way of life. Social reformers have consequently preferred prophets like Amos and Jeremiah to Solomon in all his glory. His wisdom appeals to our self-interest; he extolled diligence, temperance and chastity, and reserved all his scorn for sloth, drunkenness and adultery. This is how Solomon admonished the lie-a-bed:

> "Go to the ant, thou sluggard;
> consider her ways, and be wise"
> (Proverbs 6:6)

He ridiculed laziness with:

> "The slothful man saith,
> There is a lion without, I shall be slain in the streets."
> (Proverbs 22:13)

or with:

> "As the door turneth upon his hinges,
> so doth the slothful upon his bed."
> (Proverbs 26:14)

The drunkard too gets his share of scathing ridicule:

"Who hath woe? who hath sorrow? who hath contentions? who hath babbling? who hath wounds without cause? who hath redness of eyes? They that tarry long at the wine; they that go to seek mixed wine. Look not thou upon the wine when it is red, when it giveth his colour in the cup, when it moveth itself aright. At the last it biteth like a serpent, and stingeth like an adder. Thine eyes shall behold strange women, and thine heart shall utter perverse things. Yea, thou shalt be as he that lieth down in the midst of the sea, or as he that lieth upon the top of a mast. They have stricken me, shalt thou say, and I was not sick; they have beaten me and I felt it not: when shall I awake? I will seek it yet again" (Proverbs 23:29-35).

Still, drunkenness is often caused by the wickedness of women, and so we may read:

> "It is better to dwell in a corner of the housetop,
>   than with a brawling woman in a wide house."
> (Proverbs 21:9 and 25:24)

Or:

> "It is better to dwell in the wilderness,
>   than with a contentious and an angry woman."
> (Proverbs 21:19)

And also:

> "A continual dropping in a very rainy day
>   and a contentious woman are alike."
> (Proverbs 27:15)

But, no one can reproach the writer of the book with being a misogynist, for while the shrew aroused his most scathing scorn, the good housewife was thought worthy of the highest praise:

> "Who can find a virtuous woman?
>   for her price is far above rubies. . . ."
> (Proverbs 31:10)

All this is very well, we may say, but what is wisdom without piety, and where, oh where, is the piety of the Proverbs? No doubt they are full of the most excellently pointed morals, but where is the driving force behind them? We need not fear, however, for piety is at the root of the whole book, though the writer has seen little point in giving voice to idle repetition. Right at the beginning he tells us in few words, but clear, that:

"The fear of the Lord is the beginning of knowledge:
but fools despise wisdom and instruction."

(Proverbs 1:7)

The close relationship between fear of the Lord (piety) and virtue
is so obvious as to need no emphasis. The most inspiring sermon is
often the one in which the name of God is but rarely mentioned, nor
is he the truest Christian who for ever bandies the name of Jesus about.
And so the Proverbs simply consider wisdom an integral part of God's
world and deem the sage wise precisely because he lives in fear of the
Lord. It was the fool who said "there is no God", and we know that
"a reproof entereth more into a wise man than an hundred stripes into
a fool" (Proverbs 17:12 and 10).

Godlessness and foolishness go hand in hand, and so do piety and
wisdom. Or, to quote the Proverbs once more:

"The fear of the Lord is the instruction of wisdom;
and before honour is humility."

(Proverbs 15:33)

F. *The Age of the Prophets*

41

The Break-up of the Kingdom

WHEN Solomon died after a life of peace and prosperity, his son Rehoboam was crowned in Shechem without any of the obvious signs of trouble that marked most changes of ruler in the East. The only cloud on the new King's horizon was a deputation brought by Jeroboam to petition earnestly for some relief from the great burden of taxation. Now, Jeroboam had been one of King Solomon's most brilliant underlings, but they had fallen out when Ahijah the Shilonite had proposed crowning Jeroboam King in Solomon's stead. Though the Bible does not state explicitly that Jeroboam had agreed to Ahijah's championship, we are told that he had to flee to Egypt where Pharaoh had offered him full protection.

We need not be surprised to learn that the Pharaoh behaved so generously, for he must have been very anxious indeed about the continued expansion of David and Solomon's kingdom. The many caravans which travelled from Egypt to prosperous Mesopotamia had to pass through this kingdom, and keeping the routes open was a matter of life and death for Egypt. Any friendly pretender to the throne of Israel was therefore made more than welcome.

But now Solomon had died, and Jeroboam had hastened back home to present his petition. When, three days later, the deputation returned to the king for his answer, they were met with hostility. King Rehoboam obviously preferred the muddled advice of his younger counsellors to the voices of his sages. Now, the Bible was not opposed to autocracy on principle, for Saul and David had been autocrats too, and yet their actions had not been condemned. At worst, the Bible had admonished them when their anger was out of all proportion to the provocation they had received. But Rehoboam's case was altogether different. During the tricky period that invariably accompanied all changes of government, friendship and understanding were two prerequisites of internal peace. Yet Rehoboam's false pride was so great that, far from showing any glimmer of sympathy, he had told the deputation that whereas his father had chastised them with whips, he would chastise them with scorpions. His foolish reply was to unleash the chain of unhappy events from which Judah and Israel were to suffer for centuries. From that moment onwards, the rebellious tribes in the north refused to submit to Rehoboam's authority. They stoned their governor, and even threatened the King's life, forcing him to race back in his chariot to the safety of Jerusalem. Thenceforth Jeroboam and Rehoboam, Israel and Judah, would each go their separate ways, and all would suffer for it. Judah was the first to feel the pinch, for Shishak, the Pharaoh of Egypt, had played his diplomatic cards so well that five years later he overran her with little opposition and captured Jerusalem. Solomon's gold had long before turned the Holy City into a magnet for robbers, large and small, and Shishak, too, was out for loot. And so the golden shields which Solomon, for lack of anything better to do with his gold, had used for decorating the Temple, found a new home in the land of the Nile.

The Bible tells us that Rehoboam then replaced his father's golden shields with copper and the brilliance of Solomon's glorious kingdom finally gave way to the dull lustre of a poor substitute.

The southern tribes could never reconcile themselves to the new order, and all their writings bore witness to their longing for Jerusalem's former glory. And so began the fratricidal war in which Israel made common cause with the sons of Aram. Both Israel and Judah wasted their substance to such an extent that when the time came they fell like ripe fruit off a tree into the laps of the Assyrians and the Babylonians.

Though the Old Testament distinguishes between Judah and Israel, it is not altogether consistent. In many passages the prophets spoke of Israel, when they were clearly referring to Judah. In general, we can say that the Bible used the term "Israel" in its wider religious sense: "Israel" applied to all those who had united in worship before the one and only God. This need not surprise us, for Israel was only another name for Jacob, and Jacob was the father of all the twelve tribes, Judah among them. No wonder then that the modern Jewish state is called Israel, although most of its inhabitants are descended from the tribes of Judah in the south—at least in theory.

I should not dwell on such obvious matters, were it not that the "British Israelites" have made this distinction between Judah and

THE AGE OF THE PROPHETS

Israel the basis of their religion. They believe that the ten tribes of
Israel, having roamed about for a long time, settled finally in Western
Europe, and particularly in the United Kingdom, and that all the
Biblical prophecies about Israel can be directly referred to Britain.
You may well ask how they came to this astonishing conclusion, when
it is generally held that, after the collapse of their kingdom in the
year 722 B.C., most of the tribes simply merged with the people
amongst whom they had taken refuge, while a great many inhabitants
simply stayed put.

Indeed, there is no reason for assuming that the entire population
was expelled by the Assyrians. This misconception has led people to
declare that Jesus Christ was not a Jew, a belief that was in great
vogue among the many would-be scholars of Nazi Germany. The
fact that their "theory" was given the direct lie by the Bible never
bothered these gentlemen. But then, no one could ever have accused
them of being greatly interested in religious matters.

If you should ever visit the village of Peki'in in Upper Galilee, just
south of the Lebanese border, you may be introduced to a Jewish
family that can trace its descent in an uninterrupted line to the Israelites
who lived there before the year 722 B.C. While this is no strict proof,
it is one more bit of circumstantial evidence to prove that some
Israelites did continue to live in Galilee even after the Assyrian in-
vasion.

But what happened to the exiles? The Bible does not say, but there
are two non-Biblical sources which merit our attention. The first, an
account by the Jewish historian Flavius Josephus, who lived in the
first century A.D., makes it clear that the northern exiles were given
a chance of returning to Palestine in Ezra and Nehemiah's time, but
that they, together with many exiles from Judah, refused the offer,
preferring to continue living beyond the Euphrates. Now, though
Britain, too, lies "beyond the Euphrates", I hardly think it likely that
Flavius Josephus had her in mind.

The second source is the Book of IV Ezra. This is not in the Hebrew
Bible, but can be found in the Vulgate, whence it has come into the
Apocrypha as II Esdras. IV Ezra was written in Josephus' time, and its
thirteenth chapter tries to explain why no more was heard of the exiles
from Israel. Apparently, in order to avoid pollution through contact with
the heathen, they had moved on to the land of Arsareth, a corruption

of the Hebrew for "foreign land". The journey to that land took one
and a half years and the exiles were said to have crossed the river
Euphrates dry-foot. Even if the historical reliability of the Book of
IV Ezra were established, it would still be anyone's guess what particular country lay one and a half year's distance from the Euphrates.
Only someone with an extraordinary imagination would ever interpret
this remark as referring to Great Britain. I think I can safely say that
few trained theologians, philologists or historians would lend their
authority to so fantastic a belief.

42

Elijah and Jezebel

JEROBOAM'S son, Nadab, had ruled for only a few years when a
usurper by the name of Baasha destroyed the royal family and proclaimed himself king. Baasha's son Elah was murdered by his servant
Zimri, who, in his turn, put the entire royal house to death, only to
be ousted a few days later by Omri, his general. Omri founded a new
dynasty, which reigned in the first half of the ninth century B.C. when
the prophets Elijah and Elisha came to the fore. Now this Omri must
have been a great man, for he carried out a number of strategic and
diplomatic measures that greatly strengthened his country's position.
And Omri did this for Israel even though his name betrays his non-
Jewish origin; no doubt he was a foreign mercenary.

Omri's most important act was the founding of a new capital in
place of the insignificant and out-of-the-way Tirzah. The Bible tells
us that "he bought the hill Samaria of Shemer for two talents of silver,
and built on the hill, and called the name of the city which he built,
after the name of Shemer, owner of the hill, Samaria" (I Kings 16:24).

When we stand upon the hill of Samaria in the Arab part of Palestine
we can still understand the reason why Omri chose to found his capital
in this isolated spot. From here he controlled not only a vast stretch
of country but also the major trading routes. On a clear day, his look-
outs could follow the caravans right up to the shores of the Mediterranean. One and a half centuries later, Omri's fortress was to prove
its worth, for when the mighty Assyrians besieged it, it took them

three years to conquer the city despite their superior armaments and tremendous superiority in numbers.

But we know that Omri's fame did not rest on his founding of Samaria alone. Travelling in Trans-jordania in 1868, the German missionary F. A. Klein stumbled upon a stone with an inscription in ancient Hebrew characters. Unfortunately he could not hide his joy at this discovery from the Bedouins, who believed that the stone must surely hide a fortune, for why else should anyone be so delighted? So they made off with the stone, lit a fire beneath it and threw cold water over it until it had broken up into many fragments. How disappointed they must have been when they found it contained no gold! Fortunately a squeeze had already been taken of the surface, so that the fragments could easily be reassembled when the Arabs eventually returned them. The reconstructed stone, now in the Louvre in Paris, was originally erected by Mesha, the King of Moab in 841 B.C. to commemorate the liberation from the hateful yoke of the Israelites. In lines 5-9 we can read:

"Omri, the king of Israel, oppressed Moab many days, for the god Chemosh was angry with his land. And his son succeeded him and said: I will oppress Moab also. This he spoke in my day but I have taught him and his house otherwise. Israel has perished forever. Omri conquered the land of Medeba and oppressed it until his son had reigned forty years. Only then did Chemosh return it in my day."

This strange document gives us a glimpse of history through the eyes of an outsider, an enemy of Israel. It speaks of events that the Old Testament, for no apparent reason, failed to mention: Omri's victorious campaigns deep into Moab and right across the Jordan. The king of Moab was certain his defeat was brought upon him by the wrath of Chemosh his god, and in exactly the same way the prophets of Judah and Israel would one day explain the troubles of their own country—only the name of God was changed.

Omri was not only a great strategist but an excellent diplomat as well. Instead of wasting his energies on subjecting the southern kingdom of Judah, he made friends with its rulers and also with the mighty Phoenicians in the north-west. When Omri married his son Ahab to the Phoenician princess Jezebel, Phoenician customs began to make deep inroads into the culture of the Israelites and even into their religion. A process was begun through which Israel became enriched, but lost much of its own way of life. And so, although King Omri did so much for his country that Assyrian historians continued to speak of Israel as the House of Omri long after the fall of Samaria, the Book of Kings scorned him as one of the many kings of Israel who offended the Lord through idol worship.

Omri's son, Ahab, followed close in his father's footsteps. A warrior himself, he too preferred tact and diplomacy to war. Though he could achieve little while King Asa was still in power in Judah, he married his daughter to the son of Jehoshaphat, Asa's successor, no doubt with high hopes that this marriage would lead to the reunification of north and south. In fact the alliance must have been dominated by Ahab, for when he asked the King of Judah to join him in battle against Aram, Jehoshaphat replied very humbly: "I am as thou art, my people as thy people, my horses as thy horses" (I Kings 22:4).

In those days the people must have been torn between Jehovah, the God of Israel, and Baal, the god worshipped by Jezebel, Ahab's wife. We have a collection of ostraca, fragments of pottery, from that period, inscribed mainly with names. Now the remarkable thing about these names is the fact that one half of them contains the syllable "ja" the other half the word "baal". Those who opted for "baal" and for the Phoenician religion of Jezebel, apparently named their children in one way, while those who chose the God of Israel named theirs in another. Thus the people must have been fairly evenly divided in their religious beliefs. It was in those days that there appeared the prophet whose very name proclaimed his faith: Elijah, meaning "my God is Jehovah". He became the leading advocate against Jezebel and her henchmen. And when the great Ahab was too weak to choose between the prophet and Jezebel, the Bible condemned him as an idolater. Those who are not for the Kingdom of God must surely be against it.

Though the Phoenicians were a very religious people, they worshipped a host of different gods. Thus they had a special god of dew and rainfall, who, in times of drought, assumed a paramount place among the other gods. Such gods were called "baals", for "baal" simply meant "Lord". One such, who ruled over the flies, the baal Zebub, later fell into such disrepute that the name of Beelzebub became one of the many names of the devil. Another baal was Tamar, the lord of the palm tree, whose likeness was discovered on carvings from

Ugarit (now Ras-Shamra) that date from about the thirteenth century B.C.

But Israel knew no special god of rain and dew; she knew but the one God whose name must not be spoken. And so Elijah thundered against those who claimed that any baal could have power over dew and rain and announced that God would punish them with a terrible drought. This drought not only came, but lasted for many years, and no amount of praying to Baal brought the slightest relief. Only when Elijah called on his God, was the long spell broken at last. Thus the great drought served Israel as a warning not to worship false gods.

It was on Mount Carmel that Elijah called upon his people to make their choice. The drought had lasted three years and six months but still the people had not turned from Baal. And so Elijah challenged the four hundred and fifty prophets of Baal to a judgment of God, before the assembled multitude.

An offering would be made. The firewood having been stacked under the altar, the prophets of Baal would call on the name of their gods to light the fire, and Elijah would call on his. Clearly He who could light the fire was the one and only God. We can just picture the prophets of Baal standing round the altar in their hundreds while they called loudly from morning to noon: "O Baal, hear us, O Baal hear us!" And when this did not help, the prophets tried another well-tested means of swaying their gods—they leaped round the altar. This, too, availed them nothing, and Elijah poured scorn on them. Why not call louder, he scoffed, their god was clearly away on a long journey or else fast asleep. No one could have accused Elijah of respecting the religious feelings of others, but then he was a zealot for whom there was only one truth, only one God. All this leaping round Baal was so much hocus-pocus, and worthy of nothing but derision.

And so the false prophets shouted louder and louder, until finally, in a frenzy, they started to stab themselves so that their blood gushed out in streams. But when it was time for the evening sacrifice no answer had come. At that moment Elijah stepped forward to repair the broken altar of the Lord of Israel. He dug a trench right round the altar, stacked the wood, cut up the sacrificial bullock, and placed the sacrifice on the wood. Then he did something very strange: he poured twelve barrels of water over the sacrifice, until the altar was soaked and the trench filled with water. Now many scholars have thought

Mural from Dura Europos synagogue (IIIrd century A.D.) *illustrating the dance of the prophets of Baal.*

that this pouring of water served simply for making the miracle even more impressive, but in my opinion this interpretation is wrong. The pouring of water was a ritual act of libation before the rainy season to bring on the rain, and, in fact, during the Feast of the Tabernacles this pouring of water was a regular part of the service in the Temple at Jerusalem. Now, the Feast of the Tabernacles falls at precisely the time when rain is expected, and Elijah's action was purely ritual. If it enhanced the miracle, it did so only incidentally.

Elijah's prayer was short, but to the point: "Lord God of Abraham, Isaac, and of Israel" he began, "let it be known this day that thou art God in Israel, and that I am thy servant, and that I have done all these things at thy word. Hear me, O Lord, hear me, that this people may know that thou art the Lord God, and that thou hast turned their heart back again" (I Kings 18:36-37). And the Lord sent down his fire to lap up the burnt offering, the soaked firewood, the stones and the earth and the water in the ditch. When the people saw this they threw themselves down upon the ground and called out in fear and trembling: "The Lord, he is the God; the Lord, he is the God" (I Kings 18:39). And they took the prophets of Baal down to the brook Kishon and killed them all. Having prayed to God, Elijah then sent his servant seven times to look towards the sea. And on the seventh time the servant saw a cloud the size of a fist. The sky became cast over, the wind blew up and the sky seemed to burst open—the drought was at an end. The story goes on to say that the hand of the Lord was on Elijah, and caused him to reach Jezreel on foot long before King Ahab arrived there with all his fast horses.

But even great men can tire of their heavy responsibilities, and Elijah the prophet, too, became tired and escaped to Mount Horeb where he was safe from the threats of Queen Jezebel, who resented his hostility to her gods.

It was on this rugged mountain, where God had once given His Law to Moses, that Elijah lay down to sleep in a cave, and heard a voice calling to him: "What doest thou here, Elijah?" And the prophet answered: "I have been very jealous for the Lord God of hosts: for the children of Israel have forsaken thy covenant, thrown down thine altars, and slain thy prophets with the sword; and I, even I only, am left; and they seek my life, to take it away" (I Kings 19:9, 10). Then the Lord ordered Elijah out of his cave. "And, behold, the Lord passed by, and a great and strong wind rent the mountains, and brake in pieces the rocks before the Lord; but the Lord was not in the wind: and after the wind an earthquake; but the Lord was not in the earthquake; and after the earthquake a fire; but the Lord was not in the fire; and after the fire a still small voice" (I Kings 19:11-12).

And the Lord told Elijah to pluck up courage and to go back to Samaria and Damascus, the very cities in which his life was most threatened. No longer would he be alone, however, for God told him: "Yet I have left me seven thousand in Israel, all the knees which have not bowed unto Baal, and every mouth which hath not kissed him" (I Kings 19:18).

And so, when we meet Elijah again he has become the strong man who anoints and dethrones kings, who appoints his own successor and who plays a decisive role in the political and social life of his time. In the story of Naboth's vineyard (I Kings 21), we learn that the choice between the god of Jezebel and the God of Elijah was much more than a simple choice between two different forms of worship—it was the choice between falsehood and justice, and justice was tottering in Ahab's days until Elijah managed to resurrect it. This may help to mitigate our horror at Elijah's intolerance on Mount Carmel, where all his opponents were put to death.

His own death and ascent to Heaven were as memorable as his whole life had been. Elijah knew that his hour was come, and Elisha, his faithful pupil, knew it also. And when Elijah asked him to make his last request of him, Elisha wished for a double portion of Elijah's spirit. And while they were still talking: "there appeared a chariot of fire, and horses of fire, and parted them both asunder; and Elijah went up by a whirlwind into heaven" (II Kings 2:11).

Then the prophets of Jericho sent out fifty wise men, to seek for Elijah, and when they could not find him anywhere, they knew that he had ascended to Heaven. Meanwhile, Elisha, now wearing his master's mantle, was proving by miracles and mighty signs that he had indeed inherited a double portion of Elijah's spirit. The master's strength had passed into his mantle.

Though Elijah is dead, the children of Israel believe firmly that he will return one day. The Old Testament says simply: "Behold, I will send you Elijah the prophet before the coming of the great and dreadful day of the Lord: And he shall turn the heart of the fathers to the children, and the heart of the children to their fathers, lest I come and smite the earth with a curse" (Malachi 4:5-6). And, significantly, the Authorised Version has placed these verses right at the end of the Old Testament, thus stressing the importance of the man of God who appeared in the days of Ahab and Jezebel.

In order to appreciate how great an impression Elijah made even on later generations, we need only refer to the wisdom of Jesus, the son of Sirach (Ecclesiasticus). This sage, who lived in the third century B.C., wrote a song of praise to the Patriarchs, and he counted Elijah among them. He sang:

"Then stood up Elias the prophet as fire,
   and his word burned like a lamp.
He brought a sore famine upon them,
   and by his zeal he diminished their number.
By the word of the Lord he shut up the heaven,
   and also three times brought down fire.
O Elias, how wast thou honoured in thy wondrous deeds!
   and who may glory like unto thee!
Who didst raise up a dead man from death,
   and his soul from the place of the dead,

by the word of the most High:
Who broughtest kings to destruction,
and honourable men from their bed:
Who heardest the rebuke of the Lord in Sinai,
and in Horeb the judgment of vengeance:
Who anointedst kings to take revenge,
And prophets to succeed after him:
Who wast taken up in a whirlwind of fire,
and in a chariot of fiery horses."

(Ecclesiasticus 48:1-9)

Reading this, we see that Elijah occupied a place by the side of Moses. Moses received the Law on Mount Sinai and Elijah enforced the Law in times of greatest doubt. It is thus that the New Testament remembers him also. In its account of the transfiguration (Matthew 17) the Gospel placed Jesus side by side with Moses and Elijah, so proving in what high regard Elijah was held by the early Christians. For them, too, he was the prophet whose word shone like a bright lamp, a living and lasting token of God's nearness, and thus of immortality.

43

Elisha the Worker of Miracles

THE prophet Elisha followed faithfully in his master's path. He too was a zealot in the cause of religious purity and of the rigid application of the Law of Moses. And yet he differed radically from his great predecessor, or rather the stories about Elisha are written in quite a different strain. Everything about Elijah had been impressively great, and, moving amongst rugged mountains, he had seemed to burn with the bright flame of God.

Elisha appears to have been a character far less aloof. He did not live in deserts or rough mountains, nor was his struggle quite so hard. His story was played out in comfortable houses, in which his servant Gehazi ministered to all his needs. Actually the Biblical account of Elisha begins with a shocking episode. The prophet happened to be

K

passing through the small town of Bethel, and as he was apparently tonsured, the street urchins called after him: "Go up, thou bald head; go up, thou bald head" (II Kings 2:23). Now the prophet was not a man to be trifled with, and so he called up the bears out of the woods and they devoured forty-two of the children. The Book of Kings mentions this story without batting an eyelid, but we must surely be horrified by so much spiteful revenge.

It is not my intention to discuss all the many miracles Elisha wrought —anyone can read about them in the Book of Kings—but I should like to mention the story of Naaman the Syrian captain because it gives us an excellent idea of the times. Naaman, who was a leper, had captured a maid during a punitive expedition against the Israelites. Despite the fact that she was a slave, the maid nevertheless took pity on her master, and told him of the great prophet in her country who could cure all diseases. And so the King of Syria sent Naaman to the King of Israel with this message: "Now when this letter is come unto thee, behold, I have therewith sent Naaman my servant to thee, that thou mayest recover him of his leprosy" (II Kings 5:6). On reading this letter the King of Israel became greatly afraid. Clearly the King of Syria was asking the impossible as a pretext for falling upon Israel.

And so the king rent his clothes and exclaimed: "Am I God, to kill and to make alive, that this man doth send unto me to recover a man of his leprosy? wherefore consider, I pray you, and see how he seeketh a quarrel against me" (II Kings 5:7). When Elisha heard of the great panic at court, he had Naaman brought before him, and ordered the foreign captain to immerse himself seven times in the waters of the Jordan. Naaman was deeply offended, for to begin with Elisha had not received him personally, and now he was adding insult to injury by mocking him with that miserable river, the Jordan. He might just as well have bathed in the Abana and Pharpar, the rivers of Damascus. No, Naaman was not satisfied, and would have turned back there and then had not his servants persuaded him that he could lose nothing by trying.

And so Naaman immersed himself seven times—and was healed. Overjoyed, he returned to Elisha with silver, gold and glorious garments. But the prophet would take no fee, and again Naaman felt snubbed. However, he realised that Elisha's God was a great God indeed, and decided that he would worship Him in gratitude. Since, according to popular belief the God of Israel could only be revered on

Israelite territory, Naaman ordered his servants to fill their bags with Israelite soil, and to carry it back to Syria.

As the bags were being loaded on the mules, Naaman suddenly remembered that he was the servant of a king who worshipped another god and who would expect his captain to do likewise. His king was wont to lean upon his servant's arm when they worshipped, and so, whenever the king bowed down, Naaman would have to bow down with him. At this point Naaman had the impertinence to ask Elisha for his blessing. In our opinion, this was the time for Elisha to call the bears out of the wood. Surely, if anyone deserved to be devoured, it was not the poor urchins in the street at Bethel, but this shameless foreigner who thought he could worship both God and his old idols. What is worse: to call "bald head" after a prophet, or to ask him to give his blessing to so shameful a compromise? Yet to our utter astonishment Elisha not only blessed him but told Naaman to go in peace.

Now, Gehazi, Elisha's servant, unable to accept the fact that his master had refused the reward, caught up with Naaman and told him that Elisha had changed his mind and would now gladly accept one talent of silver and two changes of garments. Naaman was overjoyed and even gave him two talents. But Gehazi had reckoned without his master, for when he returned he was greeted with: "Went not mine heart with thee, when the man turned again from his chariot to meet thee? . . . The leprosy therefore of Naaman shall cleave unto thee, and unto thy seed for ever" (II Kings 5:26, 27). Yes, Elisha had unleashed his bears once more—this time against poor greedy Gehazi.

No, we cannot read this story without a feeling of deep dissatisfaction, and no amount of cheap philosophy can make us change our minds. Naaman, we must insist, was let off far too easily. He, who would soon be paying lip-service to the God of Israel over a heap of holy soil, while worshipping Rimmon whenever it suited his purpose, was sent away with a blessing. But the children of Bethel were cruelly punished and Gehazi's descendants were afflicted with leprosy because of two miserable talents of silver and an overcoat! But all we can say is that life itself is full of injustices and that the author of II Kings 5 merely described life as he found it. A careful perusal of the Book, however, will make it quite clear where his real sympathies lay.

44

True Prophets and False

THERE is one thing about the prophets of Israel that bothered their contemporaries and that has never been satisfactorily solved: how was it that two prophets could speak in the name of the same God and yet contradict each other so flagrantly? Only one could be speaking the truth, yet it was extremely difficult to decide which. While some of their prophecies could be tested by the events themselves, others, dealing with the more distant future, could not, and so the people were often in a great quandary. Now, chapter 22 of the first Book of Kings confronts us with just such a quandary. The reader will remember how the King of Israel, Ahab, had made common cause with Jehoshaphat, King of Judah. Before decisive battles, it was the custom to consult the gods through their prophets, and so King Ahab called together his prophets, four hundred in number, all of whom said that the Lord would be on his side. But King Jehoshaphat of Judah was dissatisfied, since he knew that one prophet, Micaiah the son of Imlah, had not been consulted. Jehoshaphat insisted on summoning him also. The Bible describes the ensuing scene with great gusto. We are shown the two kings sitting on their thrones on the road to Damascus, dressed in their ceremonial robes, while the prophets fill the air with great noise. One of these prophets was wearing horns of iron, with which he illustrated how the enemy would be mown down. Micaiah the son of Imlah, was urged not to stand out alone against all the other prophets. And, indeed, when the king asked him for his prophecy, he said: "Go, and prosper: for the Lord shall deliver it into the hand of the king" (I Kings 22:15). But apparently his voice was so sarcastic that the king could not help rejoining: "How many times shall I adjure thee that thou tell me nothing but that which is true in the name of the Lord?" (I Kings 22:16). Only then did Micaiah speak up and say: "I saw all Israel scattered upon the hills, as sheep that have not a shepherd: and the Lord said, These have no master: let them return every man to his house in peace" (I Kings 22:17). And so the kings had to decide between the two: Zedekiah the son of Chenaanah, with his iron horns, and Micaiah the son of Imlah, who saw all Israel dispersed without a leader. Who was right? Ahab and Jehoshaphat must have had a difficult choice.

The strange thing was that Micaiah, the son of Imlah, while knowing the other prophets to be liars, did not deny them the right to call themselves prophets of God, for though they were liars, he knew that they lied to serve God's purpose. In speaking of them, Micaiah made a strange pun on the Hebrew word for "spirit", a word that also means "wind", "air", or "void". The Lord had lent these prophets his "spirit", but the spirit he had sent them was in fact nothing but empty air. And Micaiah said: "Hear thou therefore the word of the Lord: I saw the Lord sitting on his throne, and all the host of heaven standing by him on his right hand and on his left. And the Lord said, Who shall persuade Ahab, that he may go up and fall at Ramoth-Gilead? And one said on this manner, and another said on that manner. And there came forth a spirit, and stood before the Lord, and said, I will persuade him. And the Lord said unto him, Wherewith? And he said, I will go forth, and I will be a lying spirit in the mouth of all his prophets" (I Kings 22:20-22).

Indeed, this is a strange story, and the strangest thing about it is the bearing it has on the idea of monotheism. Questions about true and false prophecies were quite easily resolved by all religions which believed that the world was governed by two opposing forces: good and evil, light and darkness, Ahura-Mazda and Ahriman. But this dualism is expressly rejected by the Old Testament, as we can see, for instance, from Isaiah 45:5-7: "I am the Lord, and there is none else, there is no God beside me: I girded thee, though thou hast not known me: That they may know from the rising of the sun, and from the west, that there is none beside me. I am the Lord, and there is none else. I form the light, and create darkness: I make peace, and create evil: I the Lord do all these things." Clearly then, for the Old Testament, light and darkness, good and evil, truth and falsehood, were all alike created by the one God. And so the presence of lying prophets in Israel was due to God also.

We could add drily that, this being so, the prophets' contemporaries could never be sure of anything, and we would, in fact, not be far wrong. Of course, there were some prophets who were such blatant liars that no one would ever listen to them. Yet others, whose voice was revered, would also contradict themselves. This is best illustrated by an example from the New Testament. In St. Matthew 16 we are told that St. Peter said to Jesus: "Thou art the Christ, the Son of the living God" (verse 16). Then Jesus blessed Peter, saying: "Blessed art thou, Simon Bar-jonah: for flesh and blood hath not revealed it unto thee, but my Father which is in heaven" (St. Matthew 16:17). Only a little later on, when Jesus was speaking of the suffering that was in store for him, and when Peter tried to console him, the Lord said: "Get thee behind me, Satan: thou art an offence unto me: for thou savourest not the things that be of God, but those that be of men" (St. Matthew 16:23). Strange, is it not, that one and the same chapter speaks first of all of "flesh and blood hath not revealed it unto thee, but my Father which is in heaven . . ." and then almost in the same breath ". . . for thou savourest not the things that be of God, but those that be of men"? Thus did Jesus bear witness to the fact that Peter could speak with the voice of both God and Satan, proclaiming truth and falsehood alike.

Alas, such is life, and such in particular is religious life. And for those of us who would like to see everything arranged in neat order and pigeon-holed into clear-cut systems there is a moral in the story of Micaiah son of Imlah, who like a voice in the wilderness spoke up against the four hundred prophets of Ahab.

45

The Visions of Amos

IN about the middle of the eighth century B.C., a herdsman from Tekoah in Judah came forth to prophesy by the shrine in Bethel. He was called Amos and the Old Testament has named one of its Books after him. Now, though we must not imagine that Amos himself was the author of everything written in that book, there is no doubt that his own words were well remembered by his contemporaries, and that many of his sayings were recorded for posterity.

From the Book we know why Amos had to leave his garden and his sheep to become a prophet. For when the priest of Bethel, greatly

disturbed by Amos's prophecies of doom, asked him to sell his prophecies elsewhere, Amos indignantly pointed out that he had not
learned his trade nor left his home for money, but only because God
Himself had called him out.

His visions are described in the seventh chapter of the Book. At
first God showed him a swarm of locusts falling upon the land. Amos,
realising that the Lord meant to destroy His people, prayed fervently:
"O Lord God, forgive, I beseech thee: by whom shall Jacob arise?
for he is small" (verse 2). And the Lord answered his prayer, and said
to Amos: "It shall not be." God, we are told, had repented of His
own anger. But immediately afterwards, Amos saw a second vision
in which God sent down a great fire which devoured the sea and the
land. This second vision could only mean that Israel was doomed, and
Amos exclaimed again: "O Lord God, cease, I beseech thee: by whom
shall Jacob arise? for he is small" (verse 5). And again the Lord repented.

But in the third vision Amos knew that the Lord had made up His
mind once and for all. A bricklayer was standing upon a wall and
examining the cracks. He was holding a plumbline, as God would
apply a plumbline to the people of Israel. No longer would He forgive
them all their trespasses, the idols would be destroyed, the shrines
of Israel laid waste and the House of Jeroboam laid low by the
sword.

Now, while these visions were exceedingly strange, what is stranger
still is the fact that the prophet interpreted them all as foreboding
his people's downfall, though he lived in very prosperous times when
no one else dreamt of catastrophes. For the year in which he had his
vision must have been 763 B.C. when Israel was extremely prosperous,
and when his lamentations must have fallen on very deaf ears indeed.
We may compare the situation to the turn of our own century, when
anyone who predicted the First and Second World Wars would have
been thought a lunatic. And indeed, King Jeroboam was to reign for
another successful twenty years before he died. Only in about 735 B.C.
did things begin to look serious. The Assyrians then fell upon the land
like the locusts of Amos's first vision and later destroyed town after
town like the all-consuming fire of the second vision. In 721 B.C.,
Samaria, the capital of Israel, fell after a siege that had lasted for three
years, and with it came the final collapse of the kingdom of the ten

northern tribes. Still, no ordinary mortal could have suspected anything of the sort forty years earlier.

Now Amos was not the man to have made scientific predictions
from his studies of the past. No one can do so today, and Amos could
certainly not have done so then. Each day men make quite unpredictable decisions and the sum of all their decisions makes up our history.
No one can say what decisions mankind will make tomorrow, and so
no one can ever know for certain what tomorrow holds in store, let
alone what the world will be like in forty years' time.

Nor was Amos a political genius with a clear understanding of
Assyrian motives and the ambitions of those who would one day
fulfil his prophecies. It is sheer fantasy to speak of him, as some have
done, as a widely-travelled shepherd, who knew from experience
which way the wind was blowing. No, Amos was neither historian
nor statesman—he was a visionary and a prophet, and this alone is his
greatness. All he knew was this: Godlessness invariably spells the doom
of a people. Whenever any people, flaunting God's will, decides to
take the law in its own hands, that people has called down misfortune
upon its own head, and it was this that Amos had foreseen and proclaimed even in times of prosperity.

No wonder, then, that his fellows gave him a wide berth. However,
Amos was not to be deflected from his purpose—he had absolute
faith in his visions. Thus can we still picture him rebuking Amaziah
the priest of Bethel, who had told him to sell his prophecies elsewhere,
and not to spread alarm and despondency. He cared neither for reward
nor honours but only for the future of his people. He would shake
men out of their false sense of security, their sloth and unconcern.
And when the people asked him: whence cometh your authority, with
what right do you speak to us? he answered simply: I have seen, for
the Lord has shown me, and it was for His sake alone that I left my
cattle and my country to come and prophesy in Israel.

46

Isaiah's Vision of God's Glory

To gain a clear idea of the prophets of Israel, we must remember that many of them were as concerned with the good life on earth as they were concerned with preparing the people for life hereafter. And so they were a constant thorn in the flesh of many a powerful man in the land. Few of the prophets led an easy life and many died as martyrs.

Isaiah, like Amos, was a visionary. Full of fervour, he tells us how he saw the Lord sitting upon His high and exalted throne, while the train of His garments filled the temple. Round Him stood the seraphim who sang to one another: "Holy, holy, holy, is the Lord of hosts: the whole earth is full of His glory" (Isaiah 6:3). Indeed, the sixth chapter of Isaiah is suffused with awe for the unapproachable holiness of God. As the seraphim proclaimed His glory, the doorposts trembled from the noise of their shouting, and the house was filled with smoke.

Then Isaiah exclaimed: "Woe is me! for I am undone; because I am a man of unclean lips, and I dwell in the midst of a people of unclean lips: for mine eyes have seen the King, the Lord of hosts" (Isaiah 6:5). Now the words "clean" and "unclean" must not be taken literally, but as expressing Isaiah's concern that he was too profane to be taken into the world of God without ritual or ceremony. As a result he was in fact submitted to an act of cleansing. One of the seraphim took a live coal from the altar and laid it upon the prophet's mouth. And so his lips became clean, and a voice said to him: "Lo, this hath touched thy lips; and thine iniquity is taken away, and thy sin purged" (Isaiah 6:7). Once again we must stress this did not imply that Isaiah had committed some specific sin, but simply that he was an ordinary mortal, and as such not fit to approach the Lord unprepared. Only after his purification did God's voice call out to Isaiah: "Whom shall I send, and who will go for us?" And Isaiah answered: "Here am I; send me" (Isaiah 6:8). Isaiah was the obedient servant who would go anywhere his master sent him. Yet, what was he to make of his orders when the Lord spoke to him in riddles? "Go", the Lord ordered him, "and tell this people, Hear ye indeed, but understand not; and see ye indeed, but perceive not. Make the heart of this people fat, and make their ears heavy, and shut their eyes; lest they see with their eyes, and hear with their ears, and understand with their heart, and convert, and be healed" (Isaiah 6:9-10). The whole of Isaiah's life and sermons had been devoted to precisely the opposite aim—he had tried to open people's eyes, and never tired of proclaiming the way of righteousness. Now he realised that all his prophetic preaching, all his endeavours to raise the tone of Jerusalem's political and social life during the past fifty years had been for nothing. His words had only so dimmed the people's eyes, and so stopped up their ears that after half a century they had grown more evil, more godless, more unjust than ever before.

Only despair and destruction would open up the people's eyes, and so, when Isaiah asked: "Lord, how long?" he was told: "Until the cities be wasted without inhabitant, and the houses without man, and the land be utterly desolate" (Isaiah 6:11). Then was there not a single spark of hope? Indeed, there was: God's chosen people would continue to remain His chosen people. Even though the oak is felled, new twigs shoot up from its trunk. All preaching was in vain, and yet the prophet must preach, for the Lord God, Blessed be His Name, wills it thus, and who dare run counter to His will? And so Isaiah continued to preach that the people who walked in darkness might yet see a great light, and that they that dwell in the land of the shadow of death might yet get a glimpse of His glory.

47

The Vision of Peace

PEOPLE have called the Old Testament a bloodthirsty book, possibly because it never condemned war outright. War was simply accepted as an inevitable scourge, or even as a holy duty. And war was always horrible—the enemy was given no quarter. There is no reason whatever for believing that the chosen people pursued their campaigns more gently or nobly than their neighbours, and the Old Testament made no attempt to conceal this fact. While the Bible does not revel in these wars, it does report them faithfully, and I have yet to hear of any nation's history in which no wars are reported over a period of one thousand years. No, the Old Testament is no more bloodthirsty than any other history book.

On the contrary, the Bible is imbued with a deep longing for peace. The Hebrew word for peace is "shalom", and "shalom" means far more than peace. "Shalom" is the greeting that friends exchange when they meet in the street, and "shalom" means health and happiness also. Indeed, "shalom" is not the mere absence of war, but it is the state of perfection that existed in Paradise and that will only return with the coming of the Messiah. And the more their poor little country was plagued by war, the more the children of Israel came to long for "shalom". It is this longing of theirs that inspired Isaiah's beautiful visions of peace.

One of the most famous of these is found in Isaiah 2:1-5: "And it shall come to pass", the vision begins, "in the last days." This expression did not mean at some far-off, unpredictable date, for the last day might just as well come tomorrow or the next day. It was on that day that the mountain of the Lord's house would be established on the top of all the mountains, to be exalted above the hills. Now, the house of the Lord was the Temple of Solomon, built on Mount Moriah, north of Mount Zion. Thus the eastern ridge of Jerusalem was to be exalted above all other mountains. In other words, Jerusalem was to be looked upon as the revered city, of which all the people would say: "Come ye, and let us go up to the mountain of the Lord, to the house of the God of Jacob; and he will teach us of his ways, and we will walk in his paths; for out of Zion shall go forth the law, and the word of the Lord from Jerusalem" (Isaiah 2:3). Jerusalem would become the permanent court of international justice, and with God's authority to back it. This idea of a permanent court has exercised mankind's imagination ever since, but the insuperable difficulty is and always has been that there is no one to enforce the law. And so the nations continue their bickering, and today threaten the world with utter destruction.

Isaiah's prophecies are unthinkable without a fervent longing for peace. What greater witness to peace than his: "And he shall judge among the nations, and shall rebuke many people; and they shall beat their swords into plowshares, and their spears into pruning hooks: nation shall not lift up sword against nation, neither shall they learn war any more" (Isaiah 2:4). Only a man who abhorred war from the bottom of his heart as the scourge of mankind could have spoken thus. The ideal way of life is not the heroic clash of arms, not victory in the field, but a life of peace and devotion, in which each man can till his land in peace by day and sit in the evening shade of the fig tree to talk with his neighbour. And Jerusalem was to become the guardian of this peace.

But Jerusalem must not gain its exalted position through world conquest. Dreams of such conquest might have been held in David's time, but they had meanwhile dissolved into thin air. This setback to Judah's imperialist pretensions had helped to put things in their right perspective. For Isaiah, the sword was played out and the peace of Jerusalem was not a peace upheld by well-trained legions. With God's help, Jerusalem would become the centre of international justice. Here justice would not be dispensed by the sword but by a power more absolute and much mightier than any on earth.

"For out of Zion shall go forth the law, and the word of the Lord from Jerusalem." But before this could come to pass, the house of Jacob itself would have to walk in the path of God's righteousness. For how, the prophet asked himself, could any people have faith in Jerusalem if its inhabitants failed to set an example? If only a just king would rule over Jerusalem, peace would reign throughout the world. "The wolf also shall dwell with the lamb, and the leopard shall lie down with the kid; and the calf and the young lion and the fatling together; and a little child shall lead them. And the cow and the bear shall feed; their young ones shall lie down together; and the lion shall eat straw like the ox. And the sucking child shall play on the hole of the asp, and the weaned child shall put his hand on the cockatrice' den. They shall not hurt nor destroy in all my holy mountain: for the earth shall be full of the knowledge of the Lord, as the waters cover the sea" (Isaiah 11:6-9).

With Isaiah, a new movement had come to the fore in Judah: the champions of eternal peace, and of goodwill to all men. This is how the psalmist summed up their message:

"There is no king saved by the multitude of an host:
a mighty man is not delivered by much strength.
An horse is a vain thing for safety:

neither shall he deliver any by his great strength.
Behold, the eye of the Lord is upon them that fear him,
upon them that hope in his mercy."

(Psalm 33:16-18)

And we, who continue to long for peace in the twentieth century
can only add: Amen.

48

Unto Us a Child is Born . . .

ONE of Isaiah's best-known prophecies begins with the words: "And
there shall come forth a rod out of the stem of Jesse, and a Branch shall
grow out of his roots" (Isaiah 11:1). We meet these words again in the
Christmas hymns of many nations, for the Christian Church has always
looked upon this text as prophesying the coming of Christ. "The
stem of Jesse" was the royal house of David, and though David's
dynasty had come to an end and no king ruled over Jerusalem, the
royal race itself continued, and Jesus would be born from it.

However, to discover what Isaiah himself intended with his prophecy in the eighth century B.C., it is no good looking at subsequent
Christian interpretations. We must simply try to imagine the birth of a
prince in the royal palace in Jerusalem. This happy and important
event was celebrated with much feasting and singing. The Poet
Laureate would compose songs of praise using the time-honoured
turns of phrase that were heard in every court of the East. And so the
prophet Isaiah, too, turned poet and composed these unforgettable
lines:

"For every battle of the warrior is with confused noise, and garments rolled in blood; but this shall be with burning and fuel of
fire. For unto us a child is born, unto us a son is given: and the government shall be upon his shoulder: and his name shall be called
Wonderful, Counsellor, The mighty God, The everlasting Father,
The Prince of Peace. Of the increase of his government and peace
there shall be no end, upon the throne of David, and upon his kingdom, to order it, and to establish it with judgment and with justice

from henceforth even for ever. The zeal of the Lord of hosts will perform this" (Isaiah 9:5-7).

So sang the great prophet-turned-poet. He too had to use many of the set phrases of his time, and when he called the young prince "The mighty God", "The everlasting Father" and "The Prince of Peace", he used the very titles bestowed upon the Pharaoh of Egypt. And so, the "Christian message" is but one of many songs in honour of the young prince and it is of the future king that Isaiah sang:

"And there shall come forth a rod out of the stem of Jesse, and a Branch shall grow out of his roots: And the spirit of the Lord shall rest upon him, the spirit of wisdom and understanding, the spirit of counsel and might, the spirit of knowledge and of the fear of the Lord; And shall make him of quick understanding in the fear of the Lord: and he shall not judge after the sight of his eyes, neither reprove after the hearing of his ears: But with righteousness shall he judge the poor, and reprove with equity for the meek of the earth: and he shall smite the earth with the rod of his mouth, and with the breath of his lips shall he slay the wicked. And righteousness shall be the girdle of his loins, and faithfulness the girdle of his reins" (Isaiah 11:1-5).

The song ends with the well-known prophecy that the wolf shall dwell with the lamb, and the leopard shall lie down with the kid. The king's righteousness would bring peace, not only to his own people but to all mankind—nay, even more, to the entire universe.

Now, while no one doubts that Isaiah was one of Israel's greatest prophets, we may be equally sure that the eventual turn of events must have disappointed him sorely. True, the evil that he saw did come about, but the peace and justice did not. He had aroused great hopes in his people, and thousands must have thought with deep bitterness that he had miserably failed them. What good, the people must have asked, is a poet who is of this world but whose visions are not? Uplifting words and noble sentiments are all very well, but what if we cannot apply them?

And yet his song kept haunting them. Kings would come and kings would go, to govern wisely or to govern badly, but however excellent their reign, Isaiah's hopes were never to be fulfilled. One king was strong and another weak, but however strong the king and however great his success, Isaiah's expectation had been far greater still. Setbacks, martyrdom, exile, war, and headlong flight had never been able to kill the hope he had instilled into his people. Even in the dead of night there was hope of another dawn, and when dawn broke, of another clear noon. One day he would surely arise, the great king from the House of David, and bring salvation to his people and to the world. In the fullness of time the mountains would bear peace and the hills righteousness. It is impossible to tell what secret sources of power were tapped by Isaiah's message, but the miraculous history of the Jewish people that culminated in the setting up of the modern state of Israel is unthinkable without this hope in the heart of the nation.

And once upon a time, a handful of men were privileged to witness the fulfilment of Isaiah's deepest longings. At the beginning of his Epistle to the Romans, St. Paul wrote: "Paul, a servant of Jesus Christ, called to be an apostle, separated unto a gospel of God, (Which he had promised afore by his prophets in the holy scriptures,) Concerning his Son Jesus Christ our Lord, which was made of the seed of David according to the flesh . . ." Isaiah's expectations, Paul tells us, had borne fruit in Christ Jesus. No, said the Jewish people, it has not yet come to pass, the world in which we live is still the poor thing it always was, mankind is not yet redeemed, we have still to wait. Many see here an unbridgeable gulf between Judaism as the religion of hope, and Christianity as the religion of fulfilment. Actually, the gulf is not really so great. Though the King with His crown of thorns has come, Christians like Jews still continue to hope, for the Christian faith not only preaches the message of His Coming but also the message of His Return. And Christians too recall Isaiah's songs of hope and longing. They are remembered anew each Christmas, and each Christmas they are charged with new meaning.

49

The Lord's Faithful Servant

THE twelfth chapter of St. Matthew tells us of the Lord's healing of the sick. The people came flocking to Him, but Jesus enjoined His disciples not to broadcast His cures. Matthew then explained the Lord's request by a prophecy of Isaiah: "Behold my servant, whom I uphold; mine elect, in whom my soul delighteth; I have put my spirit upon him: he shall bring forth judgment to the Gentiles. He shall not cry, nor lift up, nor cause his voice to be heard in the street. A bruised reed shall he not break, and the smoking flax shall he not quench: he shall bring forth judgment unto truth. He shall not fail nor be discouraged, till he have set judgment in the earth: and the isles shall wait for his law" (Isaiah 42:1-4).

An attentive reader may well ask himself what connection there is between the Gospel and this prophecy. Now, the prophecy was in fact the first verse of a song about the Lord's faithful servant. The whole song is made up of various parts and can only be understood if we combine fragments of chapters 42, 49, 52 and 53. In this song there is talk of a mysterious and nameless stranger, who would willingly suffer for the sin of his people. We may feel reasonably certain that the early Christians applied these verses to Jesus Christ, and that Jesus too looked upon Himself as the fulfilment of the prophecy.

We are told this stranger was a servant. Now a servant was one who belonged to his master body and soul, as, indeed, Abraham's servant had done. In Genesis 24 we are told how he journeyed into the distant land of Haran to fetch a wife for Isaac. We are not told his name, for this servant was remarkable only for his single-hearted devotion to his master's cause. Nothing could deflect him from his task, and he steadfastly refused what must have been the very tempting offer of lingering on in Laban's house and taking a welcome respite.

This idea that a servant was wholly his master's property passed into religious usage. Now, while a Babylonian king might well have called himself the servant of Marduk one day, and of Nebo the next, he who served the God of Israel could serve no other God beside

Him. No man can serve two masters, and the true servant of God was one who submitted utterly to God's will, no matter where He sent one, no matter how heavy the burden He imposed. Above all, His servant had no name, and so it is pointless to ask what actual person Isaiah had in mind. He might have been referring to Moses, to Abraham, to a king, a prophet or a priest—all of them were servants of the Lord. The moment we name him, however, we defeat the prophet's intention: to preserve the servant's anonymity.

Still, we are not kept entirely in the dark for we are told that God's spirit was upon him. Clearly then, he had the gift of prophecy, for only those upon whom the Spirit of God rested could work miracles or predict the future. Now the true prophet is quite unlike those wild enthusiasts who appeared in great throngs to prophesy noisily in the streets. And indeed Isaiah was thinking of one who went about his Master's business quietly and who did His work without clamour. The true servant does not abuse his opponents, or shout salvation in the market place. He is considerate where others are callous, and, indeed, Isaiah did well to use the wonderful allegory of the bruised reed and smoking flax which captured St. Matthew's imagination. A reed swaying in the wind is as evanescent as human life itself. Why did the prophet bother with it? And while we are still wondering, the prophet has already conjured up another image, and we see the outlines of a house in Jerusalem. Through its windows we can see the flicker of an oil lamp, with its burning wick of twisted flax. Now the oil is used up and the little lamp on the point of going out in thick smoke. Why speak of this smoking lamp, why consider its wick? Clearly because the wick, like the reed, serves to illustrate the frailty of a life that can only be tended through love, devotion and great care.

Some have interpreted the text as referring to a king as he sat in judgment over his subjects, reed in his right hand, oil lamp burning before him. If the evildoer was to be sent to his death, the king would symbolically break the reed and blow out the flame. This interpretation is tempting but not borne out by the text itself, which speaks quite intentionally of a "bruised" reed and of a "smoking" flax. And these words are in fact repeated for emphasis: the Lord's obedient servant must be careful not to let himself be bruised or befogged. He must be strong, for he is called by God to proclaim His message of salvation.

It pays us to study what else Isaiah has to say about this servant.

L

When the servant complained to the Lord that he had been left idle, and that he felt like a shaft in a quiver, impatient to be shot towards the goal, God counselled him to suffer a little longer, for not only would He bring salvation to the tribes of Judah but to all mankind as well (chapter 49). And so the servant was patient until one day, in Galilee, he went about His Master's business, gently restoring broken lives and healing broken hearts. Small wonder then that the people exclaimed: Behold, it is He of whom Isaiah said that "a bruised reed shall he not break, and the smoking flax shall he not quench".

The eighth chapter of the Acts of the Apostles shows us a courtier of the Queen of Ethiopia travelling along a lonely path between Jerusalem and Gaza. This Moor, who had adopted the Jewish faith, was returning from a pilgrimage to the Holy Temple in Jerusalem. He was a deeply religious man, and so, while he was being driven in his chariot, he chose to read the Book of Isaiah. As was then the custom, he read out aloud, for any passer-by to hear.

It so happened that Philip, one of Jesus's disciples, was passing by and asked the Moor if he understood what he was reading. The Moor admitted that he did not, and said: "How can I, except some man should guide me?" (Acts 8:31). How many of us have not felt like him, as we were puzzled by one of the more difficult passages in the Old Testament? We, too, would have been thankful had Philip offered to act as our guide as he then volunteered to do. Now the courtier had been reading about the faithful servant who "is brought as a lamb to the slaughter, and as a sheep before her shearers is dumb, so he openeth not his mouth" (Isaiah 53:7). And so he asked Philip to tell him whether the prophet was speaking, "of himself, or of some other man?" (Acts 8:34). This question could well have been made the title of a scholarly work on a problem that has bothered investigators for a whole century: the real identity of the suffering servant of the Lord who was led as a lamb to the slaughter and like a sheep was dumb before his shearer.

For Philip and the early Christians the answer was clear: He was Jesus Christ. But what did Isaiah himself and the Jewish rabbis think? The rabbis' opinion is recorded in the Targum, an Aramaic paraphrase of the Old Testament, written at the time that Aramaic replaced Hebrew as the language of the Jews. Now, the Aramaic translation differs from the original, and it is this difference which must clearly reflect the opinion of the rabbis. This is how the Targum put it: "He asked and he is answered, yea, he was heard even before he opened his mouth. And he will lead him that is mighty in the land, as a lamb to the slaughter, and as a sheep is dumb before her shearers, so no one will raise up his voice against him. He will free us of suffering and pain and the wonders which will befall us in his day, who can tell them? For he will cause the mighty of the land to lie low and to flee from the land of Israel." We note that though the words are almost the same they are turned round, and with them the sense. The suffering servant of the Lord has given way to the conquering Messiah who triumphs gloriously over the oppressor. This very difference emphasises the difference between Judaism and Christianity. Through the mouth of Philip, Christianity proclaims the message of the Saviour on the Cross, while the Targum will have no part of a suffering Messiah. And so we are back where we started, and ask once more with the Moorish courtier: of whom did the prophet speak and of whom was he thinking in his own day? If I were to quote every theory that has been propounded on this subject, I should have to write a very lengthy tome, indeed. I myself am inclined to believe that Isaiah was not thinking of any one servant in particular, but of all the true servants of the Lord, of all the men who had been the champions of righteousness and piety in Israel, and who had defended what is best in her. All carried a heavy burden; all obeyed the commandments to the letter, and by their devotion, faith and high hopes they managed to carry their people with them. Therefore the prophet could truly say: "The chastisement of our peace was upon him; and with his stripes we are healed."

The idea of the pious few withstanding the taunts of the many is found throughout the Old Testament. Nor is it dead and forgotten today, for orthodox Jews still believe in the existence of the thirty-six nameless men on whom rests the salvation of the world. No one knows them, and anyone claiming to have seen one of these saints, one of the pious and virtuous thirty-six, would be a liar, for it is their lot to remain unrecognised. And so they continue to live among us, these thirty-six, and it is for their sake alone that God continues to bear with us. The chastisement for our sins is upon them.

Philip's message, too, sprang from this belief in the thirty-six just men, but for him they had become fused into the person of Jesus Christ who took upon Himself all our suffering and all our stripes and even bore the Cross for our sake, conscious of the high office to which He was called. Jesus was at one and the same time the Master and the faithful servant of whom Isaiah had spoken, and of whom the disciples added in whispers that He was also God Himself, for only God could bear and expunge man's guilt. For the sake of His chosen people and for the world's sake also, Almighty God came down and was made man, a humble servant. And the roots of this Christian message lie embedded in Isaiah's visions whose scope was so wide that at the time no one could have foreseen their final realisation in Christ Jesus.

50

Jonah in Nineveh

MANY of us cannot think of the Book of Jonah without laughing, and our laughter is quite justified. The Bible, too, realised how small a man he was at heart, and the Old Testament spoke of him with irony. Even so, the Bible devotes a book to him, if only to emphasise that God's call makes men great despite themselves.

The story begins with the report that, when the Lord ordered Jonah, the son of Amittai, to go and preach in Nineveh, Jonah refused to carry out God's instructions. He was convinced that God's word would fall on deaf ears in that great city, for why should its mighty and cultured inhabitants listen to the words of a poor peasant from a distant land? And so Jonah preferred to run away. Now, greater men than he had balked when the call had come, but none had thought they could extricate themselves from their predicament in the stupid way that Jonah did. He simply booked a passage on a boat from Jaffa to Tarshish, in the mistaken belief that the God of Israel would have no power over him once he had fled the land of His chosen people.

But he was to be taught otherwise, for God sent a great storm upon the sea, and threatened the ship with immediate destruction. The crew, Gentiles one and all, prayed fervently and unceasingly to their respective gods, while Jonah lay fast asleep and unworried below deck. When their prayers did not avail them, the captain of the ship awakened Jonah, and ordered him to pray to his own God—in mortal danger all men grow tolerant of their neighbour's religion. But even Jonah's prayer did little towards calming the sea. Clearly, someone had deeply offended his god, and would have to be thrown overboard —but who? Only a drawing of lots could decide, and, needless to say, the marked lot fell upon Jonah.

Now the crew were very kindly people and, wanting to spare Jonah's life, they did their utmost to steer the ship to a safe harbour. Only as a last resort did they decide to surrender Jonah to the turbulent waters. And as soon as they had done so, the sea ceased its raging. There could no longer be any doubt about the might of the God of Israel, and all the seamen in gratitude brought Him offerings and pledged their lives to Him. This was the typical pattern of so many of the miracles, for miracles alone could persuade the Gentiles to live in the fear of the Lord.

And so the ship continued on its course while Jonah was left to the deep, and to the whale that swallowed him. Once inside the whale's belly Jonah had time to repent his disobedience, and he prayed unto the Lord and vowed that he would obey His commandments. "And the Lord spake unto the fish, and it vomited out Jonah upon the dry land" (Jonah 2:10). I do not wish to cross swords with those who have claimed that no fish is large enough to swallow a man and spit him out alive—for me the point of this story is simply the message of God's forgiveness. If we transgress against Him, He forces us back into the path of righteousness, and then forgives our frailty. And so God made Jonah realise that he would have to preach in Nineveh, and, in the end, preach in Nineveh he did.

The Old Testament paints the capital of Mesopotamia in glowing colours. Palestine had never known so great a city—Samaria and Jerusalem were mere villages compared with Nineveh. Yet even mighty cities have to rely upon God's mercy, as many have realised to their own great cost. His servants could take courage—they had little to fear from the great of this world.

And in fact Jonah's preaching in Nineveh bore astonishing fruit. Nineveh turned out to be quite unlike Jerusalem, which stoned its prophets to death instead of paying heed to their message of salvation. Nineveh listened, and all its citizens, great and small, poor and rich, responded to this peasant from Palestine, and turned away from the path of error. This is why Jesus praised them while condemning the people of Jerusalem who would not even listen to Him, Jesus Christ, who was so much more than Jonah. "The men of Nineveh shall rise in judgment with this generation, and shall condemn it: because they repented at the preaching of Jonah; and, behold, a greater than Jonah is here" (St. Matthew 12:41). Oddly enough the people believed Jonah even though he gave no reasons for his prophecies of doom. All the Bible tells us is that "Jonah began to enter into the city a day's journey, and he cried, and said, Yet forty days, and Nineveh shall be overthrown" (Jonah 3:4). Now, other prophets of catastrophe had always explained why God was angry. The people might have been guilty perhaps of idolatry, or of oppressing the poor, the widow and the orphan, but if the inhabitants of Nineveh had sinned, we are not told of their transgressions.

Yet, all the same, the people of Nineveh believed Jonah, and so they donned sackcloth and ashes, and proclaimed a fast, the well-tried recipes for diverting disaster. If there was a great drought—the people fasted; if there was an epidemic in the land—the people wore sackcloth and fasted; a mighty enemy came knocking at the gate—the people mourned and fasted. Yes, Nineveh fasted, even down to the cattle, which were taken off the pasture and given no water. Indeed, things had taken a surprising turn, and the prophet Jonah, instead of being thrown out of town as he had firmly expected, was welcomed as a true prophet of God.

Now, however tragic the lot of the prophet who has nothing to promise but disaster, his tragedy is small when compared with that of the prophet who promises disasters that never materialise. And this was precisely what Jonah prophesied. Truly, he had not asked to be sent into the streets of Nineveh to prophesy doom, but now that he had done his duty, he expected the Lord to fulfil his promise.

And so he went out of the city up to a hill to wait in the shadow of his hut for disaster to fall. But he waited in vain. And with bitterness in his heart, he cried out: "I pray thee, O Lord, was not this my saying, when I was yet in my country? Therefore I fled before unto Tarshish: for I knew that thou art a gracious God, and merciful, slow to anger, and of great kindness, and repentest thee of the evil. Therefore now, O Lord, take, I beseech thee, my life from me; for it is better for me to die than to live" (Jonah 4:2-3). Yes, Jonah felt that he had been a miserable failure, and so he reproached God not for His wrath but for His great mercy in saving the city. He was full of resentment against Him who was quick in anger, but quicker still to forgive. Jonah must have said to himself: I have always known God would not carry out His threats, and that is why I wanted no part of them.

But Jonah was to have even more cause for complaint and self-pity. Before his hut a gourd had shot up and its shadow had guarded Jonah from the blistering rays of the sun. But then the gourd suddenly withered and so robbed Jonah of his only protection against the hot east wind. In Israel they call this wind the *khamsin*, and people dread it like the plague. They feel faint and listless while they wait breathlessly for the wind to drop. The flowers wilt, the animals creep away. Isaiah called the *khamsin* the breath of God, when he said: "The grass withereth, the flower fadeth: because the spirit of the Lord bloweth upon it" (Isaiah 40:7).

But worse even than the *khamsin* is the heat that follows after it. I was to discover this for myself one fine day in April. The *khamsin* had begun to blow that morning, but even so I decided to pay a visit to Rishon-le-Zion to see its famous wine cellars. When I emerged from the deep, cool cellars into the light of day, the heat hit me with such force that I could only make for the nearest bench and seek what little shade a eucalyptus tree offered. It was then that I noticed that the air was absolutely still. The wind, though hot, had had a cooling effect on my perspiring skin, and now that it had dropped the air had turned as hot as an oven. Here, in the little park of Rishon-le-Zion I realised for the first time how sorely afflicted poor Jonah must have been on his hill outside Nineveh. His prophecies had come to naught, his gourd had withered and there he sat, a defeated man in the blistering heat of the *khamsin*. Clearly it was far better to die than to continue living like that.

At this point God gave him a salutary lesson. A voice said to Jonah: "Thou hast had pity on the gourd, for the which thou hast not laboured, neither madest it grow; which came up in a night, and perished in a night: And should not I spare Nineveh, that great city, wherein are more than six-score thousand persons that cannot discern between their right hand and their left hand; and also much cattle?" (Jonah 4:10-11). And so ends the Book of Jonah, but we are left wondering if Jonah was great enough to understand God's words and if he ever recovered his peace of mind. Did he find it in himself to accept his fate, the difficult fate of a prophet in the service of God the All-Merciful?

The Bible does not say, for the Bible cared little about the personal problems of Jonah, the son of Amittai. Its sole concern was to show that God Almighty reigned over all the world, from Tarshish to Nineveh, and in His great mercy caused His sun to shine even over sinful people. The Bible's message is not restricted to Jerusalem and the chosen people; the hand of the Almighty, Merciful and Omniscient Creator can be seen everywhere. And yet, however much we may agree with the writer of the Book of Jonah, we cannot help entertaining the nagging doubt that poor Jonah was cheated. What sense is there in making God's prophet preach God's judgment if His judgment is not to be carried out?

Perhaps I may be allowed to say something here that at first might sound paradoxical and far-fetched. It is this: the constant reiteration of gloomy prophecies and the constant labour of ramming them home, would be completely senseless, were it not for the implicit belief that it is never too late to change and to avert disaster. To put it even more strongly: the preaching of unavoidable disaster is the sole means of averting it. The prophet must rob us of all our easy-going optimism, for only then will we face up to our only means of salvation. Only a people on its knees will turn its back on sin. And so the prophet must hold out no hope, for every glimmer of hope is a straw at which the sinner may clutch. Of course the prophet himself must be filled with the hope that springs from faith, but he must always guard against expressing this hope. One word of solace, and the people would go back to their old ways, to procrastinate for yet another day.

And so God reveals Himself, not through honeyed words, and cheap solace, but through the words of those who prophesy catastrophe. His prophets are unlikely to find a grateful audience unless, like Jonah, they are privileged to witness the rare spectacle of a change of heart. Then, though their prophecies have not come to pass, and though the city has not been laid waste, they will thank God for His mercy. We shall never know whether Jonah, too, learned to thank God for saving Nineveh from the destruction he had prophesied. But we do agree with the writer of the Book of Jonah: far better to have a converted than a deserted city, even at the price of a prophet's happiness.

51

The Babylonian Period

JEREMIAH'S entire ministry was overcast by the shadow of Nebuchadnezzar, King of Babylon. In many ways the situation then was reminiscent of the preceding century and of Isaiah's times. In both cases Judah was sandwiched between two mighty states vying with each other for supremacy in Palestine: Egypt to the south-west and first the Assyrians and later the Babylonians in the east. Understandably enough, then, two opposing parties rose up within Jerusalem also, one favouring the cause of Egypt, and the other supporting Assyria or Babylon. Neutrality was a thing of the past, and we gain the impression that most people preferred the Egyptian yoke to Assyrian or Babylonian tyranny.

Looking back over the centuries, we cannot help feeling that with Josiah's death things had come to a terrible pass. The line of succession was broken, terrible political blunders were being committed and Jerusalem had become the dupe of stupidity and false pride. The year 597 B.C. was only one of many adverse years. Some years earlier the King of Judah had refused to pay his tribute to Nebuchadnezzar, knowing full well that the Babylonian overlord was occupied elsewhere. But now Nebuchadnezzar was knocking at the gates of Jerusalem, where an eighteen-year-old boy had just succeeded to the throne. It speaks highly for young Jehoiachin's intelligence that he realised Jerusalem was past saving. Rather than sacrifice his people in a hopeless struggle, he, together with his mother, servants, princes and courtiers went out of the city to surrender to the enemy (see II Kings 24:8-16). While the Old Testament did not thank him for his self-sacrifice, we happen to know that his people did. For in A.D. 70 Flavius Josephus, the Jewish historian, stood before the walls of Jerusalem with yet another mighty enemy. This time it was the Roman general Titus, later to become Roman Emperor, who was demanding the city's surrender. Once again Jerusalem was as good as lost and any further struggle quite senseless. But the leader of the party of Zealots, John of Gischala, would not see what eighteen-year-old Jehoiachin had once realised so clearly.

Then Josephus was ordered to go up to the city wall and to plead with John. In his book *The Jewish War* we can read that he begged John to "let the good example of our king Jehoiachin inspire you to save our city. For he, when faced with the Babylonian army, left the city of his own free will and together with his family he chose exile rather than see the Holy City destroyed by the enemy's hand, and so saved the Temple from being consumed by fire. Therefore has Jewry ever remembered his name in a hymn of praise. His memory . . . will never fade even unto the last generation. His was, indeed, a great example. . . ."

And so we know what the Old Testament never mentioned: the people looked upon Jehoiachin's surrender not as an act of weakness but as an act of heroic self-sacrifice. Not caring for his own life or honour, he was only concerned with preserving the city and protecting its people. Of course, we cannot say with certainty that his contemporaries really felt like that, and Jeremiah (22:20-30) for one spoke of the young King as an outcast who had lost favour in the Lord's eyes. But even Jeremiah was not altogether unsympathetic towards the unhappy young man. And in fact Jehoiachin's lot was sad indeed. He was taken to Babylon and kept a prisoner there for thirty-seven years, until Nebuchadnezzar's son and successor finally pardoned him.

But to return to Nebuchadnezzar's siege of Jerusalem in the year 597 B.C. When all is said and done, the King of Babylon behaved with considerable restraint. To nip any further resistance in the bud, he sent the leading citizens into Babylonian exile but he did not put an end to what small semblance of independence Jerusalem still had. He even allowed another king of David's dynasty to sit upon the throne of Jerusalem. It would be wrong, therefore, to speak of Nebuchadnezzar as a wicked tyrant and of Babylon as a typical tyrannical state. Nebuchadnezzar merely desired to resurrect Hammurabi's empire in all its former glory. Within this empire Judah and Jerusalem had every chance of an independent existence and it was up to Jehoiachin's successor Zedekiah to make the most of his chances. It was due to his political stupidity that he failed to take them.

In the fourth year of Zedekiah's reign, Jerusalem was teeming with agents from Ammon, Moab, Edom, Tyre and Sidon, all of whom conspired against Nebuchadnezzar. Now the Babylonian intelligence service was functioning perfectly, and so Nebuchadnezzar summoned Zedekiah to Babylon to account for his actions. Instead of going himself, Zedekiah sent messengers to Babylon, and apart from Zedekiah's letter, they also carried a letter from Jeremiah to the Jewish exiles there. Now these exiles had been living as if the day of their return was imminent, and Jeremiah did his best to convince them how unduly optimistic they were: "Build ye houses," he told them, "and dwell in them; and plant gardens, and eat the fruit of them; Take ye wives, and beget sons and daughters; and take wives for your sons, and give your daughters to husbands, that they may bear sons and daughters; that ye may be increased there, and not diminished. And seek the peace of the city whither I have caused you to be carried away captives, and pray unto the Lord for it: for in the peace thereof shall ye have peace" (Jeremiah 29:5-7). In other words: prepare for a very long stay and do not pray for Babylon's downfall—its welfare is your own.

We must assume that when, shortly afterwards, Zedekiah himself could no longer put off a visit to Babylon, Jeremiah implored the king to be humble towards the overlord on whose goodwill the fate of his people depended. Apparently Zedekiah heeded the prophet's advice and so managed to stave off the evil moment. But in 588 B.C. Zedekiah once again refused to pay taxes. National pride had won a resounding victory over Jeremiah's wisdom. This time Nebuchadnezzar did not tarry. Even before the rainy season had ceased, in the month of January of the year 587, he rushed his troops to Jerusalem and completely surrounded the city. For a little while it looked as if reinforcements from Egypt could stave off disaster, but the inhabitants rejoiced too soon, for in July 586, Jerusalem fell, and a month later its walls were destroyed, the Temple and palace consigned to the flames, and hundreds of leading citizens put to death. And so, by ignoring Jeremiah's warnings, Zedekiah had brought disaster upon his people, disaster that could easily have been averted had nationalism been tempered with political realism.

Babylonian captivity was a definite turning point in the history of Judah. The place of kings and prophets was taken by foreign governors, and the power of the priests and indeed, even the language changed. Before the exile the official language had been Hebrew, but now the best people would insist on speaking Aramaic.

Precisely because of this tremendous difference we may be misled into having quite the wrong conception of the period. In our mind's eye we see the entire population of Jerusalem marching in pitiful columns along the long caravan route to Babylon. Nothing could be further from the truth, for only a small part of the population was taken away, as the second Book of Kings makes perfectly clear. This Book does anything but embellish the events it describes and considers the exile an unmitigated disaster. But even so, the Book states quite emphatically that the evacuation was an orderly and strictly limited affair.

During the first exile of 597 B.C. only Jehoiachin the king, his family, his officers, his chief priests, and seven thousand of his soldiers together with a thousand smiths and craftsmen had been taken away. By depriving Jerusalem of its craftsmen, Nebuchadnezzar had deprived the city of any possibility of arming a future rebellion. We have good reason to believe that he continued to be very careful whom he left behind. No doubt, all friends of Egypt were deported, while the friends of Babylon were allowed to stay. This explains why Jeremiah was not sent into exile.

A quick calculation will show that the number of deported men was roughly eight thousand, which, together with their families, makes a total of about forty thousand men, women and children. Large though this figure is, it cannot have represented more than 10 per cent. of the total population. But even so, the remaining 90 per cent. were robbed of their leaders, their soldiers, their smiths and their priests, and without them they were helpless.

It was not Nebuchadnezzar's aim to destroy the exiles, nor even to ram Babylonian customs down their throats. The forty thousand captives were given their own territory and were allowed to settle there. This territory must have been close to the Great Canal near Tel-Aviv, but we do not know its exact location. The exiles were given every chance of arranging their social life in accordance with their own customs and laws. Many even achieved great prosperity, as was shown when excavations brought to light the archives of a Jewish family of bankers.

Among the exiles was a priest by the name of Ezekiel, the son of Buzi. He became the captives' leader and the prophet who prepared them for their return to Jerusalem. Each year a new batch of exiles was carried off from Jerusalem, and in Jeremiah 52:29 we can read that in the year 587-586, eight hundred and thirty-two souls were taken from the city. The very exactness of this figure speaks for its historical accuracy. Much less exact is a parallel report in the Book of Kings (II Kings 25:11) to the effect that the Babylonian commander carried off most of the remaining citizens, including all the friends of Babylon, leaving behind only a few poor vinedressers and husbandmen. It seems highly improbable that Nebuchadnezzar deported even his own supporters, and we had far better stick to Jeremiah's version.

The sack of the city in 586 B.C. brought freedom to Jeremiah, whom his own people had thrown into gaol. No doubt the King of Babylon knew that, though the prophet had not been actively pro-Babylonian, he had in fact played into his hands. And so he gave orders to his officers to "take him, and look well to him, and do him no harm; but do unto him even as he shall say unto thee" (Jeremiah 39:12). By mistake, however, Jeremiah was made to join the transport to Babylon. When the captain of the guard eventually recognised him, he immediately gave him the choice of either coming along to Babylon as a privileged citizen or else of returning home. Seeing his task amongst the remnants of his people, and not amongst the exiles, Jeremiah chose to return. And so he was given bread and money, found his way back to humble Mizpah where Gedaliah, the new governor, had taken up residence, and made this proclamation: "Fear not to serve the Chaldeans: dwell in the land, and serve the king of Babylon, and it shall be well with you. As for me, behold, I will dwell at Mizpah, to serve the Chaldeans, which will come unto us: but ye, gather ye wine, and summer fruits, and oil, and put them in your vessels, and dwell in your cities that ye have taken" (Jeremiah 40:9-10). When Gedaliah spoke these words, it was autumn, the time when the olives had to be picked and the grapes gathered in the vineyard. The only thing left was to pretend that nothing had changed and to carry on as always before.

For in the year 586 no one could say what the future held for Judah. Judah was still the centre of Israel, and on her the prophet Jeremiah continued to place all his hopes for the future. But fate was to decree otherwise. Not in Judah, but in faraway Babylon, was the future Jewish state being built. Indeed, the period of exile was to become of such great importance that its influence can still be felt in the Israel of today.

52

Jeremiah and the King

WE are told that Jesus asked His disciples: "Whom do men say that I the Son of Man am?" (St. Matthew 16:13). This question was answered in many different ways. Some thought that Jesus was John the Baptist, others spoke of Elijah and others again of Jeremiah. The fact that John the Baptist, Elijah and Jeremiah are mentioned in one breath, shows clearly how greatly esteemed Jeremiah was even in Jesus' day. Now, Elijah was the legendary figure whose return as the Messiah was fervently expected, and John the Baptist had taken the people of Jerusalem by storm, but why did the Lord think so highly of Jeremiah? Fortunately the prophet's sayings and thoughts were recorded by his faithful disciple Baruch, so that we can go some way towards answering this question.

Jeremiah like many of his predecessors, had never wanted to be a prophet. And so when the call came to him while he was still a young man he protested his singular lack of qualifications. "Before I formed thee in the belly", the Lord's voice told him, "I knew thee; and before thou camest forth out of the womb I sanctified thee, and I ordained thee a prophet unto the nations", but Jeremiah replied: "Ah, Lord God! behold, I cannot speak: for I am a child." Then the Lord rebuked him with: "Say not, I am a child: for thou shalt go to all that I shall send thee, and whatsoever I command thee thou shalt speak. Be not afraid of their faces: for I am with thee to deliver thee" (Jeremiah 1:5, 6, 7-8). How reminiscent of God's call to Moses! And how alike the two replies: Who are we to undertake so great a task?

And indeed the task before Jeremiah was immense. He was told: "See, I have this day set thee over the nations and over the kingdoms, to root out, and to pull down, and to destroy, and to throw down, to build, and to plant" (Jeremiah 1:9-10). How tremendous a responsibility for so young a man! His word could bring down famine and drought, and his prayer cause the heavens to open and to pour out rain over the thirsty land. His mere word could defeat the enemy—indeed, nothing was impossible for one of God's chosen prophets.

But Jeremiah did not want this power. He felt too weak to bear it, and furthermore, he knew in his heart of hearts that he would have to be God's herald of doom. The people would refuse to listen to his constant prophecies of defeat, and he would be condemned to a life of loneliness, his own friends and family deserting him one after another. The authorities would look upon him as a traitor and bind him in chains. And he, Jeremiah, loved life and prized the warm glow of friendship above all things.

Now, there are some men who seek solitude, but Jeremiah was not one of these. Then again there are the born pessimists who always look upon the worst side of things quite instinctively, but Jeremiah was not one of these either. All he was made to say and do went against the grain, and, indeed, against popular feeling, as well. Who would follow him, and see what only God could see? Small wonder, then, that the people branded him as a foreign agitator and looked upon him as a wicked and dangerous man.

Jeremiah's conflict with his king took a long time to come to a head. At first the prophet expected great things of King Zedekiah, who was, in fact, no more than a vassal of the King of Babylon. His name alone gave Jeremiah grounds for hope, for it meant "justice". Surely he would bring back justice to Judah and, in Jeremiah's eyes, justice alone could guarantee his people's continued existence. "Behold, the days come", the Lord had told him, "that I will raise unto David a righteous Branch, and a King shall reign and prosper, and shall execute judgment and justice in the earth. In his days Judah shall be saved, and Israel shall dwell safely: and this is his name whereby he shall be called, THE LORD OUR RIGHTEOUSNESS. Therefore, behold, the days come, saith the Lord, that they shall no more say, The Lord liveth, which brought up the children of Israel out of the land of Egypt, But, The Lord liveth, which brought up and which led the seed of the house of Israel out of the north country, and from all countries whither I had driven them; and they shall dwell in their own land" (Jeremiah 23: 5-8).

And so Jeremiah expected the King not only to restore Judah but to bring back the lost tribes of Israel who had been driven from their land more than a hundred years earlier. Indeed, I know of no prophecy that was less borne out by the future course of events.

Soon Jeremiah was to change his opinion about this King who had at first struck him as the righteous successor to the House of David.

In a vision, the prophet was shown two baskets of figs, one filled with good figs and the other with "very naughty figs, which could not be eaten, they were so bad". While the good figs symbolised the exiles in Babylon, whom God would protect and one day lead back home, the bad figs were Zedekiah and his courtiers. And the Lord said of his vision: "So will I give Zedekiah the king of Judah, and his princes, and the residue of Jerusalem, that remain in this land, and them that dwell in the land of Egypt: And I will deliver them to be removed into all the kingdoms of the earth for their hurt, to be a reproach and a proverb, a taunt and a curse, in all places whither I shall drive them" (Jeremiah 24:8-9). Indeed, Jeremiah had good cause to speak out against Zedekiah. The King, willing tool that he was of his wicked courtiers, failed to carry out any of the social reforms that Jerusalem so sorely needed, and in particular, he omitted to free the slaves. Meanwhile Jerusalem was hastening towards the precipice, as Jeremiah never tired of pointing out to the King. But he and his ministers had grown to hate the truth and threw the prophet into gaol. The worse things became for Jerusalem, the harsher the treatment meted out to the prophet. Thanks to a small number of faithful friends his life at least was spared. And so the tragic struggle between king and prophet continued until the day when the inevitable occurred, and Jerusalem was laid waste. Only after Zedekiah had witnessed the pitiful collapse of his town and his family, did he realise that no man can afford to ignore God's appointed prophets.

53

Jeremiah and the Temple

THE prophet Jeremiah was himself a priest, as we can see from the title of the Book that bears his name: "The words of Jeremiah the son of Hilkiah, of the priests that were in Anathoth in the land of Benjamin." Why, then, did he come into conflict with the rest of the priesthood, and particularly with the priests in the Temple of Jerusalem?

The answer is given in Jeremiah 7, where we are told that the word of the Lord ordered the prophet to stand in the gate of the

Temple, there to proclaim: "Thus saith the Lord of hosts, the God of Israel, Amend your ways and your doings, and I will cause you to dwell in this place. Trust ye not in lying words, saying, The temple of the Lord, The temple of the Lord, The temple of the Lord, are these. For if ye thoroughly amend your ways and your doings; if ye thoroughly execute judgment between a man and his neighbour; If ye oppress not the stranger, the fatherless, and the widow, and shed not innocent blood in this place, neither walk after other gods to your hurt: Then will I cause you to dwell in this place, in the land that I gave to your fathers, for ever and ever. Behold, ye trust in lying words, that cannot profit. Will ye steal, murder, and commit adultery, and swear falsely, and burn incense unto Baal, and walk after other gods whom ye know not; And come and stand before me in this house, which is called by my name, and say, We are delivered to do all these abominations? Is this house, which is called by my name, become a den of robbers in your eyes?" (Jeremiah 7:3-11). We can still picture the indignant prophet as he stood in the forecourt of the Temple, his anger reminiscent of Him who, equally incensed, would one day also liken the Temple to a den of thieves (St. Matthew 21:12-13).

Let us try to look deeper into the meaning of Jeremiah's words. The prophet did not mind the fact that the Temple was being used as a house of prayer, but he did mind the hypocrisy of those who thought that all they needed to do was to come and repeat: "The temple of the Lord, the temple of the Lord, the temple of the Lord is here." Why do you speak of threatening dangers and approaching doom? they would say to him. Why prophesy about foreign hosts that will conquer and destroy our city, and carry off its population into exile? Surely these things cannot happen to us as long as we have our Temple, the dwelling place of the Lord Himself?

Now all this sounded terribly pious, and what could the poor prophet say in the face of so much religion? His opponents invoked neither the strength of Jerusalem's walls, their military alliance with Egypt nor their number of foot-soldiers and chariots. No, they came with weighty religious arguments and the pretence of being faithful disciples of the prophet Isaiah. For Jeremiah their arguments were hollow. What if they did worship in the Temple, when they thought that by so doing they were free to oppress the poor, the widow and the orphan? What good were sacrifices when all the commandments

M

were being broken, albeit in the shadow of God's House? We can feel that Jeremiah was simply echoing Amos's pleas for justice, for Amos, too, had not objected to temples, shrines, priests and sacrifices, but like Jeremiah had known that religion was worthless if it meant that justice had to go by the board.

And Jeremiah had another excellent precedent to go by. Once upon a time, the Ark of God had stood upon the holy place in Shiloh. What could be holier than this Ark, this shrine which had been brought by the priests from the journey through the desert? But not even this Ark had been able to vouchsafe safety and everlasting peace. Eli's son had sinned and the Ark had been destroyed by the Philistines, and the people of Israel sorely defeated. Clearly, even the most illustrious temple, the most beautiful divine service, the most impressive procession of priests and Levites would avail the people nothing once they forgot what must never be allowed to be forgotten: the protection of the poor, the claims of justice and obedience to God's highest commandments.

And it was precisely their lack of social justice that showed with terrifying emphasis how the rich were disobeying the Law of Moses. Jeremiah 34 tells us of Jerusalem's last hour. The King of Babylon was standing at the gate. It was then that the people chose to remember Jeremiah's fulminations against those who had not set their slaves free after six years of service. A man would fall into debt and sometimes he would only be able to save himself by selling himself and his family into slavery. According to the Law of Moses such slaves had to be freed in the seventh year, but the rich citizens of Jerusalem had made light of this commandment. Only now, when they were being threatened with extinction, did they publicly declare their readiness to free the slaves.

But when, quite unexpectedly, the Egyptians sent reinforcements to Jerusalem's aid, the rich pretended not to have made any vows at all and at once took back their slaves. The danger was past and they had no need to heed God's commandments any longer. Then Jeremiah became so incensed that, in God's name, he proclaimed that famine and the sword would be let loose instead of the slaves. Those who knew not the value of sacred oaths were not fit to live a life of plenty.

And so Jeremiah in proclaiming God's justice, could not help attacking the priests who had so blatantly condoned the breaking of God's Laws. It was this justifiable attack which gave rise to the wrong idea that he was a violent opponent of the priesthood as such.

54

The Lamentations of Jeremiah

IN the Authorised Version, the Book of the Prophet Jeremiah is followed by Lamentations. While the Hebrew Bible does not in fact attribute this Book to the pen of the prophet, the translators into Greek and Latin felt certain that no one but Jeremiah could have written these mournful songs. And so the word "jeremiad" has come to mean a doleful complaint or a complaining tirade (S.O.E.D.). As a matter of fact most Biblical scholars are of the opinion that the Lamentations could not possibly have been written by the prophet, and that Jeremiah himself wrote quite different songs of woe. Thus he taught the women of Jerusalem to sing:

> "For death is come up into our windows,
>   and is entered into our palaces,
>   to cut off the children from without, and the
>   young men from the streets.
>
> .   .   .   .   .
>
> Even the carcases of men shall fall as dung upon
>   the open field,
>   and as the handful after the harvestman,
>   and none shall gather them."
>
> (Jeremiah 9:21, 22)

On reading these lines we must try to imagine a funeral in Old Jerusalem. Hired mourners would walk behind the bier, singing their doleful songs. Perhaps the word "singing" is an exaggeration, for what these women did was to wail in a monotonous tone, while wringing their hands in deep sorrow. Reliefs, particularly from Egypt, give us a fair idea of the scene they made, and, furthermore, until recently similar rites were performed by the Hassidic Jews in the ghettoes of

Poland. These people, so bestially murdered by the Nazis, used also to hire women mourners and pay them for their public display of sorrow.

Unlike Jeremiah's plaints, the Lamentations follow a special pattern: all the original Hebrew verses began with consecutive letters of the alphabet. Now while this specifically Hebrew form of poetry is obviously lost in translation, the tremendous power of the Lamentations is not. From the very beginning, we cannot help being deeply moved:

> "How doth the city sit solitary,
>   that was full of people!
>   how is she become as a widow!
>   she that was great among the nations,
>   and princess among the provinces,
>   how is she become tributary!"
>
> (Lamentations 1:1)

In the eyes of the poet, Judah was indeed like a mighty queen on a throne set high above the neighbouring lands. But now the queen had been dethroned, and so:

> "She weepeth sore in the night,
>   and her tears are on her cheeks:
>   among all her lovers she hath none to comfort her:
>   all her friends have dealt treacherously with her,
>   they are become her enemies."

> "The ways of Zion do mourn,
>   because none come to the solemn feasts:
>   all her gates are desolate:
>   her priests sigh,
>   her virgins are afflicted,
>   and she is in bitterness."

> "And from the daughter of Zion
>   all her beauty is departed:
>   her princes are become like harts that find no pasture,
>   and they are gone without strength before the pursuer."
>
> (Lamentations 1:2, 4, 6)

Yes, Jerusalem had been laid low, the Temple was deserted, and no longer would pilgrims walk in solemn procession to pay their homage here. Hence the sadness in the minstrel's heart, but hence also his reproach:

> "Jerusalem hath grievously sinned;
> therefore she is removed:
> all that honoured her despise her,
> because they have seen her nakedness:
> yea, she sigheth,
> and turneth backward."
>
> (Lamentations 1:8)

Now, if Jerusalem's downfall was the punishment for her sin, then there was hope, for where there was sin there could be repentance also, and a return to Him who alone could bring back Judah's lost glory. Thus the lament turns into a hymn, and a song of praise:

> "O Lord, thou hast pleaded the causes of my soul;
> thou hast redeemed my life.
> O Lord, thou hast seen my wrong:
> judge thou my cause.
> Thou hast seen all their vengeance
> and all their imaginations against me."
>
> (Lamentations 3:58-60)

> "Turn thou us unto thee, O Lord,
> and we shall be turned;
> renew our days as of old.
> But thou hast utterly rejected us;
> thou art very wroth against us."
>
> (Lamentations 5:21-22)

And so each year anew, the Lamentations of Jeremiah are remembered by Jews and Catholics alike. But while the former read them on the day their Temple was destroyed, the latter remember them during Holy Week, the week that recalls the suffering of Jesus Christ, Our Lord.

55

Ezekiel, the Prophet in Exile

I CAN imagine that the unprepared student of the Book of Ezekiel might easily become so disappointed and confused that he quickly puts it aside. Still, though the prophet himself seemed unclear about the meaning of his own visions, he spoke many truths that are valuable to this day. But these truths have to be sought with great care, for they lie hidden like rare jewels between just so much dust and rubble.

Now, while we can still picture Isaiah and Jeremiah as they walked with kings and priests, with the rich and the poor of Jerusalem and as they talked to their adversaries, the false prophets, all we know of the prophet Ezekiel is that he left Jerusalem in 597 B.C. with the first batch of exiles and that he became filled with longing for the Holy City. But like Jeremiah he accepted exile as God's just punishment, and like Jeremiah he was opposed to revolution.

Apparently Ezekiel was a great orator, though no one would think so to judge from his written pronouncements. But, in fact, God told him: "Also, thou son of man, the children of thy people still are talking against thee by the walls and in the doors of the houses, and speak one to another, every one to his brother, saying, Come, I pray you, and hear what is the word that cometh forth from the Lord. And they come unto thee as the people cometh, and they sit before thee as my people, and they hear thy words, but they will not do them: for with their mouth they shew much love, but their heart goeth after their covetousness. And, lo, thou art unto them as a very lovely song of one that hath a pleasant voice, and can play well on an instrument: for they hear thy words, but they do them not. And when this cometh to pass (lo, it will come), then shall they know that a prophet hath been among them" (Ezekiel 33:30-33).

We can just see the crowd flocking to one whose tongue might have been barbed, but whose words of condemnation sounded so beautiful that his listeners simply could not help extolling: how well you have spoken, how marvellous is your invective. And as they kept praising his great oratory, the meaning of his words ran off them like water

off a duck's back. For all their admiration, Ezekiel knew them exactly
for what they were. How gladly would he have forgone their adula-
tion and have had them behave righteously instead! Indeed, Ezekiel
preferred to remain a true leader instead of turning into one of the
sheep into which the mob so often manages to change its heroes.

But apart from being a public speaker, Ezekiel also had the rare gift
of being spirited away. He would look into remote cities and give clear
reports of what he had seen. Now, this gift was by no means peculiar
to Ezekiel. Elijah, too, had been able to transcend distance, as we can
gather from his encounter with Obadiah. Obadiah was reluctant to
obey the prophet's request to summon King Ahab, since, as he said,
". . . it shall come to pass, as soon as I am gone from thee, that the
Spirit of the Lord shall carry thee whither I know not . . ." (I Kings
18:12). And who but Obadiah would then be blamed for the prophet's
inexplicable absence?

But to return to Ezekiel. In the eighth chapter of his Book, we are
told how the Spirit took him to Jerusalem, where the prophet was to
witness that his people had begun to worship false gods in the very
Temple where the God of Israel reigned supreme.

Now, when all sorts of religions become fused into one hotch-potch,
this unholy mixture is usually dubbed with the term "syncretism",
and syncretism is generally symptomatic of a declining civilisation.
Degenerate cultures are receptive to all sorts of superstitions, and
believe that they can pick and choose what truths they like.

And this is precisely what was happening in Jerusalem between the
years 597 and 586 B.C. All the leaders, with the exception of Jeremiah,
were in exile, and Jeremiah was disliked for his gloomy prophecies.
The inhabitants had the feeling that God had left His people in the
lurch, and that the gods of victorious Babylon and Egypt must surely
be mightier than the God of Israel. Why then continue to worship a
God who had proved His impotence? And so the faith of the fathers
was going by the board, and this was what Ezekiel saw in his vision of
the Temple in Jerusalem.

First he beheld an idol which he called "the image of jealousy".
It was probably a Baal, one of the many Canaanite gods against which
even Elijah and Elisha had fought, but never with complete success.
Then Ezekiel was shown a secret door, behind which lay a dark chamber. Its walls were covered with "creeping things, and abominable

beasts", and the prophet saw that seventy of the leading citizens were burning incense here.

Unfortunately, the prophet left it at that, but even from his sparse report we gather that these men were imitating Egyptian rites. The "creeping things" could only have been reptiles, crocodiles and snakes, the very symbols of the Egyptian Osiris myth.

But when he comes to the next part of his vision, Ezekiel gives us full details. At the northern gate of the Temple he encountered a number of women, bewailing Tammuz. Excavations in Mesopotamia have made it clear that the worship of Tammuz, the divine child of the great mother-goddess Ishtar, was Sumerian in origin. Tammuz was the god of youth, and the god of spring. It was he who wedded Mother Earth and yearly gave rise to harvests and new flocks. His power waxed and waned with the seasons, and so each winter, Tammuz would be united to Mother Earth and his going down lamented by women mourners. Year after year, there would be a wedding and a quickening, a birth, and a rebirth, a death and a resurrection, and the people of Mesopotamia would give thanks and mourn in turn. Their rites captured the imagination of the people of Israel also, no matter how often the prophets had protested that only the God of Israel could bring dew and rain, and that only His hand dispensed fertility and barrenness. And so, in Jerusalem, the women were once again sitting at the gate of the Temple and lamenting the passing away of the young god. Possibly the fast on the ninth day of Ab, with which Jews to this day give expression to their sorrow about the fall of the Temple, has its mythological roots in these lamentations for Tammuz.

But his visionary tour has not yet ended. He is next taken to the innermost court of the Temple, where twenty-five men, their backs towards the Temple, were bowing down before the sun. The reader will remember what we said earlier about Akhenaten's hymn to the sun and its resemblance to the psalmist's:

> "He appointed the moon for seasons:
> the sun knoweth his going down.
> Thou makest darkness, and it is night:
> wherein all the beasts of the forest do creep forth.
> The young lions roar after their prey,
> and seek their meat from God.

The sun ariseth, they gather themselves together,
and lay them down in their dens.
Man goeth forth unto his work
and to his labour until the evening."
(Psalm 104:19-23)

What a world of difference, we exclaim once more, between
Akhenaten's attitude to Ra and the Babylonians' attitude to their sun-
god Shamash on the one hand and the conception of the psalmist on
the other! For him the sun, the moon and indeed the whole universe
are as nothing compared with God's glory and all obey His will.
But the twenty-five whom Ezekiel saw in the Temple had forgotten
the Creator of heaven and earth and were worshipping His creation in
His stead. And by upbraiding them from afar, Ezekiel kept burning the
flame of God when it was most in danger of extinction. Thus he will
always be remembered, for herein lay his greatness.

During their long years in Babylonian captivity, many of the exiles
must quite naturally have asked themselves what would happen to
their city and their country. The more pessimistic had given up all hope
of ever returning, and in fact some had made themselves so much at
home in their new land that, when the final hour of freedom struck,
they preferred to stay where they were. On the other hand some of the
exiles must have been incurable optimists and, convinced that Babylon
would fall at any moment, they must have kept their bags permanently
packed in readiness. Now the prophet, for one, knew full well that the
fall of Babylon was not imminent. According to him, the people would
first have to accept exile as their just punishment, and make the best of
life in obedience to God's laws wherever they happened to be. That
their day would come, however, the prophet knew full well, for he
was granted a vision of the new Jerusalem.

He described the plans of the new city in the last nine chapters of his
Book. Now, Ezekiel had this vision during the twenty-fifth year of
captivity, i.e. in the year 572 B.C., and thirty-three years before the
Persians were to free his people from captivity. At that time there was
no immediate prospect of liberation, and the prophet's vision cannot be
explained away by his having seen the actual plans. No, Ezekiel
was speaking the truth when he told the people that the hand of the
Lord had taken him back to Jerusalem. There, a mysterious man, a

line of flax and a measuring reed in his hand, had been waiting to show the prophet through the streets of the city and the courts of the Temple. God urged the prophet to pay careful attention, so that he could give a full report to his fellow exiles in Babylon (Ezekiel 40:1-5).

The tour itself is described in great detail. We are told how thick the walls were, how wide the gates, how large and how many the rooms. The whole story seems to be one long calculation of lengths and breadths, and it only becomes interesting when the prophet tells of God's return to the Temple. The glory of the Lord of Israel approached from the east, the very direction in which His people had been led into captivity. Ezekiel saw the return as a majestic spectacle. The Lord's voice was "like a noise of many waters" and "the earth shined with his glory". When he witnessed the awe-inspiring return of God's Majesty, the prophet fell upon his face. Then his guide took him to the innermost court of the Temple, where he heard a voice say: "Son of man, [this is] the place of my throne, and the place of the soles of my feet, where I will dwell in the midst of the children of Israel for ever" (Ezekiel 43:7). Once again, the prophet was ordered to take careful note, so that the children of Israel would know how God wanted the Temple rebuilt when the time came. And, in fact, when the time came for building the Second Temple Ezekiel's vision was to be acknowledged and realised by its architects. They may have altered some of the details, but in the main they were guided by his vision.

Another of Ezekiel's visions, that of the holy waters (Ezekiel 47), is very reminiscent of John's vision of "a pure river of water of life, clear as crystal, proceeding out of the throne of God and of the Lamb" (Revelation 22:1). At the banks of this river stood "the tree of life, which bare twelve manner of fruits, and yielded her fruit every month: and the leaves of the tree were for the healing of the nations" (Revelation 22:2). In general, one would do well to look upon John's vision as a commentary on Ezekiel's with the great difference that Jesus Christ had meanwhile come. And so when John, too, had visions of a new Jerusalem as a city of pure gold built on foundations of precious stone, his vision no longer had need of a temple, for Jesus Christ had Himself become the living Temple of God.

And so Ezekiel in addition to having been the architect of the Second Temple, was the prophet who inspired St. John's vision of the new Jerusalem, "coming down from God out of heaven, prepared as a bride adorned for her husband".

But Ezekiel's greatness lay not in his prophecies alone. There was an old proverb in Israel which said: "The fathers have eaten sour grapes, and the children's teeth are set on edge" (Ezekiel 18:1). The meaning is quite clear: the children must suffer for the sins of their fathers. We have many instances of the truth of this proverb in daily life, for, though we may think it unjust, many children, and even grandchildren, do suffer for the sins of their ancestors. But in the Old Testament the proverb meant even more than that, for we are told in the Ten Commandments: "I the Lord thy God am a jealous God, visiting the iniquity of the fathers upon the children unto the third and fourth generation of them that hate me" (Exodus 20:5 and Deuteronomy 5:9). Not only must the children pay for their fathers' sins but apparently God Himself expressly desires it to be so.

Now, this whole question is really what we currently call "collective responsibility", and in times of war people have always favoured the wholesale slaughter of the enemy. And yet it would be wrong to think of the Old Testament as the author of the idea of collective guilt. On the contrary we must marvel at those Biblical writers who dared to raise their voice against this ancient notion.

For in the Book of Deuteronomy we can also read: "The fathers shall not be put to death for the children, neither shall the children be put to death for the fathers: every man shall be put to death for his own sin" (Deuteronomy 24:16). This text was later used by King Amaziah when he left the children of his father's assassin unharmed "according unto that which is written in the book of the law of Moses" (II Kings 14:6). Thus we can see how a more humane approach was gradually coming to the fore. The prophet Jeremiah emphasised this new attitude when he spoke of the days when man "shall say no more, The fathers have eaten a sour grape, and the children's teeth are set on edge. But every one shall die for his own iniquity: every man that eateth the sour grape, his teeth shall be set on edge" (Jeremiah 31:29-30).

And Jeremiah's call was to be taken up by Ezekiel. Having quoted the notorious saying about the sour grapes, Ezekiel added: "As I live, saith the Lord God, ye shall not have occasion any more to use this proverb in Israel. Behold, all souls are mine; as the soul of the father, so also the soul of the son is mine: the soul that sinneth, it shall die"

(Ezekiel 18:3-4). No longer would the righteous son bear the guilt of the father, for while we cannot atone for another, neither can we sin for him.

But might not this new attitude place too heavy a burden on the average mortal? Might it not give him responsibilities far too heavy to bear? Ezekiel had no difficulty in answering this question, for according to him if only the sinner repented of his evil ways, all his sins are forgiven him. "Have I any pleasure at all that the wicked should die? saith the Lord God: and not that he should return from his ways, and live?" (Ezekiel 18:23). These words of Ezekiel anticipated those of Jesus Christ, who proclaimed: "I say unto you, that likewise joy shall be in heaven over one sinner that repenteth, more than over ninety and nine just persons, which need no repentance" (St. Luke 15:7).

And so, collective responsibility, with all its terrible consequences, was roundly condemned. And here a new problem arose: that of the good man who is yet sorely afflicted. No longer can his suffering be explained by the transgressions of one of his forefathers, or even of one of his compatriots. Why then does he have to suffer at all? And it is this burning question which became the central theme of the Book of Job.

G. *Exile and Return*

56

Portents of Freedom

LIKE all great events, the fall of Babylon in the year 539 B.C. cast its shadow before it. Even while Nebuchadnezzar's proud empire had still seemed inviolable, a watchful observer could not have helped noticing the cracks that were fast appearing. The first to read the signs were the Jewish exiles, who realised that Nebuchadnezzar's successor was anything but a worthy heir to his father's throne. Now Hammurabi's empire had gone down for the same reason, a thousand years earlier, and Nebuchadnezzar, who was Hammurabi's great admirer, had done his utmost to prevent a repetition. But, alas, his son Evil-merodach turned out to be a weakling who was overthrown after a reign of only two years. Evil-merodach was succeeded by Neriglissar, who managed to keep his throne for four years. Since Jeremiah had mentioned him for the part he had played in the conquest of Jerusalem, it is reasonable to assume that he must have been a very old man indeed by the time he came to power. His son, Labashi-Marduk, ruled for only a few months to be ousted by Nabonidus, one of the strangest figures in ancient history. Nabonidus was neither soldier nor diplomat—he was an antiquarian, of whom a great deal is known from ancient Babylonian clay tablets. Now, amazing though it is to read about a king who was interested in antiquity as long ago as 550 B.C., we must remember that Babylon had by then existed for two thousand years. Even so it was rather dangerous for a king to be more interested in excavations than in battles and ceremonial, a thing that antagonised his all-powerful priests. As King of Babylon, Nabonidus was expected to pay public homage to Marduk, the god whose second name was Bel. At the beginning of the New Year, the statue of Bel would be carried in procession along a hallowed route, and it was the king's task to walk alongside it touching the statue's hand. When Nabonidus refused point-blank to carry out this traditional duty, he initiated a struggle with his priests which was eventually to lead to his country's downfall.

To make things worse, Nabonidus deserted his capital for an oasis in the Arabian desert. Scholars have never been able to agree why he went into the wilderness, some regarding it as yet another sign of his characteristic contrariness, others believing that he went out to build a new bulwark against the ever-growing might of the Persians. However, all we know with certainty is that Nabonidus left Babylon and that he handed over the reins of government to his son Belshazzar. Meanwhile Cyrus, the mighty King of the Persians, was inexorably drawing closer.

It is against this background that we must read the story of King Nebuchadnezzar's dream, a dream that God had revealed to Daniel so that the prophet could say: "Thou, O king, sawest, and behold a great image. This great image, whose brightness was excellent, stood before thee: and the form thereof was terrible. This image's head was of fine gold, his breast and his arms of silver, his belly and his thighs of brass, his legs of iron, his feet part of iron and part of clay. Thou sawest till that a stone was cut out without hands, which smote the image upon his feet that were of iron and clay, and brake them to pieces. Then was the iron, the clay, the brass, the silver and the gold, broken to pieces together, and became like the chaff of the summer threshing-floors; and the wind carried them away, that no place was found for them: and the stone that smote the image became a great mountain, and filled the whole earth" (Daniel 2:31-35).

Those of us who know anything about Babylonian history will have little difficulty in interpreting the dream. What better description of Nebuchadnezzar's empire than a "giant with feet of clay"? What finer way of characterising its decline than to speak of gold, silver, brass, and iron in just that order? What more telling symbol for King Cyrus' invincible army than the rolling stone that smashed the giant's feet of clay? Hence Daniel's interpretation: "Thou, O king, art a king of kings: for the God of heaven hath given thee a kingdom, power and strength, and glory. And wheresoever the children of man dwell, the beasts of the field and the fowls of the heaven hath he given into thine hand, and hath made thee ruler over them all. Thou art this head of gold" (Daniel 2:37-38).

Soon the prophecy was to come true. The fifth chapter of Daniel describes the night in which Babylon was conquered by the army of Cyrus, King of the Persians. The watchmen were fast asleep while their betters were busily disporting themselves at a feast. Suddenly, a hand appeared out of nowhere and began to write a mysterious message

Ruins of the great city of Babylon, built by
King Nebuchadnezzar.

Plate 7

Ruins of the old wall of Samaria, built by Omri.

Shoval Settlement in 1950. Ploughing with a tractor.

Bedouins near Shoval Settlement (Negev, 1951).   *Pla*

on the wall of the king's banqueting chamber. Neither the king nor his sages could decipher the message, and, deeply perturbed, they sent for Daniel, who had proved himself a solver of riddles and an unraveller of mysteries. And in fact, Daniel was able to interpret the writing so plainly that not one of those present was left in any doubt about its meaning: God had numbered the days of their kingdom, He had weighed them; He had divided them and given them over into the hands of the Persians.

From this interpretation we must assume that the original Aramaic words read: Menah, tekal, peras, paras, i.e. He has numbered, He has weighed, He has divided, the Persian. Now, why was it that Daniel could read the text while the king and his sages could not? Surely, if they immediately recognised the justice of Daniel's interpretation, they ought to have been able to understand the writing by themselves. Many scholars have dwelt on this question, and some have suggested that the message was an anagram, the solution of which demanded a great deal of mental ingenuity. I do not agree with them, and feel sure that the message must have been written in straight Aramaic, just like the rest of the chapter. However, written Aramaic, like written Hebrew, had no vowels, and so the writing on the wall must have read: mnh, tkl, prs, prs. Now, instead of adding the vowel "a", the king's sages must have added the vowel "e", thus reading the message as: meneh, tekel, peres, peres—three measures of weight!

In that case we cannot really blame them for failing to understand the message. Which of us would be able to fathom the divine meaning of a message that said one ton, one stone, one cwt., one cwt.? But Daniel, simply by filling in the correct vowels, and reading the writing as "menah, tekal, peras, paras" had no difficulty in interpreting it correctly: God has numbered your days, he has weighed you and found you wanting, he has divided your kingdom to give it to the conqueror who is already knocking at the gate, the King of the Persians. In its Biblical rendering of mene, mene, tekel, upharsin, the writing has once again become meaningless, for in transliterating the vowel-less sounds the whole point of the story was necessarily lost.

It cannot be said that our interpretation diminishes from the story of the writing on the wall. They who served the false gods of gold and silver, brass and iron, lead and stone, were deaf to God's voice, precisely because their thoughts dwelled exclusively on gold and silver, on brass and iron. Used as they were to counting their possessions, they could read measures and weights, but not the word of God.

It was to these greedy men that Daniel was called. He who served but the one God, in whose name the prophets had preached righteousness and justice, knew at once that if God revealed Himself, He would not speak in riddles or in anagrams. When God spoke, He could not possibly be reciting so many weights of gold and silver. Steeped in the religious traditions of his people, Daniel understood immediately what the sages of Babylon had been too blind to see. His wisdom was not derived from a study of magic, as Nebuchadnezzar's courtiers must have thought, but from the wisdom of a heart that is guided by God.

57

The Rule of the Persians

AND so the giant with feet of clay, Nebuchadnezzar's mighty Babylonian empire, came tumbling down. Cyrus, the King of the Persians, took Babylon without encountering any resistance—he had appeared as suddenly as the rolling stone in the king's dream. Yes, Daniel had been a true prophet—Babylon had been weighed and found wanting, and now it was the Persian's turn. The Persian empire was enormous, and Judah but one of its many provinces.

At first sight we might be inclined to say that things had not changed very much for the better. The Jews were not given back their independence—they simply had a change of master. However, there is a tremendous difference between one overlord and another, as the people of Europe know only too well. There are some empires whose spirit is akin to ours and others which are so tyrannical that we feel compelled to fight them tooth and nail. And this was roughly the difference between the Babylonians and the Persians. Under the Babylonian yoke, the Jews had suffered so much that most of them looked back on their enforced captivity as a time of deepest despair. On the other hand, the Persians had come as welcome liberators, and their customs and even their religion were not altogether unlike those of the Jews. Thus, while Isaiah could call Cyrus a shepherd, and even one of

God's anointed (Isaiah 44:28 and 45:1), the Kings of Assyria and Babylon had always been looked upon by the prophets as scourges in God's hand. Through them God had wanted to punish His people for their sin, but they had gone much further in their retribution than God had demanded. King Cyrus, however, was quite unlike them, for the Lord had told Isaiah: "I will loose the loins of kings, to open before him the two leaved gates; and the gates shall not be shut; I will go before thee, and make the crooked places straight: I will break in pieces the gates of brass, and cut in sunder the bars of iron: And I will give thee the treasures of darkness, and hidden riches of secret places, that thou mayest know that I, the Lord, which call thee by thy name, am the God of Israel. For Jacob my servant's sake, and Israel mine elect, I have even called thee by thy name: I have surnamed thee, though thou hast not known me" (Isaiah 45:1-4).

Clearly Isaiah thought very highly of this great King, whose wisdom and understanding were the mortar that held his mighty empire together. No doubt, many Jews had been deeply disappointed to learn that no seed of David would grace their throne, but even so they felt God knew best what they needed. "Woe unto him," the prophet said, "that striveth with his Maker! Let the potsherd strive with the potsherds of the earth. Shall the clay say to him that fashioneth it, What makest thou? or thy work, He hath no hands? Woe unto him that saith unto his father, What begettest thou? or to the woman, What hast thou brought forth?" (Isaiah 45:9-10). Yes, the true believer must follow wherever God leads him, and be truly grateful when the Lord allows him to return to His Holy City. And he must be doubly grateful for being allowed to rebuild the Holy Temple in Jerusalem, albeit with Persian help.

The Jews must have felt much sympathy for the Persian religion. The Persians were apparently disciples of Zarathustra who had taught that on earth there were two forces, locked in deadly struggle, which would remain so until the end of all time: Ahura-Mazda, the god of light and Ahriman, the god of darkness and evil. Now the worship of Ahura-Mazda had much in common with the worship of the Jews. Unlike the surrounding nations, the Persians did not make images of their god, and so the Persian religion escaped the scathing scorn of Israel's iconoclastic prophets. Nor was there all that much difference between Moses' and Zarathustra's ethical laws. In fact there was a great deal of mutual understanding and friendship between the two peoples, and therefore an exchange of religious ideas. All our distinctions between God and Satan, heaven and hell, light and darkness, date back to the Persian era, for the Jews adopted them and handed them on to early Christianity.

But we would be wrong to think that the Jews renounced their own religion for that of the Persians. On the contrary, they were fully conscious of the difference between Persian dualism and their own idea of the one God who created light out of darkness, and life out of chaos. This specifically Jewish attitude was summed up by Isaiah's: "Thus saith the Lord . . . there is none beside me. I am the Lord, and there is none else. I form the light, and create darkness: I make peace, and create evil: I the Lord do all these things" (Isaiah 45:1, 6-7). With this classic refutation of dualism, the Jewish people bore witness to the fact that they had not lost their heritage. Friendship and prosperity may often prove more dangerous to our spiritual integrity than times of oppression, and so it is not really surprising that the Jews remained faithful to their own way of life under the Babylonian yoke. What is surprising is the fact that they remained steadfast even under the wise, tolerant and benevolent régime of the Persians, and that they continued to put their trust in Him who had taught them to say: "Hear, O Israel: The Lord our God is one Lord" (Deuteronomy 6:4).

58

Haggai and Zechariah

IN about 520 B.C. a strange Messianic movement arose among the Jews. Its spokesman was the prophet Haggai who proclaimed that the House of David would be restored in all its glory and the people of Judah return to the splendour of Solomon's day. Actually the movement is mentioned in only a few lines at the end of the Book of Haggai, but it is well worth our while to pay careful attention to these lines, particularly since very little else is known about the period immediately after the liberation.

We are told that the word of God came to Haggai, saying: "Speak to Zerubbabel, governor of Judah, saying, I will shake the heavens and the earth; And I will overthrow the throne of kingdoms, and I will destroy the strength of the kingdoms of the heathen; and I will overthrow the chariots, and those that ride in them; and the horses and their riders shall come down, every one by the sword of his brother. In that day, saith the Lord of hosts, will I take thee, O Zerubbabel, my servant, the son of Shealtiel, saith the Lord, and will make thee as a signet: for I have chosen thee, saith the Lord of hosts" (Haggai 2:21-23). Haggai's mysterious reference to Zerubbabel must be read in conjunction with the date on which the prophet had this vision: the four and twentieth day of the ninth month in the second year of the reign of King Darius.

Now we know from Herodotus that King Darius had great difficulty in asserting his authority. Darius' claims to the crown were contested by one Gaumata who claimed that he was the son of King Cyrus and whose supporters were so numerous that they shook the whole Persian empire. No doubt the subject states must have had the fleeting illusion that the empire was tottering, and Judah, too, must have preferred independence to being a mere province in however perfectly organised an empire. It is against this background that Haggai spoke of overthrowing the throne of kingdoms, and of bringing down the chariots and those that rode in them. Judah would be freed by Zerubbabel, the son of Shealtiel. Now, the name of Zerubbabel was mentioned also by Zechariah, Ezra and Nehemiah as the man to whom the Persians had entrusted the task of repatriating his people. He must have proved himself so capable that he was later appointed governor of Jerusalem. His compatriots had every reason for being delighted at this appointment, as Zerubbabel, the grandson of King Jehoiachin, was one of King David's direct descendants. Once again the House of David ruled over Jerusalem, while the overlords were busily fighting amongst themselves. We need little imagination to realise what great hopes his people placed in him, the chosen servant of the Lord, of whom Haggai had spoken as the Lord's own.

Little else is known about him. Darius managed to suppress the rebels, the storm abated and peace returned to the Persian empire. Whether he killed Zerubbabel for his insubordination, as some have thought, is a matter of conjecture, for it is equally possible that word of Zerubbabel's Messianic movement never reached the king at all.

In any case, why should Darius have shown any consternation if a handful of Jews saw fit to look upon the governor of one of his cities as the Messiah?

And so the clarion call to liberation gave way to the muted sounds of regret. The Temple continued to be a mass of rubble and, to make things worse, the harvest that year was so poor that Haggai had to exclaim: "Ye have sown much, and bring in little: ye eat, but ye have not enough: ye drink, but ye are not filled with drink: ye clothe you, but there is none warm; and he that earneth wages earneth wages to put it into a bag with holes" (Haggai 1:6). A bag with holes—how better describe the dangers of inflation! The scarcity of goods and the lack of food had sent prices soaring so high that the people felt that their money was fast being drained away.

Dejection about the harvest was so general that both farmer and vinegrower complained in unison: "Since those days were, when one came to an heap of twenty measures, there were but ten: when one came to the pressfat for to draw out fifty vessels out of the press, there were but twenty" (Haggai 2:16). Though all this misfortune was brought about by enemies which had threatened Palestine since time immemorial, drought and plant diseases, Haggai knew that these scourges were sent down by God. For the Lord had told him: "And I called for a drought upon the land, and upon the mountains, and upon the corn, and upon the new wine, and upon the oil, and upon that which the ground bringeth forth, and upon men, and upon cattle, and upon all the labour of the hands" (Haggai 1:11). "I smote you with blasting and with mildew and with hail in all the labours of your hands; yet ye turned not to me, saith the Lord" (2:17).

Sentiments worthy of Amos, these! Adversity is but a call to return to God. God has a purpose in whatever He does, and misfortune serves to remind man of his failings. Amos knew full well what was missing in his time: righteousness; but Haggai's answer was quite different: all her misfortunes were due to the fact that Israel had failed to build a new temple. And when the people said: "The time is not come, the time that the Lord's house should be built" (Haggai 1:2), the prophet rebuked them in the Lord's name: "Is it time for you, O ye, to dwell in your cieled houses, and this house lie waste? . . . Go up to the mountain, and bring wood, and build the house; and I will take pleasure in it, and I will be glorified, saith the Lord" (Haggai 1:4, 8).

I can understand how ridiculous the thought of solving economic problems in this way must sound to modern man. Far from relieving the pressure, he will point out, the building of a temple is a costly affair and furthermore a temple, once built, would swallow vast sums for its upkeep. But if the modern sceptic were to imagine himself back in Haggai's time, he would quickly change his mind. For the Temple was Jewry's spiritual centre, and without such a rallying point the gigantic task of rebuilding a devastated country was unthinkable.

And Haggai for one was quick to realise this. In his own expressive way he spoke of each man running about his own house while the communal house lay in ruins. In the year 520 B.C., there was no co-operation, no consultation, no communal feeling, let alone organised teamwork, and so Haggai's apparently childish solution was the only right answer for his time and day. No wonder, then, that it differed from that of the earlier prophets who had minimised the importance of the Temple. Where they had demanded a direct return to righteousness—a Temple without righteousness was anathema to them—Haggai looked upon the Temple as an essential first step towards this goal.

Luckily Haggai could count on the support of Zerubbabel the governor, and Joshua the high priest. And so, on the twenty-first day of the sixth month in the second year of Darius' reign, i.e. in the year 520 B.C., the work was in fact begun under their guidance. Once the rubble had been cleared Haggai adopted a new tone. The granaries might have been empty, the vine, the fig, the pomegranate and the olive barren, but everything would now change. From now on, God would bless the land again, yea, heaven and earth would share in man's salvation.

Scarcely four years later the work that Haggai had begun was completed, thanks largely to the generous assistance of the Persian authorities. And so when God's Temple shone in Israel with renewed glory, it was because of help from worshippers of Ahura-Mazda—one of many paradoxes in Israel's history.

The new Temple was much larger than Solomon's had been. We know a great deal about its compass both from the Old Testament and also from the first-hand account of a traveller who visited Jerusalem at the time of Alexander the Great. The building itself was of cubical form, its sides about 90 feet long. The temple was surrounded by a wall some 500 feet long and about 140 feet wide. It was an impressive building indeed that had arisen opposite the Mount of Olives. The priests and prophets had good reason to be well satisfied.

The Book of Ezra tells us that "many of the priests and Levites and chief of the fathers, who were ancient men, that had seen the first house when the foundation of this house was laid before their eyes, wept with a loud voice; and many shouted aloud for joy" (Ezra 3:12). Their weeping on such an occasion must have been ritual rather than sorrowful. Ritual tears are mentioned also in the Psalms, where we can read:

> "They that sow in tears
> shall reap in joy.
> He that goeth forth and weepeth,
> bearing precious seed,
> shall doubtless come again with rejoicing,
> bringing his sheaves with him."
>
> (Psalm 126:5-6)

And so while some people wept before the New Temple, the better to be able to rejoice afterwards, others "shouted with a loud shout, and the noise was heard afar off" (see Ezra 3:12-13).

The New Temple differed from Solomon's not only in size, but in that its Holy of Holies remained empty. In the place of the Ark a great rock marked the spot of what is today the beautiful Kubbet es Sakhra, or "Dome of the Rock", the Mohammedan shrine dominating the Temple Mountain. The Talmud called this rock "the foundation stone of the world", but its presence was by no means the most significant difference between the two temples. The chief distinction was the way in which the distance between the ordinary Jew and the Holy of Holies had grown since Solomon's time. Now Levites as well as priests stood between him and the altar, and no longer did God address His people directly through the mouths of His prophets; indeed God had withdrawn to His Heaven and the distance between the ordinary man in Israel and His shrine was symbolic of this change.

We have already stated that Haggai looked upon the rebuilding of the Temple as the beginning of a new era. The drought and bad harvest would come to an end, and everything would be rosy again. It was in this spirit that the prophet Zechariah exclaimed: "There shall yet old men and old women dwell in the streets of Jerusalem, and every man with his staff in his hand for very age. And the streets of the city shall be full of boys and girls playing in the streets thereof" (Zechariah 8:4-5). Here the prophet emphasised the difference between the life of the pioneer who works among rubble heaps, and the settled existence of people in a well-ordered society. Only in such a society can the aged bask in the sun and the children play safely in the streets. Once again, the prophet added, the seed would thrive, the vine bear fruit in plenty, the land yield its harvest and the heaven give its dew. Indeed optimism must have run wild as the people felt that they had passed the worst crisis in their history and that they were rising rapidly to new heights.

But very soon dissenting voices were heard. The New Temple exacted a great deal of tribute from the people. Before the exile, the king himself had borne all the costs of its upkeep, and even afterwards the Persians had continued to meet most of the expenses. But when they finally asked the Jews to look after their own Temple, and to supply all the burnt offerings, the people were very displeased. How much this was the case can be gathered from the prophet Malachi's exhortation: "And if ye offer the blind for sacrifice, is it not evil? and if ye offer the lame and sick, is it not evil? offer it now unto thy governor; will he be pleased with thee, or accept thy person? saith the Lord of hosts" (Malachi 1:8). Things had come to a sorry pass indeed, when the people dared to bring offerings to their God that they would have been loath to offer to the governor. Once again His people were on the point of deserting Him, even though they had built Him an impressive house.

Nor was that all. While Jerusalem had lain low, other cities had grown from strength to strength. One of these was Jerusalem's old rival, Samaria, and the Samaritans were filled with jealousy as they watched the new city rising out of the rubble. And so, a new time of struggle lay ahead, a time in which there was great need for strong leaders. Fortunately such leaders did come to the fore, and two of them, Ezra and Nehemiah, were to lend their names to two Books of the Old Testament. It was they who guided their people during the dark moments that were to come.

59

Ezra's Task

It was Ezra who, in Biblical times, left a lasting mark on Judaism. The Jewish refusal to merge with the nations is, in fact, the direct result of Ezra's work.

A priest by birth, Ezra could trace his descent back to Aaron, the brother of Moses, and his official title: "Scribe of the law of the God of Heaven" (Ezra 7:12 and 21), makes it probable that the Persian authorities looked upon him as their adviser for Jewish affairs. And Ezra did in fact obtain far-reaching powers from King Artaxerxes, who proclaimed to the Jews: "I [i.e. Artaxerxes] make a decree, that all they of the people of Israel, and of his priests and Levites, in my realm which are minded of their own free will to go up to Jerusalem, go with thee. Forasmuch as thou art sent of the king, and of his seven counsellors, to enquire concerning Judah and Jerusalem, according to the law of thy God which is in thine hand" (Ezra 7:13-14). Armed with this authority, Ezra made his way to Jerusalem. He refused a military escort, for on this journey to Jerusalem he would trust in God alone.

On his arrival there, Ezra was shocked to see that more and more of his people were contracting mixed marriages, and that even the priests had taken to marrying alien wives. Ezra's indignation had no historical roots, for we know that Hagar, Abraham's concubine, was an Egyptian woman, and that Moses took an Ethiopian wife with God's blessing. On searching through the Five Books of Moses, Ezra might, however, have come across the following passage in Deuteronomy 7:1-4: "When the Lord thy God shall bring thee into the land whither thou goest to possess it, and hath cast out many nations before thee, the Hittites, and the Girgashites, and the Amorites, and the Canaanites, and the Perizzites, and the Hivites, and the Jebusites, seven nations greater and mightier than thou; And when the Lord thy God shall deliver them before thee; thou shalt smite them, and utterly destroy them; thou shalt make no covenant with them, nor shew mercy unto them: Neither shalt thou make marriage with them; thy daughter thou shalt not give unto his son, nor his daughter shalt thou take unto thy son. For they will turn away thy son from following me, that they may serve other gods: so will the anger of the Lord be kindled against you, and destroy thee suddenly."

On the other hand, Ezra may not have troubled to find Biblical sanction, since his motives in opposing miscegenation were anything but religious. Had they been, he could have averted a great deal of misery and suffering by insisting that the women become converted to Judaism rather than deporting them. But Ezra was concerned with racial purity alone, though his underlying reason may well have been the conviction that the faith of Abraham could only be preserved if his seed were kept unpolluted.

The better to drive home his point, Ezra rent his garments and plucked out the hair from his head and beard and sat down "astonied". His weird behaviour quite naturally aroused the curiosity of the crowd, who gathered round him in great number and patiently waited for an explanation. Only when it was time for the evening sacrifice, did Ezra rise up and proclaim that all Israel's misfortunes were the result of intermarriage.

Then the mob, infected by his denunciations, broke out into loud wails. A man rose up from among them, and said: "Now therefore let us make a covenant with our God to put away all the wives, and such as are born of them . . ." (Ezra 10:3). And Ezra made the leaders of Jerusalem swear an oath and he summoned all the people to do like-wise. "Then all the men of Judah and Benjamin gathered themselves together unto Jerusalem within three days. It was the ninth month, on the twentieth day of the month; and all the people sat in the street of the house of God, trembling because of this matter, and for the great rain" (Ezra 10:9).

The Book of Ezra concludes with a list of those who had contracted mixed marriages. We may be fairly certain that this list is incomplete, for miscegenation had become widespread among the people. We do not know what happened to Ezra afterwards, for the Bible does not say, and other sources contradict one another. According to Josephus he was given a state funeral in Jerusalem, and according to another source he returned to Babylon to be buried in a town that bears his name to this very day. One thing alone is certain: Ezra's actions must have caused a great upheaval among his people.

Though Ezra was a loyal servant of Artaxerxes, his loyalty did not prevent him from remaining faithful to his own people also. Realising that insurrection would have been sheer madness, he did his utmost to plead the cause of Jewry before his king. The Talmud tells us that it was Ezra who introduced the modern square Hebrew characters. This report fits in well with what else we have learned of Ezra's character—the holy seed must be distinguished from the surrounding heathen even by having its own alphabet. But the introduction of new characters is an innocent pastime when compared with the rigorous application of principles of racial purity. No doubt Ezra was a harsh man, but we must quite frankly admit that without him the Old Testament might never have been handed down to posterity.

60

Esther and the Feast of Purim

THE Book of Esther tells an exciting story in the best Eastern tradition. But while it is full of dramatic highlights and suspense, no one could really call it a deeply religious book. God's name is not so much as mentioned once and it seems odd that the book was thought fit for inclusion in the Bible. And in fact, in Jesus' day, neither this book nor the Song of Solomon was considered Holy Writ, and so neither is quoted in the New Testament. Originally, the Book was read as a Festal Roll during the Jewish feast of Purim. To this day the chanting of the Roll of Esther, accompanied by the shouts of the congregation which greet every mention of Haman, the arch-anti-Semite, is one of the events of the Jewish year. The feast of Purim is celebrated with that mixture of joy and seriousness that is so characteristic of all the Jewish High Festivals.

In order to understand the profound meaning of Purim, we must try to appreciate the feelings of resentment that must necessarily fill a people that has suffered centuries of senseless persecution. Nowadays we have little difficulty in understanding what the Jews must have gone through, and so we are armed against accepting Martin Luther's denunciation of the Book of Esther. Luther deemed the Book to be too Jewish in spirit and expressed the wish that it had not been written at all.

The main plot of the story concerns Haman's colossal threat to all the Jews in the Persian empire. Now it can be shown that such a dangerous situation actually existed at the time that Artaxerxes II (405-359 B.C.) introduced his religious reforms.

Though the doctrine of Zarathustra had long been practised, particularly by the Persian aristocracy, the old popular and idolatrous religion had never really died out. So, as we know from the great Babylonian historian, Berosus, Artaxerxes II had little difficulty in persuading people to return to their ancient idol-worship, and to order statues of Anahita, the goddess of love and fertility, to be erected in Babylon, Susa, Ecbatana, and other great cities of his empire. Quite possibly he made the worship of these images a measure of his people's loyalty, in which case he might have been the very king who caused the three young men, Shadrach, Meshach and Abednego to be thrown into a furnace (see Daniel 3). Though Daniel's king was called Nebuchadnezzar, Daniel might very well have referred to Artaxerxes II. In Daniel's story, the king asked his officials to prove their loyalty by bowing down before the idol. It goes without saying that pious Jews would not obey this order, and Daniel 3 must be considered as a call to persevere in the face of death—God would save His faithful even from the flames of the furnace. Read in conjunction with Berosus' account of Artaxerxes' return to idolatry, the story takes on a new significance. Jewish courtiers—and their number was legion—must have withdrawn their services, and anti-Semitism reared its ugly head once more.

The famous story of Daniel in the lions' den shows clearly that Jewish ministers and courtiers were persecuted even when the king himself had been there to protect them. But now that the king had turned against the Jews, the anti-Semites felt they could make short shrift of their hated enemies. Idol worship once again emphasised the gulf between Jew and Gentile, and Haman, the arch-anti-Semite, set to work.

Only when seen against this historical background does the Book of Esther cease to be merely an exciting story without any religious meaning. Now we realise how terribly wrong Luther was in not realising that the story of Esther was really the story of a people that refused to worship any other god. By denying and betraying their own principles, they could have saved face and fortune, and this no doubt is what many Jews must have done. But the vast majority kept faith with their religion and willingly bore all the ardours of isolation, degradation and martyrdom, for their faith's sake. And so they lived through the crisis, and the Book of Esther bears witness to their miraculous salvation. Haman was not only defeated but turned into the unwitting spokesman for Mordecai, his mortal foe. The Jewish people had been saved by a miracle. Why then did the Book of Esther fail to explain this miracle in the only way that would have assured it canonical repute? Is it perhaps because the author, by deliberately refraining from mentioning God by name, wanted to show that there are other ways of proving our faith in Him? Those who would have this Book expunged, might well ponder this point.

61

A New Conception of History

THE Book of Chronicles is not everyone's favourite Bible reading, and in the Hebrew Bible it did in fact take last place, though the Authorised Version puts it immediately after the Book of Kings. Its first nine chapters are devoted to tracing the line of the kings of Judah back to Adam and Eve, and the rest to a repetition of what we already know from the preceding books, and particularly from Kings. The only significant difference is the fact that Chronicles describes the events from the point of view of the priests in about 400 B.C.

Conscious of writing the history of God's chosen people, the author begins with the creation of the world. The ending is practically identical with the beginning of Ezra, but originally Chronicles included both Ezra and Nehemiah. After Ezra had been split off, the author no doubt wanted to avoid ending his book with the fall of Jerusalem, and so he repeated himself. But it must have been his original intention to describe the whole of Judah's history from the creation of the world to the restoration of Jerusalem. The theme of the Book of Judges is here strictly applied to all history: all misfortunes are due to man's transgressions against God's commandments. A good example of this approach is shown in the treatment of the story of Manasseh. While II Kings 21 has little good to tell of him, II Chronicles 23 stresses only his good points. True, he had been guilty of idolatry, but after being punished by the Assyrians he repented and so was allowed to reign happily for another twenty-five years. Manasseh's long reign had somehow to be explained away despite his many faults, and the same argument is applied to Rehoboam, Asa, Jehoshaphat, Joash, Amaziah and Uzziah. Defeat, sickness, untimely death, famine—all were explained by the sins of the victim, and particularly by his disobedience to God's laws.

A second characteristic of Chronicles is a corollary of the first: all history is made by God alone; man's decisions have little bearing on it. Men can only influence history indirectly by prayer and pious song. This is best shown by the account of Jehoshaphat's victory over the Moabites and Ammonites. When the king was told that a mighty foreign army was drawing nigh, he prayed fervently: "O our God, wilt thou not judge them? for we have no might against this great company that cometh against us; neither know we what to do: but our eyes are upon thee" (II Chronicles 20:12). And while the whole of Judah, women and children included, stood reverently before His altar, a Levite, moved by the spirit of the Lord, called out: "Be not afraid nor dismayed by reason of this great multitude; for the battle is not yours, but God's" (II Chronicles 20:15). Only then did the people go out to face the enemy without fear, and strong in the Lord. Men in festive garb placed themselves at the head of the army while the people sang praises to the Almighty. Meanwhile, the armies of Moab and Ammon had begun to quarrel amongst themselves, and when Jehoshaphat approached he found the entire enemy army already destroyed. "And the fear of God was on all the kingdoms of those countries when they had heard that the Lord fought against the enemies of Israel."

Similar accounts are given of Abijah's victory over Jeroboam of Israel (II Chronicles 13) and of Asa's triumph over the Ethiopians (II Chronicles 14). Neither bravery in the field nor strategy decided the issue, God alone vanquished the enemy.

Another important theme of the Book of Chronicles is its emphasis on the Temple, the service, the Levites and religious song. This is clearly seen from its attitude to King David. While the Book of Samuel spoke of David as a great general, a brave fighter and a brilliant politician, the Book of Chronicles sees him exclusively as a great temple builder. Almost eight chapters are devoted to this subject, and reading them one might think that David had never done anything other than build a house of worship.

Thus the Book of Chronicles, while lacking historical accuracy, gives us remarkable insight into the minds of the priesthood. No doubt they did violence to the facts, but we cannot deny that they were filled with an unequalled zeal to keep the flame of righteousness burning, and to extol the Lord in all His glory.

H. *Wisdom*

62

Satan versus Job

IN Job we meet a man as pious and virtuous as any man could be. But God-fearing and upright though he was, Job was yet more sorely afflicted than any other figure in the Bible.

His troubles began with a meeting of the Heavenly Council, during which Satan cast doubt on the possibility of human goodness. Though the devil had met Job, and though the Lord was right in thinking him an upright man, God-fearing and humble, Job was not really a good example. "Hast not thou made an hedge about him, and about his house, and about all that he hath on every side?" Satan asked the Lord. "Thou hast blessed the work of his hands, and his substance is increased in the land. But put forth thine hand now, and touch all that he hath, and he will curse thee to thy face" (Job 1:10-11). No one could have missed the grain of truth in Satan's remarks—how characteristic of the devil and all his works, to produce half-truths! Rank prevarication and unmitigated lies are usually recognised as such, but when it comes to half-truths people often think that where there is smoke, there must be fire. And so Satan implied that riches and personal happiness made it easy for man to put his trust in God, though he could equally well have claimed that wealth and smugness are certain roads to perdition. But let us see how Job responded when he was suddenly stricken with a great many misfortunes.

In quick succession, Job lost all his cattle and donkeys, his sheep were consumed by the fire of God, his camels stolen by the Chaldeans and his sons and daughters buried under the ruins of a house. But as each of these devastating reports reached him, Job simply arose, rent his mantle, shaved his head, fell down upon the ground and prayed: "Naked came I out of my mother's womb, and naked shall I return thither: the Lord gave, and the Lord hath taken away; blessed be the name of the Lord" (Job 1:21). Clearly Job had passed his test with flying colours—he had uttered not a single curse against the Almighty. And so God turned to Satan and asked him: "Hast thou considered my servant Job, that there is none like him in the earth, a perfect and an upright man, one that feareth God, and escheweth evil? and still he holdeth fast his integrity, although thou movedst me against him, to destroy him without cause" (Job 2:3). Surely this is one of the most remarkable things the Almighty ever said, so much so that one of the rabbis commented in the Talmud: "Were not these words written in the Bible, I should never have believed them to be true." Here God had frankly admitted that He had listened to Satan's hollow arguments, and that He had persecuted an innocent man. And to make things even worse, God went on paying attention to the devil's arguments. True, Satan argued, Job had passed his first test, but would he also pass the crucial test? Man's health was his greatest treasure, more precious even than riches and children. "Skin for skin," the devil concluded, "all that a man hath will he give for his life. But put forth thine hand now, and touch his bone and his flesh, and he will curse thee to thy face" (Job 2:4-5).

And so, poor Job, terribly afflicted though he already was, was now smitten "with sore boils from the sole of his foot to his crown". And he sat down amongst the ashes to scratch himself with a potsherd, one of his few remaining possessions. Surely, if ever any man had the right to curse his Creator, it was Job. But when his wife told him so, Job rebuked her: "Thou speakest as one of the foolish women speaketh. What? shall we receive good at the hand of God, and shall we not receive evil?" (Job 2:10). Once again, Satan had been defeated but once again, he persevered. And all the previous misfortunes were as nothing compared with what was yet to come.

Actually, Job's whole problem was no more and no less than the problem of life on earth where happiness and misfortune and good and evil are dealt out in a measure that man's reason cannot fathom. It is not true to say that our chickens invariably come home to roost, for there is a great deal of undeserved misfortune, and equally undeserved happiness.

Now the Book of Job does in fact try to offer a solution to this problem. The pious man is made to suffer so as to strengthen his faith and to deepen his piety. Perhaps Job had been too smug in his righteousness and had to be humbled before he was repaid with interest for his sufferings. If we look at it this way, then Satan is no longer the fallen angel who goads God into doing evil, but God's special instrument for strengthening man's resolve. In the Book of Job, the worst punishment was not so much the undeserved misfortune as the doubt that went with it.

But even as Job was being pushed towards the precipice of doubt, God Himself had no doubt about the final outcome, just as He had never doubted the outcome of Abraham's crucial test. And so it was really Satan, the arch-doubter, who had lost the struggle—even before it was begun.

63

Job's Argument

THE beginning and end of the Book of Job are written in prose, the remainder in lovely verse. The first piece of prose ends with the moving account of how three of Job's friends, Eliphaz, Bildad and Zophar, came to console him in his pit. When they realised how truly pitiful he had become, they could only rend their mantles, sprinkle dust upon their heads and weep. Their carefully prepared speeches were out of place—that they knew—and so they sat down for seven days and seven nights without saying a word. To my mind Job's friends could not have been described more sympathetically: their compassion for Job was so great that they were stricken dumb. Nothing could have made their sincerity more obvious.

It is important to stress this fact, since the author of the Book of Job makes them out to have been men with much too complacent a conception of God's righteousness. "My wrath is kindled against thee", God is made to say to Eliphaz, "and against thy two friends: for ye have not spoken of me the thing that is right, as my servant Job hath" (Job 42:7). Presuming to judge Him by human standards, the friends felt that God could not possibly have punished Job without good reason. Still, they kept their own counsel and waited patiently for Job to speak out first.

When he did, it was only to cry out in anguish:

> "Let the day perish wherein I was born,
>   and the night in which it was said,
>   There is a man child conceived.

Let that day be darkness;
let not God regard it from above,
neither let the light shine upon it."
(Job 3:3-4)

Yes, Job cursed the day of his birth, but not his God who had brought all these misfortunes upon him. Still, he did question God's wisdom in having shown the light of day to one whose destiny it was to live in misery. What was the point of letting man be born if he was destined to a life of sorrow and regret? And during his long conversations with his friends, Job kept harking back to this theme. Not that he cursed God; far from it, he merely professed his utter lack of understanding.

And here we come upon one of the many unexpected and surprising moments, so characteristic of the Book of Job: God did not seem to mind at all when Job, a mere mortal, dared to argue with Him. To understand this, we must take an example from every-day life, not, it must be emphasised, to bring God down to our own level, but simply because this is the only way in which we can try to understand His actions. And God, in His infinite wisdom, did in fact make allowances for our inability to rise beyond the visions of this earth, when He came down to be as one of us. Let me try and illustrate this by considering two intimate friends. If only their love be great enough, they will be very careful not to bear each other any grudges. If one happens to offend the other for no apparent reason, the other can do one of two things: he can either say nothing at all and so create an unbridgeable gulf between them, or else he can take his friend to task. In so doing he may say many bitter and even irresponsible things that he will later regret, but all his remarks, however harsh, are meant to heal the breach. Surely, frank argument is always better than sullen silence, for silence breaks the bond, while words heal the breach.

It is in this sense, but of course on quite another plane, that we must look upon Job's arguments with God. Nor was Job the only good man in the Old Testament to have argued thus. Jeremiah, too, complained bitterly when he was made to live in solitude amidst his relatives and friends. Had he spared his words, he would surely not have been the prophet we know him to have been. He realised full well that God knew what He was doing, but even so he argued and murmured.

We must dwell on these facts a little longer, the more so since they do not tally with our conventional ideas of piety. We think that it is truly pious to say Amen to everything God chooses to send us: good and evil, happiness and misfortune. Our ideal of such piety is best epitomised by Job's saying: "The Lord gave, and the Lord hath taken away: blessed be the name of the Lord", or his: "Shall we receive good at the hand of God, and shall we not receive evil?" Still, in our heart of hearts, we must admit that such piety would be quite beyond us, and, indeed, that it is a little unnatural. Were everything that happened to Job to happen to us also, we should never have it within our hearts to find so much devotion and humility. And so we feel a little easier when we read not only that Job protested, but that for doing so God set him above the three friends who had never so much as raised their voices. From the Book of Job we may learn that God invites us to be frank with Him. In our talks and prayers to Him, we need not hide anything—not even our innermost doubts. Everything can be said so long only as our argument remains an argument with God. True wickedness is not to argue with God, true wickedness is to keep sullen silence. For sullen silence implies that we recognise no one to whom we can unburden ourselves and in so doing find salvation.

This cannot be emphasised enough, because, as a parson, I have witnessed on more than one occasion how easily people collapse in the face of misfortune. Unable to confide their doubt in God's wisdom to anyone, their doubt choked their faith, and with it their will to live. Had they but argued like Job, the Lord would surely have listened to them and eased their burden. This is the greatest lesson to be learned from the Book of Job.

64

The God of Job's Friends

THOUGH Job's three friends came to him with the best of intentions, they only served to add to his difficulties. Wishing to console their friend, they ended their long silence by insisting that the Lord was a righteous God, and that Job must surely have sinned to have been punished so severely. And so they enjoined him earnestly to confess his sin before God. But Job would not agree with them. He knew perfectly well that he was as imperfect as any man, but he also knew that his misfortunes were not of his own making. All round him the wicked were thriving—there was no justice on earth. God was omnipotent, that he knew, but clearly He was not just.

It is on this subject that Job carried on long and tiresome conversations with his friends. They, who must have been prosperous men, had every reason to believe in God's justice, for had not their own lives borne it out? Good Jews that they were they did not believe in reward and punishment in the hereafter. Justice had to be meted out here on earth, and in man's lifetime. This made Job's complaints doubly heart-rending, and his friends' arguments doubly out of place. And this is why the Lord rebuked Eliphaz with "Ye have not spoken of me the thing that is right, as my servant Job hath". In other words, the author of the Book sided with poor rebellious Job against the friends who had so nobly and logically defended God's righteousness. It is not as if the writer had tried to ridicule them, by contrasting their sham piety with poor Job's misery. No, he remained faithful to reality, and reality is not usually made up of black and white but of a great many intermediate tints.

And so the Book of Job gave honour where honour was due. The three friends were made to say many worth-while things, even though they were quite wrong to believe that God's righteousness was reflected in man's just reward. Let us look at Eliphaz's opening remarks. He reminded Job how he had been wont to encourage others, only to become embittered himself at the first sign of personal misfortune. And who could gainsay Eliphaz? How easy it is for us to preach to others, and how difficult to persevere ourselves! The value of our sermons must be tested in our own experience, as Eliphaz so rightly pointed out. And he was equally justified in praising the purging effect of misfortune. It is simply not true that our happiest have always been our most blessed days, for as Eliphaz pointed out:

> "Behold, happy is the man whom God correcteth:
> therefore despise not thou the chastening of the Almighty:
> For he maketh sore, and bindeth up:
> he woundeth, and his hands make whole."
>
> (Job 5:17-18)

And Bildad, Job's other friend, was made to speak in a similar vein, when he recalled the struggles that previous generations had been forced to make before God had revealed His light to them:

> "For enquire, I pray thee, of the former age,
>   and prepare thyself to the search of their fathers:
> (For we are but of yesterday, and know nothing,
>   because our days upon earth are a shadow).
>   (Job 8:8-9)

And so Job's friends defended a religious point of view which commands respect, albeit with great reservations. The error they committed is one they shared with most of us, no matter of what religion: the moment we have felt God's presence, we have an irresistible urge to turn our experience into a system or a dogma. Now God's unpredictable actions just will not fit into any system whatsoever. We have difficulty in accepting this fact, for, poor mortals that we are, we feel helpless and lost without cut-and-dried creeds. And this is what the author of the Book of Job wanted to bring home to us: our articles of faith, our dogmatic assertions and what we have learnt from our catechism all are shattered into a thousand fragments when they come up against such terrible experiences as those of Job. His friends were like us in that they held fast to their precious watertight system, even in the face of incontrovertible evidence that something was wrong with it. They could not live without their props. This does not mean that they were plaster saints or dishonest men, but it does mean that they lacked real depth. Job in his direst need rose up to harangue his God. And in breaking with the little God who is found only in man's little systems, he discovered the real God whose actions pass human understanding.

65

The Answer in the Storm

As we have seen, the Book of Job is full of surprises. One of these is found at the beginning of chapter 32. Job had avowed his innocence for the last time, and his friends had come to the end of their tether.

Obviously Job had lost all sense of proportion. He was no longer in a frame of mind to repent, and had best be given up for lost. At this point, a fourth friend, Elihu, turned up quite unexpectedly. Many are of the opinion that the author added this fourth friend as an afterthought when he revised the Book. Now it is extremely difficult to reconstruct the story of Job's life, but it is a fact that Elihu's appearance added an entirely new element to the story, though his message fits in perfectly with the magnificent conception of the rest of the book. At first Elihu merely repeated what the three friends had already told Job:

> "Therefore hearken unto me,
>   ye men of understanding:
>   far be it from God, that he should do wickedness;
>   and from the Almighty, that he should commit iniquity.
>   For the work of a man shall he render unto him,
>   and cause every man to find according to his ways.
>   Yea, surely God will not do wickedly,
>   neither will the Almighty pervert judgment."
>
> (Job 34:10-12)

But then Elihu introduced a new note: God's majesty and mysterious power. Asking Job to look upwards, Elihu told him:

> "Hearken unto this, O Job:
>   stand still, and consider the wondrous works of God.
>   Dost thou know when God disposed them,
>   and caused the light of his cloud to shine?"
>
> (Job 37:14-15)

And then there follows the climax of the whole Book, for God Himself now appeared out of the whirlwind and addressed Job:

> "Who is this that darkeneth counsel by words without knowledge?
>   Gird up now thy loins like a man;
>   for I will demand of thee, and answer thou me.
>   Where wast thou when I laid the foundations of the earth?
>   declare, if thou hast understanding.
>   Who hath laid the measures thereof, if thou knowest?
>   or who hath stretched the line upon it?
>   Whereupon are the foundations thereof fastened?

or who laid the corner stone thereof;
When the morning stars sang together,
and all the sons of God shouted for joy?
Or who shut up the sea with doors,
when it brake forth, as if it had issued out of the womb?
When I made the cloud the garment thereof,
and thick darkness a swaddlingband for it,
and brake up for it my decreed place,
and set bars and doors,
And here shall thy proud waves be stayed?"

(Job 38:2-11)

This long quotation is only a small fragment of God's long answer, the whole of which is reported in chapters 38-41, four chapters that proclaim God's majesty in unequalled verse.

In general I am not the man to stress the beauty of Biblical writing, for to do so might well detract from its central importance. The Bible does not speak to us that we may admire its poetic perfection, but that we may draw closer to God. And so I, for one, do not commend the Bible as an example of fine writing. In fact, some parts are far from elegantly written, but as regards chapters 38-41 of the Book of Job, there is no doubt that, seen from any point of view, they must be counted among the best that Eastern literature had to offer. Their poetic imagery, for one thing, has no equal in the whole literature of antiquity.

Yet, I can well imagine how irritating some readers might find these chapters. Man on earth is frail and pitiful enough and visited by so many misfortunes that there is truly no need to drive this point home at great length. And this is precisely what God is made to do in these chapters. From His exalted dwelling-place, God the Almighty assails poor Job with crushing question after crushing question: knowest thou? . . . hast thou perceived? . . . canst thou? . . . where wast thou . . . ? What other answer could he have given but: I know not . . . I have not perceived . . . I cannot . . . I was not there . . . ? Still, it would be quite wrong to think this was the main point of God's message to Job.

It is important that we realise that all God's words had one central theme. This theme runs through the entire Old Testament, and can be summed up in a few words: the fear of the Lord is the beginning of all wisdom. This fear is no cowardice, and no one need be ashamed of it. It is the reverent submission to Him whose hidden Glory and Majesty passes all understanding, and whose real essence we can never discover. Sometimes we may be inclined to dismiss this fear of the Lord with John's inviting comment: "There is no fear in love; but perfect love casteth out fear: because fear hath torment. He that feareth is not made perfect in love" (I John 4:18). Far be it from me to deny the truth of these words, for piety is not mere fear and trembling, it is confident faith and hopeful trust also. But we usually move halfway between fear and safety, between anxiety and love, and no perfect love is possible that has not stood the test of fear. Fear alone can protect us from contemptuous familiarity with God, and from the mealy-mouthed piety of the friends who thought they had to find a good reason for Job's misfortunes.

And so, when God asked:

"Shall he that contendeth with the Almighty instruct him?
he that reproveth God, let him answer it,"

(Job 40:2)

Job was ready to reply with humility:

"I know that thou canst do everything,
and that no thought can be withholden from thee.
Who is he that hideth counsel without knowledge?
therefore have I uttered that I understood not;
things too wonderful for me, which I knew not.
I have heard of thee by the hearing of the ear:
but now mine eye seeth thee.
Wherefore I abhor myself,
and repent in dust and ashes."

(Job 42:2-3, 5-6)

Thus the story is brought to its quite unexpected conclusion. Job's friends had believed in a God who was easy to understand, a God who rewarded virtue and punished sin, a God who was very close to them. But Job was given an answer by a God who is far away, a God who causes his sun to shine on good and evil alike, who causes his rain to fall on both the righteous and the wicked. It was this God who had humbled Job, who had taught him to keep faith even in adversity.

Greek dramatists frequently used the device of catharsis, the purging of the hero. Just like them, the author of the Book of Job had his hero purged by hell-fire. A broom had swept away every last trace of Job's belief that piety must needs lead to personal happiness, to teach him that virtue is its own reward.

66

Job's Vindication

MANY readers have felt that the ending of the Book of Job is not in keeping with the rest. They think that the happy ending spoils the whole point of the story. God had spoken from the whirlwind and poor Job had repented. Why say any more? Why revert to the pedestrian prose of the beginning?

And why did Job's life have to take a sudden turn for the better and why was he given back a double portion of what he had lost? Why in fact, the conclusion:

"So the Lord blessed the latter end of Job more than his beginning: for he had fourteen thousand sheep, and six thousand camels, and a thousand yoke of oxen, and a thousand she asses. He had also seven sons and three daughters. And he called the name of the first, Jemima; and the name of the second, Kezia; and the name of the third, Keren-happuch. And in all the land were no women found so fair as the daughters of Job: and their father gave them inheritance among their brethren. After this lived Job an hundred and forty years, and saw his sons, and his sons' sons, even four generations. So Job died, being old and full of days" (Job 42:12-17).

As we read this, we feel that nothing fundamental in Job's life had changed at all. His camels, cattle and asses had doubled in number, and once again he had ten children. He had become so rich that he could give an inheritance even to his daughters, although he had no legal obligation to do so. He had reached what the writers of the Old Testament must have considered the height of human happiness: great riches, many children and a ripe old age.

And so, as we have said, the curtain fell on a very happy ending. Was it in order to please his reading public that the author finished his book in this way? Many people find it difficult to believe that the same man who wrote so conventional an ending should have written the moving chapters that went before, and so they claim that the book was based on an old folk-tale.

This folk-tale, they believe, told the story of a pious man whom Satan had asked God to put to the test, and who remained faithful even when his wife and his friends had deserted him. For his faith he was rewarded with riches much greater than he had ever known. This, in brief, was the plot that the author of the Book of Job was supposed to have modified, the better to emphasise his own point of view. The happy ending was so well known that the author dared not change it, for fear his readers might reject his entire message.

This theory sounds very feasible. The only difficulty is that no trace of the original story has ever been discovered. However, we do know that the prophet Ezekiel mentioned the name of Job in one breath with those of Noah and Daniel (see Ezekiel 14). This Daniel was not the Daniel of the lions' den who, according to the Bible, was a contemporary of Ezekiel, but a man who, together with Noah, had lived at the time of the Flood. Now stories of the Flood had been told also by the original Canaanites in whose midst the Israelites had pitched their tents. What little we know of the literature of these Canaanites from such finds as were made in the ruins of the ancient Phoenician town of Ugarit (thirteenth century B.C.), makes it quite likely that they were in fact the originators of this tale. Even so, by including their ending, the author did violence to his story. In my opinion, he had to run this risk if he was to be heard at all. Job was right to persevere in his faith, even in the face of injustice, and how right he was could only be brought home to the reader in the traditional form. In reality, Job's persistence in the face of adversity needed no justification, and his friends had been wrong all along the line even though they were keen theologians, and shrewd dogmatists. Their very intellectualism had helped to estrange them from reality. But Job, with his bitter experiences, was part and parcel of reality. He knew what it meant to argue with his God, and yet to bow down in humility before Him.

67

Ecclesiastes, or the Preacher

EVEN though Ecclesiastes makes easier reading than many other books of the Old Testament, it is full of pitfalls. Its tenor is very much in keeping with our own times, and the beauty of its polished style, and the poetry of its sounds—which can only be truly appreciated in the original Hebrew—reflect the mind of a highly cultured man. But who was he in real life?

According to Ecclesiastes 1:1 he was the son of King David, and according to 1:12 he himself was king over Israel in Jerusalem. Accordingly, he could have been none other than Solomon, though he speaks of himself as Koheleth. In Ecclesiastes 12:9-10 he is called a wise preacher who taught the people knowledge, who gave good heed, who sought out and set in order many proverbs, and who found fitting words for writing what was upright and truthful.

We do not know whether Koheleth was a title or a proper name. Even the oldest translations reflected both points of view, though in the end the name was translated as the Preacher, one who addressed the "kehillah", the congregation. Yet Koheleth did not really preach. On the contrary, we feel that he must have been soliloquising with never a thought for an audience.

He did a great deal of soul-searching, for such was his nature. Nor did he consider his search for truth an unmitigated joy, but as a sore travail that God had given to the sons of man to be exercised therewith (1:13). Some of his sayings have become household words and we know perfectly well what he meant when he said that "In much wisdom is much grief" (1:18), that "there is no new thing under the sun" (1:9) and that "what is crooked cannot be made straight, and what is wanting cannot be numbered" (1:15). The Preacher was no social reformer. According to him, wisdom was no surer way to happiness than foolishness. The building of houses and the planting of vineyards, the laying out of parks with pools and trees, the service of slaves and of singers—none of these brought lasting satisfaction. It was much better not to bustle about to reform the world but to leave everything to God. The Preacher knew full well that joy and sorrow came from His hand alone. No matter how hard we try to store up spiritual or material treasures, all our efforts are in vain, if we do not find favour in His eyes. God has little use for bourgeois respectability.

With almost deliberate monotony, the Preacher insisted that all things had their season. By this he did not mean that everything was evanescent but rather that everything that happens on earth is ordained by God. It depends on Him whether we kill or heal, construct or demolish, love or hate (3:1-15). God's work passes all understanding, and so we had best stop worrying and rather eat, drink and be merry, while God allows us to do so.

Above all, there is no reason for counting on a life hereafter, for nothing is known about it. Just like the beasts so do men die also. Some might say that the spirit of men goes upwards, and the spirit of the beast goes downwards, but who could be certain? All we do know is that we return to the dust from which we were made.

And meanwhile, we, like the Preacher, must love life with a deep passion. Not for him a life of solitude and self-denial, but one by his neighbour's side:

> "Two are better than one:
> because they have a good reward for their labour.
> For if they fall, the one will lift up his fellow:
> but woe to him that is alone when he falleth;
> for he hath not another to help him up.
> Again, if two lie together, then they have heat:
> but how can one be warm alone?
> And if one prevail against him, two shall withstand him;
> and a threefold cord is not quickly broken."
> (Ecclesiastes 4:9-12)

Yet this self-same man, who had sung such praises to friendship and marriage, had also discovered that the woman "whose heart is snares and nets, and whose hands are as bands" is more bitter than death. Good women were scarce and "one man among a thousand have I found; but a woman among all those have I not found" (Ecclesiastes 7:28). Even so, "live joyfully with the wife whom thou lovest all the days of the life of thy vanity, which he hath given thee under the sun, all the days of thy vanity: for that is thy portion in this life, and in thy labour which thou takest under the sun" (Ecclesiastes 9:9). And, furthermore: "Go thy way, eat thy bread with joy, and drink thy wine with a merry heart; for God now accepteth thy works. Let thy garments be always white; and let thy head lack no ointment" (Ecclesiastes 9:7-8).

With profound understanding, the Preacher admonishes his readers not to go to extremes, for it is just as reprehensible to be too righteous and too wise as it is to be too wicked and too foolish (7:15-18). The rabbis, in trying to get to the bottom of this saying, felt that the Preacher must have referred to too narrow an interpretation of the Law. The classic example of such narrow-mindedness is the story of the deeply religious man who would not rescue a drowning woman, because it was sinful to touch any woman other than one's wife. The Preacher's plea was for the middle way, for the golden mean, and the wisdom that realised that there is no life without compromise.

In general, the Preacher's word must be looked upon as a cry from the heart against the commonplace belief of his day that money, children, and long life brought the greatest happiness. Riches themselves were no proof of God's favour—the only proof of that was the opportunity to enjoy these riches. Hence these aphorisms of the good life: "A good name is better than precious ointment; and the day of death than the day of one's birth. It is better to go to the house of mourning, than to go to the house of feasting. . . . Sorrow is better than laughter. . . . It is better to hear the rebuke of the wise, than for a man to hear the song of fools. . . . Better is the end of a thing than the beginning thereof. . . . Say not thou, What is the cause that the former days were better than these? for thou dost not enquire wisely concerning this" (see 7:1-10).

Sometimes we gain the impression that we are being told the very things against which we feel sure the Preacher would have argued with all his force. This is due to the fact that—in common with all Biblical writing—the Book makes no clear distinction between the different speakers in it. And so, while one verse says that the wicked will not be punished, another says that it shall not be well with them.

Be that as it may, the Preacher keeps harking back to the vanity of our life that passes by like a shadow. Make hay while the sun shines, for the days will soon be upon you when you will say: "I have no

P

pleasure in them." Rarely has death or the fear of old age been taken as seriously as in this book,

> "In the day when the keepers of the house shall tremble,
> and the strong men shall bow themselves,
> and the grinders cease because they are few,
> and those that look out of the windows be darkened,
> And the doors shall be shut in the streets,
> when the sound of the grinding is low,
> and he shall rise up at the voice of the bird,
> and all the daughters of musick shall be brought low."
>
> (Ecclesiastes 12:3-4)

Then, while the mourners go about the streets, the silver cord will be loosened and the golden bow smashed; the pitcher will lie broken at the fountain, and the wheel at the cistern. And then the dust shall return to the earth from which it came, and the spirit to God who created it. Now this "spirit" was not the soul, which the Greeks thought could leave the prison of the body to become truly free only after death. The Preacher took death so seriously, precisely because he thought that when man died he perished body and soul. Life was as precious as gold and silver, and as rare as an oasis in the desert. Yet precious though life be, it is not complete without love of God. Not because virtue was rewarded in this world, or because the pious might expect rewards in the world to come, did the Preacher ask man to remember his Creator in the days of his youth (12:1). No, to taste life to the full was in itself an acclamation of God's Glory, albeit the scribes and learned rabbis said otherwise. Man needed no props apart from his faith, and the Preacher, for one, had more than his share of that.

I. *The Songs of Israel*

68

Religious and Secular Songs

LIKE all other Eastern people, the children of Israel were very fond of song. Airs were whistled by the young men in the street, sung by grown men at their work or in the taverns, chanted by the women grinding the corn and piped by the shepherds in the field. When the harvest was gathered in the spring, or the grapes picked in the autumn, the mountains of Judah would resound with the song of old and young alike. We know only a minute fraction of their music, for the Bible ignored most of their popular songs, and only in those rare cases when secular music had also a religious significance, or when it dealt with historical events in Israel's history, did the Old Testament regard it as worthy of mention.

The centre of communal life in those days was the well, for everyone would come there to draw water. Here, as day would change into sudden night, the people would gather round to sing songs like:

> "Spring up, O well;
>   sing ye unto it:
>   the princes digged the well,
>   the nobles of the people digged it,
>   by the direction of the law-giver,
>   with their staves."
>   (Numbers 21:17-18)

We also know some of the songs that the women sang as they went out to meet their victorious men with psalteries and dancing. The reader will remember how they greeted David with "Saul hath slain his thousands and David his ten thousands" (I Samuel 18:7). In Hebrew these lines not only scan but they rhyme also. Hebrew words can be made to rhyme very easily, since in Hebrew all possessive pronouns are suffixes. A good example is found in Judges 16:23-24, which tells how the Philistines gathered for a great feast in honour of their god Dagon, and how they praised their great fortune in having rid themselves of Samson. In Hebrew these lines rhyme by virtue of the suffix "enu", meaning "our". Transliterating the original, we get:

> "Natan eloh*enu* et oyev*enu*
> ve-et machariv arts*enu* va-asher hirba et-halal*enu*."

In translation: "Our god hath delivered into our hands our enemy, and the destroyer of our country, which slew many of us" (Judges 16:24), much of the original poetry is lost.

Songs were also part and parcel of family life, all arrivals and departures being heralded by music. Thus, when Laban realised that Jacob, his son-in-law, had fled, he rode out after him to reproach him not so much for having escaped, as for having escaped in secret, so preventing him from sending his daughters off with mirth and songs, with tabret and with harp (Genesis 31:27).

The popularity of tavern songs, again, can be gathered from Isaiah's denunciation: "Woe unto them, that rise up early in the morning, that they may follow strong drink; that continue until night, till wine inflame them! And the harp, and the viol, the tabret, and pipe, and wine, are in their feasts: but they regard not the work of the Lord, neither consider the operation of his hands" (Isaiah 5:11-12). Their song was a variation on the age-old theme: "Let us eat and drink; for tomorrow we shall die" (Isaiah 22:13). No wonder that Amos, too, decried these frivolous songs (Amos 6:4-6), and that the Old Testament did not think them worthy of reporting.

Quite a different attitude to song was evinced by Jesus, the son of Sirach, or Ecclesiasticus:

> "Pour not out words where there is a musician,
> and shew not forth wisdom out of time.
> A concert of musick in a banquet of wine
> is as a signet of carbuncle set in gold.
> As a signet of an emerald set in a work of gold,
> so is the melody of musick with pleasant wine."
>
> (Ecclesiasticus 32:4-6)

This quotation not only emphasises the difference between the words of the prophets and the sayings of the sages, but also makes clear that they moved in quite different circles.

While we can have no more than a rough idea of the melodies, we can be reasonably certain that the lyrics of many of their secular songs were not so very different from ours. One central theme, then as now, was man's love for woman, and it so happens that a whole book of the Bible is devoted to this subject.

69

The Song of Songs

THE Song of Solomon is also called the Song of Songs to stress the fact that it was Solomon's most beautiful poem. This claim is not exaggerated, for few songs in ancient literature tell of love with greater poetry or with more inspiration. Its period is the ever-new season of love—spring. Winter with its cold showers is past, and once again the sun caresses the earth out of a bright blue sky. Now and then a final cloud pours out its mild gifts on the drying soil. And so the lover calls to his beloved:

> "Rise up, my love, my fair one,
>   and come away.
>   For, lo, the winter is past,
>   the rain is over and gone;
>   The flowers appear on the earth;
>   the time of the singing of birds is come,
>   and the voice of the turtle is heard in our land;
>   The fig tree putteth forth her green figs,
>   and the vines with the tender grape give a good smell.
>   Arise, my love, my fair one, and come away."
>   (Song of Solomon 2:10-13)

And she calls back to him:

> "My beloved is mine, and I am his:
>   he feedeth among the lilies.
>   Until the day break, and the shadows flee away,
>   turn, my beloved,
>   and be thou like a roe or a young hart upon the mountains of Bether."
>   (Song of Solomon 2:16-17)

What a lovely description of a young girl's reveries, as she lies down on her couch to dream of her beloved! She is asleep yet her heart keeps watch. Is this her lover knocking at her door? In her dreams she rises up, to find that he has vanished. Desperately she goes out to search for him:

> "I sleep, but my heart waketh:
> it is the voice of my beloved that knocketh, saying,
> Open to me, my sister, my love, my dove, my undefiled:
> for my head is filled with dew,
> and my locks with the drops of the night.
> I have put off my coat;
> how shall I put it on?
> I have washed my feet;
> how shall I defile them?
> My beloved put in his hand by the hole of the door,
> and my bowels were moved for him.
> I rose up to open to my beloved;
> and my hands dropped with myrrh,
> and my fingers with sweet smelling myrrh,
> upon the handles of the lock.
> I opened to my beloved;
> but my beloved had withdrawn himself, and was gone:
> my soul failed when he spake;
> I sought him, but I could not find him;
> I called him, but he gave me no answer.
> The watchmen that went about the city found me,
> they smote me, they wounded me:
> the keepers of the walls took away my veil from me."
>
> (Song of Solomon 5:2-7)

It would be wrong to look upon this Book as a series of different love songs, for it is held together by a central thread. In the beginning (1:6) the girl complains about the harsh treatment she has suffered at her brothers' hands. In appointing her keeper of their vineyards, they left her no time to look after her own. And the Book concludes on the same note:

> "M   vineyard, which is mine, is before me:
> thou, O Solomon, must have a thousand,
> and those that keep the fruit thereof two hundred."
>
> (Song of Solomon 8:12)

This central thread holds together all the lovely songs of love and joy that have made this Book so rightly famous. Fear of love is expressed by this injunction:

> "I charge you, O ye daughters of Jerusalem,
>   by the roes, and by the hinds of the field,
>   that ye stir not up,
>   nor awake my love, till he please."
>   (Song of Solomon 2:7)

This verse is repeated in 3:5 word for word, but in 5:8 we can read that desire has conquered fear of love:

> "I charge you, O daughters of Jerusalem,
>   if ye find my beloved,
>   that ye tell him, that I am sick of love."
>   (Song of Solomon 5:8)

With a small variation 2:7 is repeated in 8:4 also. The verse:

> "His left hand is under my head,
>   and his right hand doth embrace me."
>   (Song of Solomon 2:6)

is repeated in 8:3. The song builds up to a tremendous crescendo:

> "For love is strong as death;
>   jealousy is cruel as the grave:
>   the coals thereof are coals of fire,
>   which hath a most vehement flame.
>   Many waters cannot quench love,
>   neither can the floods drown it:
>   if a man would give all the substance of his house for love,
>   it would utterly be contemned."
>   (Song of Solomon 8:6-7)

As we read the Song of Songs we marvel not only at its lovely poetry but also at its positive attitude to sensuality. Now this very fact would most likely have precluded the Song of Songs from canonisation, had not the commentators attributed an allegorical character to it. Each carnal reference was interpreted by them as having a symbolic meaning. Thus the love between man and woman was said to be symbolic of God's love for His chosen people. Other interpreters have read the whole song as a paean of praise to Jerusalem, the beloved city. No doubt, all such interpretations are highly flattering but all are equally unlikely, since in all of them the burning passion of the actual song is forgotten. And the song does unquestionably sing the praises of carnal love, of man's love for woman which in its intensity reflects man's love for God. No wonder that Rabbi Akiba said that no day in history was as important as the day in which we were given the Song of Songs. And the rabbi enjoined the people not to profane this song by singing it in the taverns. Those who did, the rabbi added, would have no share of the world to come.

We have only to read Hosea or Ezekiel 16 to realise that they, too, saw God's love reflected in man's erotic passion. When the Christian Church applied this love to Christ and His Church, it did no more than follow in the footsteps of the prophets.

Now we can also understand why the Song of Songs is recited in the synagogue during the Passover celebrations. The Festival of Passover takes place in spring, and the Song of Songs sings of the joys of spring when both love and nature have quickened. But Passover is no longer a primitive festival; it has become the historical feast-day to mark the Exodus from Egypt. Now, what is the connection between Exodus and man's carnal desire? Once again we must open Hosea and Ezekiel to find that both looked upon the Exodus and the sojourn in the desert as the time of Israel's honeymoon. Then all was well between Israel and their God, and God found the people of Israel: "like grapes in the wilderness; I saw your fathers as the firstripe in the fig tree at her first time" (Hosea 9:10). And so it would be again. In order to appreciate why Rabbi Akiba thought the Song of Songs God's greatest gift to the world, we need only savour the pure sensuality of Hosea's, "And I will betroth thee unto me for ever; yea, I will betroth thee unto me in righteousness, and in judgment, and in lovingkindness, and in mercies. I will even betroth thee unto me in faithfulness" (Hosea 2:19-20).

J. The Wording of Holy Writ

70

Our Bible

WHEN we compare the Vulgate with the Authorised Version, we see that the latter has dropped quite a few books of the Old Testament, and relegated others to the Apocrypha. The Greek Orthodox Church again, while retaining some of the apocryphal books, has scrapped others. Different churches have thus different ideas of what is Holy Writ. While the Catholics have followed the Alexandrian traditions, we have kept more closely to the original Hebrew text.

Protestants, realising that the Old Testament was quite exclusively the property of Israel, went back to the real sources, and so Luther and Calvin, deliberately ignoring other versions, referred directly to the Hebrew original which Jewish scribes had preserved through the centuries. Those Greek translations of the Old Testament for which no Hebrew original could be found were denied canonical status. The reformers were willing to look upon them as inspiring literature, but that was all. Even such books as Ecclesiasticus and Tobit which must certainly have been written in Hebrew, since Hebrew fragments of both books have recently come to light, were said to lack the authority of the other books. Paradoxically enough then, the Protestant Churches in deciding which books of the Bible were to be considered canonical had to mould their Bible before they could allow the Bible to mould them.

Now, apart from references to the Law of Moses, the Prophets and the Psalms (Luke 24:44), the New Testament also contains references to "the holy scriptures" (II Timothy 3:15), all of which Jesus and the apostles accepted as authoritative. While we know perfectly well what the disciples meant by the Law of Moses, and the Prophets, we do not know precisely what they referred to as "holy scriptures".

The status of the Books of Esther, the Song of Solomon and Ecclesiastes had been the subject of long arguments, and we can well understand why the rabbis were so diffident about them. Only in about A.D. 100 did the rabbis agree what part of holy scripture was to be included in the Jewish canon. It is said that this question was authoritatively settled at the Synod of Jamnia, although it seems probable that no such Synod was ever convened and that the final decision was the culmination of a very long process—we know neither when nor how. Now a final decision had become imperative at a time when Jewry was being threatened by Christianity from without and syncretism from within. The extent of the Law, the Prophets and "holy scriptures" (in Hebrew the "Tenach" which is an abbreviation of their initials) had to be quite deliberately restricted, if a continuous tradition was to be ensured. The rabbis must have used a very simple criterion: they assumed that the prophetic era had ended with Ezra and Nehemiah. Everything that belonged to this period or that had any claims of belonging to it was declared holy scripture, and the rest rejected.

The Reformers kept to this rabbinical restriction, but followed the Christian tradition when it came to the actual order of the books. Thus Ruth gained her place after Judges, Esther after Nehemiah, Lamentations after Jeremiah, the Song of Songs and Ecclesiastes after Proverbs; Chronicles was moved up from the end of the Bible to its place after Kings, and Daniel was given a more honourable place immediately following the Prophets.

By continuing to adhere to the rabbinical dictate as strictly as she has done, the Church has invited a great deal of justified criticism. Recent and even less recent discoveries have made a rediscussion of this question imperative. What is the Church to make of the new manuscripts, for instance a manuscript of Isaiah dating from the second century B.C.—if they differ from the more recent texts sanctioned by the rabbis? Must these differences be ignored? In any case the Church ought certainly to have discussed them quite frankly. However, it must be remembered that, in opting not for the most recently discovered text but for that approved in A.D. 100, the Church maintained the distinction between a classical text, which scholars could translate as they wished, and a text that had been authenticated by the Church as Holy Writ.

So far we have dealt with two important phases in the process of canonisation: the Synod of Jamnia and the Reformation. But what about the earlier phases, lost in the distant past? All we can do here is speculate. We may be reasonably certain that the Bible originated from an oral tradition. This need not have militated against the faithfulness of the tradition, if only because the memories of the people had not yet been ruined by notebooks and filing systems. In any case it would be wrong to compare oral tradition in the ancient world with the fabrication of village gossip.

The moment a saying was recognised as coming from a higher source, it was treated with great reverence and care and meticulously repeated from generation to generation. Whenever one and the same saying existed in two different versions, say, in Jerusalem and in Samaria, both were reported together, no matter how much they contradicted each other. The problem of the so-called mutual contradictions in the Old Testament can usually be explained in this way.

In very rare cases we actually have some knowledge about the first written texts. Thus Jeremiah 36 tells us how the prophet dictated all his sayings to Baruch, the scribe, and the very style of Ezekiel makes it reasonably certain that the prophet wrote down rather than recited his visions. But in general it is very difficult to say where oral tradition ended and where written tradition began. Again it is the style of the text that makes us think that the Books of Moses were the first to have been committed to paper, and that the Prophets came next. But we have no idea how far this process had been completed even in Ezra's day.

71

The Manuscript

IN the summer of 1947 a remarkable discovery was made in the desert of Judah. The newspapers were full of it—overnight the Old Testament had become a topic for breakfast discussions. In a cave near the Dead Sea a number of scrolls were found which, according to a preliminary view, must have originated in the second century B.C. Among these manuscripts was found a complete version of the Book of Isaiah with all its sixty-six chapters. While the report made a stir even among the average newspaper readers, it fell like a bombshell among Biblical scholars.

Now the possibility of discovering old manuscripts in Palestine had never been seriously entertained. The humidity of that area is such that written material undergoes relatively quick decomposition—both parchment and papyrus are attacked by the atmosphere. Only in the dry desert sand of Egypt do leather and papyrus have a long life, and so there was no reason to expect that we should ever unearth old manuscripts in Palestine. And yet, in these scrolls, we have recovered manuscripts of more than two thousand years ago.

There is yet another reason why this find was so sensational: the oldest other manuscript of Isaiah's prophecies dates from roughly A.D. 900. If we assume that Isaiah lived in Jerusalem in about 750-700 B.C., there is a difference of sixteen centuries between his original work and the oldest manuscript known before 1947! Clearly during those sixteen centuries the scribes must have committed all the many mistakes that we may expect a normal human, and thus fallible, scribe to commit. Overnight this gulf of sixteen centuries had now been lessened to one of only five centuries.

Today this manuscript can be read by all who are interested. An American scholar has published an excellent photographic reproduction, so that anyone placing the two texts side by side can see what changes the scribes have made in the text in the course of eleven centuries, and what errors or omissions they have been guilty of. Actually, most of the discrepancies can be reduced to differences in spelling which are of interest only to philologists. But even so the jubilation of orthodox circles over the small number of differences between the Isaiah manuscript from the Dead Sea and the Massoretic text is not entirely borne out by the facts.

Things are very much worse in the case of Jeremiah's prophecies. There is a tremendous difference between the tenth-century Hebrew text and the fourth-century Greek translation, and these differences cannot be attributed to the negligence of the translators. For this reason it will be only if the Hebrew manuscript of Jeremiah is ever discovered, that we shall be able to assess with what accuracy the written tradition has been handed down. In the face of recent discoveries, such a find cannot be ruled out, and it seems probable that Biblical scholarship has entered, or is about to enter, a new chapter with unpredictable consequences.

Now, though the scribes were meticulous when it came to writing down what was thought to be God's revealed Word, they must have been a little careless when it came to other writing—hence the many discrepancies. The Talmud makes it quite clear with what circumspection the true word of God was customarily treated by the scribes: "While I was still a pupil of Rabbi Akiba," a rabbi wrote, "I used to pour vitriol into the ink. Later I came to Rabbi Ishmael and he asked me what my work was. When I had told him that I was a scribe, he admonished me thus: 'My son, be careful at your work, for it is a labour of God, and if you omit or add but a single letter, you may destroy the whole world.' I answered him: 'I am greatly experienced in the writing of all words, but to make certain that not even a fly will settle on the stroke of a ד ["daleth"] thus turning it into a ר ["resh"] I always pour a few drops of vitriol into my ink.'"

In order to appreciate this story to the full, we must remember that until A.D. 700 no written vowels were known in Hebrew or Aramaic. Now, until vowels came into use—and they certainly had not in Rabbi Akiba's day—the consonants were doubly important. What happened when the letter ד ("daleth") was accidentally changed into a ר ("resh") by omitting just one part of the stroke was exemplified by a famous example. In Deuteronomy 6:4 we can read the Israelite creed: "Hear, O Israel: The Lord our God is one Lord." Now the Hebrew for "one" is "echad" and if the "daleth" is accidentally changed into a "resh" the result, in the absence of vowels, becomes "acher" meaning a "stranger". The creed then reads: "God is a stranger." Small wonder then, that in copying the text, all sorts of precautions were taken, so that "till heaven and earth pass, one jot or one tittle shall in no wise pass from the law" (St. Matthew 5:18). The jot (Hebrew "yod") was the smallest letter in the alphabet, and the tittle a minute writing sign. Even the smallest mark mattered because it, too, was part of Holy Writ. To make doubly sure all the sentences, and indeed even the letters, were counted, the number of sentences recorded at the end of each Book, and the halfway mark shown. Hence we need not be too surprised to learn that an Isaiah manuscript from the second century B.C., i.e. from a time when his sayings had long been canonised, does not essentially differ from one a good thousand years later.

And so as we open the Old Testament on our pulpits, we know that

Q

it was handed down by two fallible human methods. It was the synagogue and the church that decided which of the writings were to be Holy Writ. But long before the Synods gathered, and before the translators set to work in Worms, in Zurich or in Alexandria, the old scribes were bending over their parchment, prepared from the hides of consecrated animals. No one can deny that some mistakes did creep into their writing. The differences between the various manuscripts make it clear that it was not always the hand of God Almighty that guided their pens. But even so, we may rest assured that they worked with an almost superhuman thoroughness.

72

The Translation

WHENEVER we read the Bible in translation we see the world of the Old Testament through a glass darkly. Finer shades of meaning may escape us altogether if we do not read the text in Hebrew; the beauty and meaning of all original works are unavoidably dimmed in translation, but particularly by translations from an ancient Semitic tongue into a modern European language.

To start with, the point of most puns must necessarily be lost completely. Take Isaac's name, to the Hebrews reminiscent of laughter. We are told that, when Isaac's birth was announced to Abraham and Sarah, Sarah responded with laughter (Genesis 18:12-15). God asked Abraham why she had laughed, but Sarah denied that she had. And God said, "Nay; but thou didst laugh." Now if we read this passage in Hebrew we observe what we miss in translation, namely that these four references to Sarah's laughter are in fact also references to Isaac. Similarly the name of Jacob meant heel-catcher, for Jacob had caught his twin-brother Esau by the heel at their birth.

But perhaps, after all, it would be better to have spoken not of seeing through a glass darkly but of looking through different-coloured spectacles. Each translator had his own idea of the text—depending on whether he was Jewish, Catholic or Protestant. Try as he would, he could not help imposing his own bias on his work. And so the translators not only handed down the text but their own attitudes to it also, and this is even more true of unannotated Bibles than of those which restricted their comments to the margin. I should like to illustrate this point by just a few examples.

The Authorised Version renders Exodus 22:25 as: "If thou lend money to any of my people that is poor by thee, thou shalt not be to him as an usurer, neither shalt thou lay upon him usury." In fact, the Hebrew original spoke of interest, and not of usury at all. All we can say in the translator's justification is that in the East the rate of interest was often usurious in the extreme. In any case the Revised Standard Version has correctly altered "usurer" to "creditor" and "usury" to "interest".

Each translation represents a particular point of view. The Authorised Version reflects the Anglican tradition, and this becomes quite evident from its rendering of Isaiah 7:14: "Behold, a virgin shall conceive, and bear a son." The original "almah" meant both "virgin" and "young woman", and the choice of the former, together with pointed references to Matthew 1:23 and Luke 1:31, speak for the translator's belief that Isaiah must have referred to the Virgin Mary. The Revised Standard Version, in choosing "young woman" is, of course, much closer to the Jewish tradition.

I hope that these few examples have illustrated my point. But while there are not many of us who can read the Bible in the original, we have to make do with what translations there are. Still we must always remember that however beautiful a translation may be, it must needs be only a poor substitute for the real thing.

73

And the Word was Made Flesh

MOST readers of the Bible are so used to reading the Old Testament in their own language, that they fail to realise that the very fact of their being able to do so involved a most important principle. There were many who considered any translation of Divine Revelation as blasphemous, holding as they did the view that reverence for the Book involved that not the slightest change in its language or contents was admissible.

The Jews have coped with this problem by teaching their young to become so proficient in Hebrew that, at the age of thirteen when, according to the synagogue he has reached his majority, a boy is capable of reading and interpreting the original texts. Many rabbinical pronouncements warn specifically against the danger of translation. Thus the treatise known as Sopherim states emphatically that the day on which the Greek translation of the Torah first appeared in Alexandria was as sad a day as that on which the Israelites worshipped the golden calf in the desert. In another treatise Meg. Ta'anith, Rabbi Jehudah, referring to the same event, speaks of the world being cloaked in darkness for three days.

Nevertheless even the Jews were eventually forced into translating the Old Testament, if only to give their version to the world. A Yiddish version appeared in Amsterdam as early as the seventeenth century, and a famous German translation by Martin Buber and Franz Rosenzweig has recently attracted a great deal of attention. Rosenzweig showed his profound wisdom when he justified his translation by saying: "If the Bible lacked the mysterious power of changing our error into its truth, this translation would have been even more impudent an undertaking than in fact it was." This assertion implies a dynamic conception of the Bible which freed the authors from the shackles of the mere letter of the word.

Unlike the Jews, the Christian Church has never demanded a knowledge of Hebrew and Greek from its members as a prerequisite of Biblical study. Only theologians were expected to know these languages, the better to interpret the Divine Message. The Church has never objected to any faithful translations, since it did not look on the Old Testament as a book that was written in Heaven.

The unqualified condemnation of all translations is characteristic of Islam and some minor sects. The Muslims are in fact the only people to have drawn the full consequences of a static approach to Holy Writ, and therefore the faithful will not read the Koran in any other language than Arabic. True, the Koran has been translated, but only for the sake of infidels and not for good Muslims. And so Islam is the book-religion *par excellence*. Only one standard text of the book may exist and in only one language; not one letter may be changed, not a single word be omitted. Fortunately neither orthodox Jews nor Christians share this rigid point of view, though the Samaritans go even further than the Mohammedans. They worship only a particular manuscript, the famous Scroll of Abisha, which is said to have originated in the year 625 B.C.!

A scholar of comparative religion has formulated the difference between Islam and Christianity in a few words: for the Muslim the Word has become a book, while for the Christian the Word was made Flesh. The consequences are tremendous. We must state this fact with emphasis since far too many Christians still hold rigidly to such texts as Deuteronomy 4:2 and 12:32, Proverbs 30:5, Ecclesiastes 3:14, all of which enjoin them not to add to the word or diminish aught from it. If only they read these words in their context, they would soon realise that they have a strictly limited meaning. Those in Deuteronomy refer to God's Commandments alone, and the Preacher was merely speaking of God's works and not about the Book when he said: "I know that, whatsoever God doeth, it shall be for ever: nothing can be put to it, nor any thing taken from it."

Only in the apocalyptists do we meet the conviction that every word they wrote is sacrosanct. Thus we can read in Revelation: "For I testify unto every man that heareth the words of the prophecy of this book. If any man shall add unto these things God shall add unto him the plagues that are written in this book: And if any man shall take away from the words of the book of this prophecy, God shall take away his part out of the book of life, and out of the holy city, and from the things which are written in this book" (Revelation 22:18-19). But these lines can hardly be applied to the Bible as a whole nor were they meant to do so, even though we gladly admit that if everyone had added to or diminished from the Book at will there would have been no Bible at all. When we say that Jews and Christians alike originally tried to adapt the message of the Bible to their time, we do not mean that every heretic is at liberty to justify his heresy by reading into the Bible what he likes. Nevertheless, I believe that each one of us who genuinely wishes to live in truth and sincerity by the Bible need only heed Franz Rosenzweig's injunction to let the Bible change our errors into truth. Then no interpretations or typologies can ever detract from its central message. This, according to my Christian conviction, applies particularly to those who know that the Word was made Flesh.

Their Bible is always the Book of Him who in order to speak to mankind, came down to earth to be as one of us.

Our journey along the byways of the Old Testament has come to an end. We have been unable to solve the mystery of the origin of Israel's religion. Still, there is no doubt that Abraham, when he left Ur, set out towards Western civilisation, for Western civilisation would have been unthinkable without Judaism and Christianity. This explains why the Bible so often poses the burning problems of our own time, and why the Old Testament is no "older" than the New. Each of us must never tire of formulating its message anew for himself and for his own generation. I am perfectly conscious of the fact that many will disagree with me, but surely no one can gainsay that wrestling with the Bible, here and now, is always wrestling with a truth that alone can free us and reveal the meaning of life. If then we try to understand the Bible, neither bogged down by traditional nor yet by anti-traditional prejudices, we may once again make the Bible a living book, and help to fashion a truly religious community which, living by God's Word, can go out to face the future as bravely as Abraham did when he left Ur to go into the unknown.

FINIS

Index of Biblical References

OLD TESTAMENT

APOCRYPHA

NEW TESTAMENT

General Index

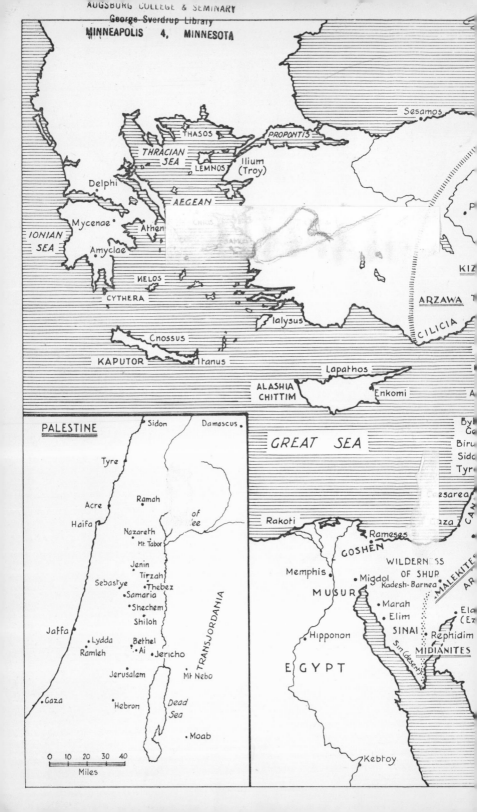

THASOS

PROPONTIS

THRACIAN
SEA

LEMNOS

Ilium
(Troy)

Delphi

AEGEAN

Mycenae

Athen

IONIAN
SEA

Amyclae

MELOS

CYTHERA

Ialysus

KIZ

ARZAWA

CILICIA

Cnossus

Itanus

Lapathos

KAPUTOR

ALASHIA
CHITTIM

Enkomi

PALESTINE

Sidon

Damascus

GREAT SEA

By
G

Tyre

Biru

Sid

Tyr

Ramah

Acre

of
ee

Caesarea

Haifa

Rakoti

aza

Nazareth

CAN

Mt. Tabor

Rameses

Jenin

GOSHEN

WILDERNESS

Tirzah

OF SHUP

MALEKITE

Sebastye

Thebez

Memphis

Migdol

AR

Samaria

Kadesh-Barnea

MUSUR

Shechem

Marah

Ela

Shiloh

Elim

(Ez

Jaffa

SINAI

Rephidim

Lydda

Bethel

Hipponon

Sin (desert)

MIDIANITES

Ramleh

Ai

Jericho

Jerusalem

Mt Nebo

E G Y P T

Gaza

Hebron

Dead
Sea

Moab

TRANSJORDANIA

0   10   20   30   40

Kebtoy

Miles